can i
have
my
ball
back?

RICHARD HERRING

can i have my ball back?

SPHERE

SPHERE

First published in Great Britain in 2022 by Sphere

1 3 5 7 9 10 8 6 4 2

A CIP catalogue record for this book
is available from the British Library.

ISBN 978-0-7515-8576-6

Typeset in Palatino by M Rules
Printed and bound in Great Britain by
Clays Ltd, Elcograf S.p.A.

Papers used by Sphere are from well-managed forests
and other responsible sources.

Sphere
An imprint of
Little, Brown Book Group
Carmelite House
50 Victoria Embankment
London EC4Y 0DZ

An Hachette UK Company
www.hachette.co.uk

www.littlebrown.co.uk

For Dick, Matt, Tony and Thalia

Prologue

In 2002, I was on the worst holiday of my life.

I was in Barbados with my girlfriend of a few months, staying in an exclusive boutique hotel right on the beach. I admit that, so far, this doesn't sound like the worst holiday of my life, but bear with me. This always-rather-dramatic relationship was about to explode. Unbeknownst to me, my girlfriend had spent the night before we left with her ex, who had taken the opportunity to propose to her.

She had decided to come on holiday with me anyway, but was mulling over the offer and secretly ringing her ex/ potential husband from the telephone in our room when I was sunbathing. (The worst part of that is that I was paying for everything, including these international calls from a hotel room. I was getting billed for this cuckolding.) Things were a bit weird and tense, though I, of course, didn't know why.

On the second or third day, I went for a paddle in the sea. I don't like taking risks, and am not into surfing or paragliding or scuba-diving – or even just swimming in the ocean, really. I was literally just trying to cool off in the shallow water. I was maybe five metres from shore, the water not even up to my swimming trunks, when the swelling sea decided to swell a bit more, and I was sucker-punched by a wave that sent me somersaulting off my feet, turning me 180 degrees and causing my head to smash down on the stony sand beneath.

I was winded and confused, and fierce waves were now crashing around me and threatening to pull me out into the depths. I somehow scrambled the tiny distance to the safety of the shore and lay on the beach, breathing heavily, considering how close I had come to death (not very) and how pathetic a death that would have been (very).

My head and shoulder had taken the brunt of the impact, but I felt like I'd been through the spin cycle of a washing machine and my stomach was sore. More worryingly, over the next few hours, my right testicle swelled up to about three times its regular (not inconsiderable) size. It probably goes without saying, at least to fifty per cent of the readership, that this was extremely uncomfortable. It was also bamboozling. How could a bang on the head have such an impact on my gonad?

My girlfriend didn't seem too concerned that fun sexy times were now off the menu; if anything, there was a palpable sense of relief on her part. While I recuperated, she headed off to experience the local nightlife on her own. Maybe she was out cheating on me *and* her potential fiancé, although it doesn't really matter. None of the central players in this story were ready for a committed relationship.

I struggled through the rest of the week. Sometimes I left the room, unknowingly giving her the opportunity to carry on her transatlantic conversation, but whatever I did, the discomfort was constant.

That was nothing, though, compared with what I would go through on the plane ride home. My swollen testicle, still continuously throbbing with pain, was able to gauge changes in atmospheric pressure. As the craft went higher, the agony became ever more excruciating. Every metre we climbed was a kick in the ball. Perhaps airlines could get rid of expensive altimeters and instead employ big-bollocked men to let the pilot know their exact height based on the intensity of their screams.

Looking back, I have wondered why God was punishing me when *I* was the one who had been wronged. (Admittedly, I had also cheated on my girlfriend a couple of times in the 'relationship', but that's hardly the point.)

We broke up in the cab home from the airport (my girlfriend and me, not me and my testicle, though I'd happily have jettisoned it over the ocean). I only found out about the proposal a couple of weeks later, from a friend of her friend. My girlfriend denied it, but I rang the number that kept appearing on my itemised hotel bill – and guess who answered?

In case you're wondering, their engagement didn't work out, and a couple of months later my ex and I briefly hooked up again, because we were both idiots who thrived on the excitement and the wrongness of it all.

I also went to the doctor about my inflated love-egg. He thought that I'd probably ripped my stomach lining in the tumultuous sea. As there are nerves that connect your stomach to your acorn-hammock, he said this trauma was the cause of my testicular mishap. I don't really remember what happened next. He must have given me some pills; my genitals certainly returned to their regular (breathtaking) size, and I got on with my life.

My broken heart healed as quickly as my pumped-up beachball, and I moved on. This became an amusing anecdote of doomed love and damaged goolies. But fate, that ultimate court jester of the human condition, was already percolating a punchline that would be twenty years in the making.

Comedy is tragedy plus time, then a bigger tragedy.

1

Grow some balls

Balls.

They're a symbol of strength, yet they are the weakest and most vulnerable part of the human body.

They represent masculinity, and yet with a well-placed kick – or even a firm poke – the feeblest child can reduce a muscle-bound jock to a squirming heap on the floor.

If we are cowardly, we are told to grow some; if we're brave, we're said to have huge ones; if it's cold, they are liable to fall off – even if you're a brass monkey.

If we're in trouble, someone will threaten to break them; if we have to work hard, we might very well bust them; if we're in somebody's thrall, then they've got us by them.

Balls are a euphemism for something useless and mendacious – unless they belong to a dog, in which case, for some unfathomable reason, they are the best thing ever.*

They are possibly the least attractive external body part,

---

* For my money, dogs' bollocks are some of the least appealing bollocks out there – and given how awful bollocks are in general, that's really saying something.

resembling two kiwi fruits bulging in a hairy shopping bag. They are not even symmetrical. And yet, even in this age of plastic surgery, hardly anyone elects to have the things snipped off to make their undercarriage more aesthetically pleasing.

They are often neglected and ignored, very much the backing singers in the band that is the male genitalia, overshadowed by the charismatic front man. They are the equivalent of the two blokes who stood at the back in East 17, making weird shapes with their hands.

Even those of us who have them don't think about them too often, unless they are in peril.

Yet there, hanging between the legs of roughly 50 per cent of the human beings on the planet (and let's not forget all the animals, birds and fish that have them too), are one or two (or occasionally more) of the most magical, almost fantastical, god-like Genesis machines on the planet, spewing out potential new lives at an improbable rate.

A pair of functioning human testes, in their prime, produce 1,500 sperm every second of the day. That's something like 525 billion sperm cells churned out of these weird, gristly clumps of tubules in a human lifetime. An estimated 21.5 gallons of semen – enough to fill half a bath.*

If half a bath is a bit of a let-down for a lifetime of spunk production, remember that, with the help of an enthusiastic and determined friend, you could fill your tub to the brim – although if you're planning to have a bath in your lifetime's worth of jizz, you might want to be careful about filling the thing that high. Remember the work of Archimedes. In some ways, it's better to luxuriate in half a bath of gametes than to

---

* Andrew Fiouzi, 'How much cum do you throw away over the course of a lifetime?', www.melmagazine.com.

send a volume equivalent to your own mass spilling out on to the bathroom floor.

Five hundred and twenty-five billion sperm! That's a lot of potential people. Given that most men will father somewhere between zero and three children in their lifetimes, there's a huge volume of sex-mess going to waste. If God is serious about every sperm being sacred, every man who has ever lived is in an awful lot of trouble. Though to be fair, it's God who has made us have so much of the stuff, and so this is, at the very least, entrapment.

Even someone like Genghis Khan, who allegedly fathered thousands of children (and to whom we are all almost certainly related), wasted essentially the same number of tadger-tadpoles as any other man in percentage terms.

If there was only one testicle in the universe producing this amount of latent life, it would be worshipped as a god – or at least appear in an episode of *Star Trek* shooting terrifying giant space-fish at Captain Kirk (who I think might secretly like it). Yet this miraculous gobbing globule is so commonplace that it hangs between the legs of approximately four billion living humans (as well as having been possessed by maybe another fifty billion dead ones). Even if you're the only cojones-owner in the room, you (usually) have two of the things. Their ubiquity makes them ordinary, and the willingness of most owners to liberally share the contents of their testes means there is never any danger of scarcity. Consequently, rather than being revered, this pair of hairy deities in our pants are regarded as comical and ridiculous, like a slightly less wrinkly version of the Chuckle Brothers.

As if the production of 130 million spermatozoa isn't enough for you, these great balls of fire also produce testosterone: assisting the development of the genitals, firing up the process of puberty and prompting muscle and bone growth, as well as creating libido and the ability to maintain erections. That's some serious multi-tasking, which, even on a non-divine level, we should be grateful for.

For me, though, the most remarkable fact about the McSquirter Twins* is that if they are transplanted from one person to another, they will continue to manufacture the sperm of the *original owner*. For this reason, testicle transplants are very rare indeed, and are only carried out in extraordinary circumstances between identical twins, to avoid the moral quandary of somebody fathering another person's child. If you get someone else's heart, you don't start to love the things they loved (except in fanciful horror films); if you are given someone else's kidney, you don't start to wee their wee; even someone else's blood will become yours once it's in your arteries. Aside from the even more magical ovaries (which I – admittedly wrongly – like to think of as the super-testicles of a superior species) there is only one other organ of the human body that, one would assume, would refuse to give up the identity of its originator if it were to be successfully transplanted: the brain. People talk about men having their brains in their pants, but in this sense we do. We have a pair of organs so loyal that they remain ours and keep shooting out our progeny even if they migrate to a different ballbag.

Like a sort of anti-Borg, they refuse to be assimilated.

Yet most pod-possessors are so blasé about our human glue factories that we can't really be bothered to just check them over once a month to ensure there are no lumps or bumps. I get it. About fifteen years ago, I took part in a campaign to encourage men to have a little (non-sexual) feel every now and again, and even I didn't really bother to check my own. It was

---

* A euphemism that sadly will be lost on anyone who didn't watch the British TV show *Record Breakers* in the 1970s.

embarrassing and weird, and if there was something wrong, I didn't want to know about it. If I didn't know about it, then it couldn't hurt me.

Anyway, that kind of stuff only happens to other people ...

ON THE BALL

As well as sharing my own personal story, I also want to use this book to give you a flavour of balls throughout history: their function, their cultural and artistic significance, and how they have become associated with particular attributes (some real, but many imaginary). These bulbous additions will dangle between each chapter as a little amuse-bouche or palate-cleanser. I hope you enjoy my gobbets.

Why the low-hanging fruit?

> 'I've always felt that the placement of a man's testicles is an eloquent argument against intelligent design.'
>
> **– Mark Lawrence**

The big question about balls that needs answering straight away is this: Why the hell are they outside the body and not sealed deep within us, shielded by the same kind of armour that you see on rhinos, but also studded with diamonds and including some kind of built-in missile system to repel attackers?

I'd always understood that it was to do with temperature: ideal sperm production occurs at thirty-five degrees Celsius, but the inside of the body is thirty-seven degrees

Celsius, and so our balls have descended out of our abdomens and into this stupid, ugly unprotected sack in an effort to stay cool, like two little Fonzies.

Wait a minute, though. Elephants and birds have a higher body temperature than we do, but still have internal balls. Furthermore, whales, dolphins and seals don't leave their balls dangling behind them in the nice cool ocean – perhaps for fear of them acting as bait for fish or sharks. Theirs are neatly tucked inside too. Has science lied to us?

The temperature theory was first proposed in 1890 by Joseph Griffiths, who tried to prove his point by pushing dogs' bollocks back into their abdomens and sewing them in place so they couldn't pop out. Luckily for him, he was a scientist, so this kind of behaviour was acceptable and not an indication that he would soon be going on a terrible killing spree. After a few days, Griffiths discovered that the pushed-back, sewn-up bollocks had degenerated – what a surprise – and sperm production had more or less ceased. He decided that this was due to the higher temperatures inside the body, and not the stress and shock he'd caused by messing around with canine genitals.

Some academics have offered other theories, with the most fanciful being a suggestion that our vulnerable plums might be somehow equivalent to peacock feathers. Peacocks are much more susceptible to prey because of their colourful tail plumage, but that disadvantage is outweighed by the fact that peahens get moist for those crazy feather displays. Thus, some scientists have genuinely argued, maybe vulnerable balls are also some kind of ornamental display intended to wow the ladies. As Jesse Bering puts it: 'If the organism can thrive and survive while still being hobbled by a costly, maladaptive trait such as elaborate, cumbersome plumage or (in this case) vulnerably drooping gonads, then it must have some high-quality genes and be a valuable mate.'*

Even the people who came up with this theory thought it was unlikely. Besides, if it was such an evolutionary advantage, then ballsacks would have evolved to come down to our knees and be brightly coloured, and maybe placed between two massive cymbals that would pulverise them every time our legs knocked together.

Also, I think it's fair to say that if this theory were true, women would be much more interested in balls than they are. There would be young men with their balls out on page three of tabloid newspapers, dildos would come with huge, dangling appendages, and balls would be greeted with gasps and reverence rather than mockery and scarcely hidden disgust.

The position of human balls probably *is* to do with temperature, but maybe not for the reasons originally posited. Some have argued that cooler temperatures might stop DNA from mutating, while evolutionary psychologist G. G. Gallup proposed the activation hypothesis, which states that sperm are kept cooler than body temperature so that once the lucky ones find themselves in the warmer vaginal canal, they know they're about to get a chance to fulfil their purpose and get turned on (maybe in both senses of the word), increasing their mobility so they have a chance to get to their goal before the hot female body fries them. Or, to quote the more scientific Gallup: 'Descended scrotal testicles evolved to both capitalise on this copulation/

---

* Jesse Bering, 'How are they hanging?', www.psmag.com, 26 April 2013.

insemination contingent temperature enhancement and function to prevent premature activation of sperm by keeping testicular temperatures below the critical value set by body temperatures.'*

I think the way I put it was better.

Whatever the reason, I still have to ask, couldn't the balls be outside the body *and* have diamond-studded rhino-armour that fires missiles at intruders? Or how about a nice rounded cup made of bone to act as a nest for these precious eggs? Would that have been too much to ask for, evolution, you massive prick?

* Gordon G. Gallup, *et al.* 'On the Origin of Descended Scrotal Testicles: The Activation Hypothesis.' *Evolutionary Psychology*, October 2009.

2

I can't imagine what that would be like

To say the least, 2020 had been a bit of a distracting year.

Not only was there the lingering fear of illness and death from Covid-19 hanging over us all, but with the NHS stretched to its limits, it had struck me pretty quickly that this would also be a terrible time to get ill with something else. *Imagine being unlucky enough to get cancer NOW,* I thought, never considering the possibility that it might happen to me. I was fifty-three, and come from hardy stock: my parents are in their mid-eighties and still fit, while my grandparents had all made it to seventy-five, with my grandma finally deciding to give the bucket a toe-punt when she was 102. I'd never spent a night in hospital (except when my kids were born, but I don't think that counts)* and there was no indication that anything was wrong with me at all.

---

* It didn't seem fair that my wife got a bed, while I was supposed to sleep in a very uncomfortable chair. Yet when I complained, my wife seemed annoyed, and even called me selfish!

Well, not with my body.

Lockdown had already brought about one surprising self-discovery. I had chanced across a social media post that asked me to visualise an apple with my mind's eye. I closed my eyes, fully expecting to see a nice ripe Golden Delicious hovering around in my brain space. But there was nothing.

However hard I tried, only empty blackness. The exercise was literally fruitless.

Apparently, many people can bring to mind a 3D image of an apple in full colour. Adam Buxton boasted to me that he was a mental gymnast who could make his apple spin around – the show-off. Others see a dimmer version, maybe in 2D, maybe without colour.

But I see nothing. Not a sausage. And, more pertinently, not an apple.

I'd even be happy if I could see a sausage when I'm trying to see an apple. But I can't see a thing.

Before seeing that social media post, I'd had no idea that I couldn't produce mental images. I'd always imagined that I could. (Although when I imagined that, it turns out, I wasn't actually *seeing* myself imagining it. Because I can't imagine.)

My point is that before this revelation (or perhaps non-revelation), I would confidently have told you that I could visualise, but now I realised that the way I think is much more abstract.

If I am called upon to imagine an apple or a tree or the faces of my children, I think of the word and then get a vague sense of the object or person, along with the briefest of flashes of a suggestion of an image, like a fractured reflection on water, that still remains somehow behind my field of vision.

If I try to think of the colour 'blue', I know what blue is, but I *see* no blue whatsoever. The only thing I can think of is the empty blackness that must come with death.

It turns out that I have aphantasia. My mind's eye is blind.

I still see images in my dreams, and sometimes vague and uncontrollable random ones fly into my brain as I drift off to sleep, but nothing else.

It was quite demoralising to discover that I was missing out on something that others took for granted. It's not a nice feeling to be deficient, even if you didn't know that you were until that moment. I wished I'd never found out; until I discovered that I couldn't see mental images, I had assumed that I could, that my way was the way everyone experienced thought.

Of course, by telling you this, I have just made about one in a hundred readers aware of their own aphantasia. I wish I could picture your horrified faces.

My mind was on my mind, but my balls were not. Did I even get an inkling that something might be going on in my nutsack?

Perhaps I had noticed a slight change in the way things were hanging. But I put this down to middle age. In my most recent stand-up show, *Oh Frig, I'm 50!*, I had discussed the fact that gravity takes its effects on men's bodies in ways that aren't usually talked about. I revealed that in your fifties, there's a genuine chance that you might sit on your own testicles. I pretended that I had a system where I'd get my balls swinging from side to side like pendulums, using centrifugal force, and once they touched at the zenith of their arc, I'd know I was safe to be seated.

None of this was true. I'd never even come close to sitting on my balls when I wrote that routine, and as I entered my sixth decade in 2017, everything was hanging tight. Maybe fate wanted me to pay for my comedic mendacity, because in the autumn of 2020, life imitated art, and as I went to sit down on my bed, my nut nudged its way under my buttock – and would have taken the full weight, had I not leapt to my feet at first contact. It still smarted.

I was surprised and upset, but it was surely karma. I had joked about this, and now it had happened, so I assumed that middle age had caught up with me. Similarly, if my ball seemed heavier in the bath, it must be the same deal. Just another of the awful effects of getting older: horrible hanging conkers dangling down around your knees, there to make it absolutely clear to you (and anyone unlucky enough to catch sight of them) that you're no longer a sexually desirable entity.

In any case, I didn't have time to worry about it at this point. I was all caught up in home-schooling, wondering when I could perform live comedy again, starting up an insane live-streamed ventriloquism show in my attic and unsuccessfully trying to cure my blind mind's eye.

It wasn't until January 2021 that I began to idly wonder if something was wrong. The ball wasn't merely heavier, it felt like it was getting larger and maybe a bit harder than I remembered. Or was I imagining it? Was I capable of imagining anything? I certainly didn't tell anyone about it. Not even Catie, my wife.

There were no lumps or bumps on my magic bean, which is what I understood you were supposed to look out for. Everything seemed to be functioning as normal; the only things coming out of my balls were the things that were meant to come out. Maybe in less impressive quantity than twenty years ago, but again, that's middle age.

The ball did undoubtedly feel weird, though. It was a bit scary. The kind of scary where you decide not to look into it, in case you find out something you don't want to.

Eventually, I was concerned enough to google my symptoms. I can't remember what I searched for, or exactly what page I ended up on, but I know that I was satisfied from this search that I didn't have anything to worry about.

How that is possible is a mystery to me now, because every subsequent time I have googled the issue, all results have said something along the lines of what you'll find on the NHS website:

> Lumps and swellings in the testicles can have lots of different causes. Most are caused by something harmless, such as a build-up of fluid (cyst) or swollen veins in the testicles (varicocele). Sometimes, they can be a sign of something serious, such as testicular cancer.
>
> Don't try to self-diagnose the cause of your lump – always see a GP.

Did I stop reading after the second sentence? Did I see what I hoped I would see? Or was I simply feeling embarrassed or frightened? Whatever was going on in my trouser-brain, I did not go to see my GP.

I didn't want the distraction, either, because amazingly, I had actually got some work. In lockdown. I know!

I was heading to Wales to take part in a feature film. This kind of thing doesn't happen to me very often/ever, and I didn't want to have a doctor tell me I'd have to cancel the trip and with it my chance of becoming a movie star.

Instead, I let my swollen ball keep on swelling, maybe hoping it would deflate on its own. Instead, something weirdly symbolic (symbollock?) was on the horizon.

ON THE BALL: The origin of the testes

Ever wondered where your favourite bits of bollocky slang might have started? Here are a few possibilities.

The dog's bollocks

I have researched the subject quite thoroughly, but have been unable to find out why this term became a synonym for outstanding.

The phrase 'the dog's bollocks' was originally the nickname given to a typographical construction consisting of a colon followed by a hyphen, like so:

:-

Why that was thought to resemble a dog's bollocks when it is similar to the male genitalia of many species (including humans) and clearly includes a penis, I can't tell you. Surely the colon alone should signify bollocks. The phrase was used as early as 1949 by etymologist Eric Partridge, so let's blame him. I can only assume that he spent a lot of time looking at dog genitals, and so when he saw a colon followed by a hyphen, that's what leapt to mind.

This doesn't explain why it became a synonym for excellence. Perhaps the printers who popularised the term thought that this early crack at an emoji was so brilliant that it could double up to mean something was outstanding?

According to the *Oxford English Dictionary* (*OED*), the earliest recorded use of 'the dog's bollocks' as a superlative is from a 1986 version of *The Gambler*, a musical by Peter Brewis, Bob Goody and Mel Smith, first staged at Hampstead Theatre, London. It includes the line 'When it comes to Italian opera, Pavarotti is the dog's bollocks.'

Unsurprisingly, another early adopter of the phrase was the hilarious and pioneering adult comic *Viz*, which always has its ear to the filthy ground searching out poetry of the gutter. If you have never read their *Roger's Profanisaurus*, one of the most important literary works of our age, I strongly recommend it. Their 1989 compilation edition is called *Viz: The Dog's Bollocks – The Best of Issues 26 to 31*.

That takes balls

Testicles have long been associated with courage, with Greek and Roman medical writers very literally seeing balls as the sources of male bravery. Medieval writers picked up the ball and it continues to represent valour to this day. It's impossible to identify the person who originally made this connection, but my guess is that it was a caveman with massive knackers who managed to spin his unfeasibly large testicles into something positive.

To give someone a bollocking

The *OED* gives the earliest meaning of 'bollocking' as 'to slander or defame', and suggests that it entered the English language thanks to the 1653 translation of one of Rabelais's works, which includes the Middle French expression '*en couilletant*', translated as 'ballocking'. The earliest printed use in the sense of a severe reprimand is, according to the *OED*, from 1946. Presumably, the verb here implies a violent act upon one's testicles, hence the negative association.

3

Bursting my bubble

Being a movie star did not turn out to be as glamorous as I had expected.

We were filming in a rainy South Wales in January 2021 (though including 'rainy' in that sentence is practically a tautology). The United Kingdom was basically shut down, but actors were, for some reason, allowed to work – as long as we were regularly tested and stayed in our bubbles. I guess this means we were on the front line. Nothing is more important than the continuation of independent films. Why weren't people banging pots on their doorsteps for actors?

Setting off from my Hertfordshire home, I found that the motorways were eerily quiet. I felt conspicuous and criminal, and was concerned that I would be stopped by the police and imprisoned for contravening lockdown. I had an 'official letter' (an easily forgeable print-out of an email) to show to the authorities in the event of my capture. This was (hopefully) the closest my generation would get to being in *The Great Escape*.

It's quite rare that I get acting work, and I was keen to make a good impression. I also have a pathological fear of being late, so I had set off early and arrived with over an hour to spare. I was tired from the journey – it was, after all, the first time in over a year that I had driven this kind of distance – and I was keen to get my first all-important Covid test over with and have some dinner.

The sat nav took me to a lorry loading bay with closed barriers. I was told over an intercom that I had come to the wrong entrance. Well, duh. The voice gave me directions, but they washed over me, and the minute I'd turned around, I was confused and lost. I pulled over to see if I could ring anyone, but every number I tried went straight to voicemail. I'd got an email saying that the Covid test was now happening at a different venue, and fed the new postcode into my sat nav.

It was getting dark and, as so often happens when you only have a postcode, my electronic guidance system (which I rely on, because for some reason I am unable to picture maps in my mind), led me to a desolate location where there were no buildings at all. I drove back and forth a few times before taking a punt on a sign for a tourist attraction, making my way up a long, winding driveway.

A couple of hundred metres along, there was a group of men in high-viz jackets. They seemed to know about the filming and waved me on. There was a car park round the corner and signs indicating a Covid facility, so I parked up, assuming, not unreasonably, that I had arrived at the testing site.

A scattering of people were heading towards the building, so I followed them and found myself in the large hall of a stately home. There were medical staff behind a desk, but they had not heard about the filming. I soon established that this was a vaccination centre, not a testing one. The staff said the only place that they knew of that was doing tests was the crematorium – which seemed a bit on the nose, but I guess that way they could deal with the severe Covid cases in one visit.

Why were all the details I'd been given wrong? Why couldn't I get through to anyone on the phone? Was this all an elaborate prank by Jeremy Beadle? Had he gone to the trouble of faking his own death thirteen years earlier to lull me into a false sense of security?

I was now officially late and getting fraught. Without thinking things through, I decided to try and find the crematorium. I got back into my car and drove past the men in high-viz jackets, not thinking to ask them for clarification, but instead hoping they didn't see me and question why I was leaving. As I got to the main road, I had to drive over one of those one-way spike devices that burst your tyres if you go over them in the wrong direction. I was going in the right direction, so it wasn't a problem.

I immediately got lost again. Panicking, I disconnected the logical part of my brain and started running on adrenaline-soaked instinct. I decided that the testing centre couldn't be at the crematorium or the stately home. My brain might have been screaming, *Then how come the high-viz jacket guys knew about the film?*, but I wasn't listening – or maybe I just assumed that they were all Jeremy Beadle wearing a false beard over his real beard so I wouldn't recognise him.

Like a headless chicken, I took the next right and ended up in a tiny lane that tapered down to a car's width and then hit a dead end. Never a fan of reversing long distances, I had to do a fifty-eight-point turn to get my large VW Sharan facing back in the right direction.

I drove back up the main road, trying to find an alternative venue, almost weeping with the stress of it all. I had burned up another half an hour and gone back and forth three or four times, looking for a turning that wasn't there, going back up the long driveway and then turning round because I couldn't face talking to the high-viz men and admitting that I was lost. Manly pride meant that I would be emasculated if I asked for help.

Finally, hungry, angry and bewildered, I had to admit that the high-viz men were my only hope. I went back up that driveway for the third time. Someone – maybe another lost and confused actor – had parked their car right by the gate, and I had to drive around it. In my heightened emotional state, I may have been driving faster and less accurately than I should have been.

Suddenly, I became aware of an unpleasant thudding and flapping sound. Was my car tilting? I'd had so much bad luck already that driving the wrong way over a one-way spike device would surely be too much to add to my plate. Even I couldn't pretend that the car wasn't noticeably listing as it bumped its way along the road. I'd clipped the edge of the spiky thing on my way round the parked car.

The men in the high-viz jackets were observing my progress with a mixture of concern and barely contained glee. As I wound down my window, one of them observed, 'I think you might have a flat tyre there, mate.'

'Yeah, I know,' I said, trying to make it sound as if this had been a choice rather than an error. They let me park up in an empty car park and said they'd keep an eye on the car. I told them I was lost, and they explained that I was meant to have taken a right up the hill before the vaccination centre car park, which would have brought me to the castle. It would have been nice if they'd said that the first time. Or if they had said it, it would have been nice if I had listened properly. Either way, it was their fault.

I took my suitcase and suit bag and laptop bag out of the boot and set out to walk to the castle. It couldn't be that far.

It was that far.

And then a bit further.

Once I'd rounded a bend, I could see the dimly lit castle in the distance. The road seemed to go on forever and get steeper with each step. As I got closer, I fancied I could take a shortcut across the grass. I stepped in unseen muddy puddles and water seeped into my shoes and socks. The gates on this side of the building were all locked, so I squelched my way back to the road. I was so far beyond the end of my tether that I considered lying down and dying right there, and it didn't seem like the worst option. I summoned up some residue of inner strength and pushed onwards. Finally, I rounded a corner and saw parked cars and human beings. I was where I was meant to be – and where I could have been a good ninety minutes earlier if only I'd asked for clearer instructions.

All my fear of being unpunctual had been for nothing, as the production was in enough chaos of its own. We were meant to be sleeping in a nearby student outdoor adventure centre, but the central heating had broken, so the crew were desperately trying to find a local hotel that could accommodate the thirty people in the cast and crew, while keeping us in our bubble. On top of this, Covid tests were taking forever, as each person had to wait for their result before the next one could be tested, which meant we were going through at a rate of one every thirty minutes. Exhausted and hungry and unpleasantly damp, I was fifth in the queue.

When I finally got to the front, my first ever Covid test was a trial by fire. The man giving the tests must have been new to it (we all were at this stage): he pushed the stick so far up my nostril that I'm surprised it didn't come out with a bit of brain on it. It was agony, but he insisted he was doing it right. He was wrong about that, but none of us would know it until someone else tested us.

Even once I'd run that gauntlet, I was not in the clear. After waiting for test results and the minibus, we were taken to the freezing student centre for dinner, which turned out to be a tin-foil container holding a weird dish made of cabbage and potato, with roast potatoes on the side. I don't *think* it was intended as a parody of Soviet-era cuisine. Why not have potatoes with potatoes? Potatoes are nice. I could have done with a third kind of potato instead of the cabbage. A group of cold and shell-shocked actors ate this lampoon meal under harsh strip lighting, unsure of where we'd be sleeping tonight, what the hell we'd got ourselves into, or if we were all in fact being Punk'd. One of us was still smarting with embarrassment over the fact that he'd driven the wrong way over a one-way spike. I am hardly a macho man, but I experienced the burning shame of making such an unmanly, unforced and basic error in driving. I was mortified, and the only good thing about it was that I was playing a deeply unhappy, inadequate and angry man in the film (I don't know why I only get parts like this), so I could use this festering self-hatred for my performance.

As much as I have tried to distance myself from clichéd notions of masculinity in my life, this whole incident was a perfect illustration of the almost unshakeable insecurities that come with being a 'man', from the reluctance to ask for directions, through the inability to control my emotions, to struggling up that hill in the dark, and right up to the lingering sensation that I had failed because of a minor driving error. All of this after choosing not to visit the GP despite having an exponentially expanding plum. I was a walking cliché – and with my car out of action, I would now have to walk everywhere.

I was so tired that I couldn't face travelling to a hotel and so decided that I would take my chances staying in the fridge-like conditions of the student centre. I could wash myself with water from the kettle. I was shown to my room and had the choice of four tiny bunks that a thousand schoolchildren had almost certainly wanked in. The extra blanket I had procured did little to keep out the cold, and the seemingly solid rain pelted against the roof and walls, while the harsh wind did its best impression of the howling souls of the millions of Welsh people who had perished in dreary conditions such as these, after feasting on cabbage and potato and more potato.

And there was no kettle.

I lay there, sadly feeling my balls (unlike every other occupant of this bed, not for my own sexual gratification – or not only for my own sexual gratification; I'm only human) and wondering what was wrong with them. At least there was a chance that my problems would be solved, as tonight I was likely to freeze those bad boys right off. It was possibly the most miserable time I would endure in the whole of 2021, and without wishing to give too many spoilers, that is quite an admission.

The next morning, after sleeping for maybe sixty disconnected minutes, I went down to look at the car in the cold light of day. It sat sad and alone in the muddy car park, its rear driver's side tyre sagging and empty. I didn't know it then, but this was a presage of the weeks ahead for me, where my own right-hand-side rear wheel would end up in a similarly deflated state.

A couple of days later, a Welsh man in a van came and replaced the tyre with a new one. This was less of a presage of what would happen to me, though I wouldn't have minded it. He was very efficient and he made my car as good as new. His solution wasn't to simply hack off one of my car's wheels, but I guess that's why mechanics are more sophisticated than surgeons.

ON THE BALL: Always mind your bollocks

'Bollocks' has always been my favourite testicular euphemism. When it comes to describing bollocks, bollocks is the dog's bollocks. But where did the word originate?

'Bollocks', meaning testicles, is first recorded in the thirteenth century as 'ballocks'. It derives from the old English *bealluc*, meaning ball. An early source for it is Wycliffe's Bible from way back in 1382, in which Leviticus 22:24 reads: 'Al beeste, that ... kitt and taken awey the ballokes is, ye shulen not offre to the Lord ...' (Or, in more modern English: 'Any beast that has been cut and the bollocks taken away, you shall not offer to the Lord.') So kids, it's OK to say bollocks – it's in the Bible.

In the late nineteenth century, 'bollocks' had come to mean 'nonsense', and because priests and religious folk were (however unfairly) perceived to waffle on about a load of palpable old bullshit, bollocks quickly became a synonym for the clergy, too. Weirdly, this association became a key argument during the obscenity trial directed against the Sex Pistols album *Never Mind the Bollocks*.

Professor James Kinsley, Head of English at the University of Nottingham, was called by the defence, and argued that 'bollocks' was not obscene because of its alternative definitions: clergyman or nonsense. The chairman of the hearing was forced to sum up:

Much as my colleagues and I wholeheartedly deplore the vulgar exploitation of the worst instincts of human nature for the purchases of commercial profits by both

you and your company, we must reluctantly find you not
guilty of each of the four charges.

Satisfyingly, in a study of UK swear words conducted
by the BBC in 2000, 'bollocks' was rated the eighth-most-
severe word, right between 'prick' in seventh place and
'arsehole' in ninth. Exactly where it belonged.

4

Teenage dirtbag

Even with the central heating fixed, the student centre was freezing. For the five nights I slept there, I pulled my thin blankets over my mutating body and spent sleepless hours nervously ball-fondling. Was it just my imagination or was my right bollock bigger than it was yesterday?

What if it kept growing? I could become more bollock than man. The bollock might take over and turn me into *its* bollock to see how I liked it.

I've always neglected the balls. Not only in checking them for lumps and bumps, but even in the more fun times. Why hammer away at the oversensitive buttons when you have a joystick that can really take a bashing?

Was this all revenge for taking my baby-batter-makers for granted? Finally, I had to pay some attention to my Jedwards.

I tried to push these concerns to the back of my mind and to concentrate on the job, but each night became more nightmarish. It wasn't only the appalling Welsh weather that was trying to permeate my four-bunked fortress of solitude. Like a demented Kate Bush, my rain-drenched bollock was banging at the windows in my brain, demanding my attention.

When I got home, I once again turned to Google. This time, however, everything I read seemed very insistent that, while it was probably nothing to worry about, I must immediately contact my GP.

Covid was hitting its post-Christmas peak, and I was reluctant to clog up the system for those in real need, but I knew I couldn't keep putting this off. If the ball got much bigger, it might explode and take out half the houses in the street, and I wasn't convinced my home insurance would cover that.

I presumed that I'd very much be at the back of the queue for appointments, so I was surprised, and not a little concerned, when they arranged to see me within thirty-six hours of my call.

They were taking this seriously. Too seriously. Like this could only mean one thing ...

I had a day and a half to ruminate about the worst-case scenario and wallow in the possibility that I might be checking out sooner than I had intended. I hugged my kids and told Catie that I wanted her to find love again once I was gone. It was play-acting. I knew that the chances of it being something really serious were slim. It was like going on a scary fairground ride. It looks like it might kill you, and when you're on it, you experience the sensation of fear, but you know that you're practically certain to walk away in one piece.

That said, the knowledge that it's still possible that something could go horribly wrong gives the pretence a little tinge of genuine danger. In a perverse way, there's an element of fun to it. The ever-present threat of death is, of course, what makes so much of life exhilarating. How dull things would be if we were immortal.

Once you reach your fifties, every visit to the doctor comes with the extra jeopardy that this might be the one where things get serious. It might still be years away, but it might be months away. Right now, it might be thirty-six hours away.

Unless you are taken suddenly and unexpectedly, that moment where the doctor pauses, all stern-faced, about to deliver your own personal bombshell, is coming to us all. You just kick the can down the road and hope it's not coming too soon.

I'd had scares in the past. About fifteen years before, a medical had thrown up the possibility that there was something wrong with my heartbeat. The medical staff looked ashen-faced and told me that the heart-monitor graph had a beat that went down when it should have gone up. They didn't need to tell me that this could be serious, as I was immediately sent to hospital for tests and to have my heart properly scanned.

Everything was fine. That's just the way my heart beats: to its own rhythm. My body likes to do things differently, whether it's pumping blood in an unusual way or failing to visualise thoughts or trying to grow a testicle that might one day make it as a prize-winning pumpkin.

A few years later, I had some test results that suggested I had a very mild thrombocytopenia and borderline splenomegaly, which would have been scary if it hadn't sounded like those were conditions made up by a four-year-old child. I went to hospital again and they extracted samples from my bone marrow. They found a very small population of cells compatible with hairy cell leukaemia (and surely the only way you can make leukaemia not sound like awful news is to put the words 'hairy cell' in front of it). While probably nothing to worry about, they wanted to keep an eye on me. I went in to see an oncologist annually for the next four or five years, but the blood tests always came back fine, and eventually he agreed that the thrombocytopenia had corrected itself (probably because it was a made-up condition). After I told him I'd run a half-marathon and set a personal best, he said I was clearly fit and there was no need for me to see him again.

So, I'd experienced that rug-being-pulled-from-under-the-feet sensation of thinking that my time might be nearly up, only to have the reassurance that it was a false alarm and life would go on. It's always a false alarm, kick the can down the road.

A big bollock isn't as scary as a heart defect or dubious cells in your marrow. While I had to consider my mortality again, it was from a position of near certainty that I'd be fine. I was able to indulge myself and almost enjoy the unfolding tragedy of an unlikely timeline where everything went wrong, like a sort of perverse *Schadenfreude* where an unfortunate potential version of myself was the target of my glee. Look at stupid possible future Richard Herring, crying over the fact that he won't see his kids grow up and that in five years his wife will be married to someone else, who will be the only dad his son remembers and who will drink all that nice whisky that dead old Richard Herring had been saving for a special occasion that never came. What an idiot!

It's human to project in this way: to imagine the worst possible outcome and slightly enjoy this personalised horror movie. I think most of us believe that envisioning the most nightmarish eventuality somehow prevents it from ever coming true. Every time I've got on a plane, I've stated that it's definitely going to crash, yet none of those planes have crashed, because fate hates to be predictable. No need to thank me, fellow passengers, I had your backs. I only feel sorry that nobody on all those planes that have crashed thought to take the same precaution.

I am also a comedian, and that meant an additional layer of mad thoughts. There was a part of me that was thrilled that something was wrong. In a way, wouldn't it be quite good if this turned out to be serious or even terminal? Imagine the Edinburgh Fringe show I'd get out of that! It might have to be performed by a hologram of me, but if the show sold out, then who cares?

This is the mindset of the professional comic: as long as something doesn't instantly kill you, every awful experience is material. I was already thinking of potential titles and ideas for jokes, and imagining the awards I'd win for my challenging show about my suicidal testicle. I might even get a book out of it. It would be amazing.

In idle moments, I've often thought of the jokes I might write if I lost a leg or was blinded. I have never been so committed to the material that I have decided it's worth purposefully maiming myself. I suppose it's a way to try and look on the bright side. I have been in the middle of terrible events – a fight, a humiliating sexual encounter, a mugging, a lot more humiliating sexual encounters, a plane seemingly on fire* – and every time, a voice in my head has been saying to me, *Think of the jokes we'll get out of this*. In a sense, it's part of what humour is about: finding the light side of tragedy; being able to laugh in the face of life's horrors. Even when we are powerless, it gives us the illusion of power.

I admit, though, that it is deeply weird to be slightly wishing for something awful to happen to you for the lols.

Come on, though, if there was something seriously wrong with my testicles, what a gift that would be! Balls are absolutely the funniest body part. In terms of generating laughter,

---

* I'd only imagined it crashing, not going up in flames, so fate got me on that one.

there couldn't be a better organ to go wrong. You try writing a joke about liver cancer – it's possible, but you'd need to really work at it. Your balls trying to kill you, though? That show would write itself!

It'd be just my luck if this whole thing turned out to be nothing. I might get a solitary routine out of a ball-based false alarm, but that would hardly be a consolation.

Sure, if it was serious, I could die, but at least my kids could read my five-star reviews and believe that their dead and half-forgotten dad had been a success.

You can think a lot of crazy shit in thirty-six hours, and I was relieved to get to the time of the appointment, so we could sort this all out one way or the other.

I hadn't been to the village GP's practice since 2019, and things were starkly different to how they'd been on my last visit. First, there was a brand-new young GP there, who I'd be seeing for the first time. Secondly, Covid restrictions made the usually mundane and respectable task of visiting a doctor feel underground and illicit.

The front door was locked. I buzzed the intercom and a voice told me that I needed to wait by a side door, and the doctor would let me in when he was ready. Shady!

As I stood in the drizzle, someone arrived to pick up their prescription from reception. This time, the front door opened far enough for a rubber-gloved hand to emerge, holding a small wooden tray. The patient put their money on it, then the door shut. Shortly after, the tray reappeared with the drugs (and the change), and the deal had gone down.

It was as if I was in a terrible student sketch that imagined what it would be like if practising medicine was illegal. However, as with so many situations in this weird year, it was soon going to turn into a poorly written sitcom.

After maybe ten minutes, the door opened, and I saw the youthful face of the new doctor for the first time. I was smiling behind my mask, but he looked confused.

'Who are you?' he asked.

Who was I? Had this man not watched TV in the 1990s? To be fair, my show was probably on after his bedtime (and most adults didn't watch it, either), but that's hardly the point.

'I'm Richard Herring,' I said.

'You can't be,' he insisted.

'I'm pretty sure I am.'

'I was expecting a sixteen-year-old,' he said, and I was a little put-out that he presumed I wasn't a teenager. Maybe one who lived a pretty high-octane life, but was it really beyond the realms of reality? We were not getting off to a great start.

We stood awkwardly for a moment, seemingly having reached an impasse. But then he decided to let me in anyway, even though I wasn't me.

In his room, he checked his computer. 'Ah, yes. Sorry. I had the wrong notes up.'

That was reassuring.

'I've had four people in with the same issue as you this week.'

'It's an epidemic!' I replied. 'No one will even remember Covid when everyone's hobbling around with giant testicles.'

'At least that can only affect fifty per cent of the population.'

'No, everyone! That's why it's so scary.'

He laughed. He was a little scatty and nervous, but in very good spirits for a man coping with Covid, along with four men in one village having larger than expected testes.

I told him that my ball had been feeling a bit big and hard for the last couple of weeks, and he asked me to take down my trousers and pants so he could examine me.

As his gloved hand met my clammy ballsack, it struck me that this was the quickest I've ever gone from meeting someone for the first time to them cupping my balls. (There had been a girl at university who had run him close, and she didn't put a dampener on things by asking weird questions. That said, I think she was sick out of a window soon after.)

'Have you had any pain?' he asked.

'Not at all.'

'Any blood in your urine or your semen?'

'Not that I've noticed ... I think I would have noticed.'

'Did your testicles descend properly when you were a kid?'

'As far as I know. How far were they meant to go?'

'Just into your scrotum.'

'Oh yeah, that's where they stopped. I was imagining them being like yo-yos.'

'Any history of cancer in your family?'

'No ...'

That was a bit of a concerning question. Was that what this was?

The doctor told me not to worry and to get dressed. He agreed that the ball did seem rather hard and enlarged, but quickly reassured me: 'The good news is, I don't think this is cancer.'

I let out an audible chuckle of relief and exhaled. I had been more worried than I'd realised.

'If I was a betting man,' he continued, 'I would say that this is epididymitis ... Now. I know you're going to be googling that when you get home.'

I was actually wondering which bookmakers would have taken such a weird bet. And what odds they'd have given.

'The epididymis is the coiled tube at the back of the testicle ...'

I knew this already. I didn't want to show off to the doctor, but I am the author of a seminal (pun-intended) book about male genitalia, *Talking Cock*,* and so I already knew the name and function of every part of male genitalia, and had in fact renamed it all to make it more accessible to the layman.† I scanned the shelves of the surgery to see if my book was among the other academic tomes, but couldn't spot it. He'd probably lent it to one of his other big-bollocked patients.

Meanwhile, he continued to inform me about epididymitis.

'... it can become infected by bacteria or get blocked and become inflamed. This can also affect the testicle in something that is called epididymo-orchitis ...'

'So, is it treatable?'

'Yes, it's nothing to worry about at all. Just to be sure, we have to send you into hospital for a scan. We don't mess around with things like this.'

I briefly wondered which illnesses GPs might consider messing around with: 'It's just piles – but let's tell them they've got two hours to live!'

'Someone will be in touch with you in the next couple of days,' the GP said.

I left the practice with a weight lifted. I was genuinely elated, and realised I had been even more scared about all this than I'd let myself believe. I was walking on air, breathing deeply and cherishing each delicious, life-giving breath, listening to birdsong, smiling and giving a cheery hello to the villagers I passed – even the lady who voted for UKIP and liked to mention it at every opportunity.

I was ALIVE.

My death sentence had been commuted. I might live to see

---

* Available wherever you get your eBooks.
† I called the epididymis 'the cat's cradle'. I've also tried to get the aperture at the end of the penis renamed 'the Herring's eye', though with limited success so far.

my kids grow up – and, more importantly, I should live to polish off all the whisky. As disappointed as I was about the loss of my heartbreaking and brave one-man show (and I was still quite disappointed), I was happy to not be dying. I had the scarcely believable revelation that my continued existence was more important to me than comedy.

This was a big turnaround for me.

I'd been given a second chance, and from now on was going to live every second to the full.

At least, just as soon as I'd got through the tricky level I was stuck on in the *Homescapes* game on my phone.

ON THE BALL: Testicular maladies

You've seen that my big ball was initially diagnosed as epididymitis. If you notice a change in the size of your testicles or have a lump or bump, don't worry too much – it might well not be cancer. That's not to say that the thing it might be is a walk in the park either, but here are some other possible causes of swelling and bumps.

Testicular torsion

All right, this one is pretty bad, and might end up with you losing a testicle, but it's still preferable to cancer. Testicular torsion is the delightful occurrence where one of your balls twists, and your spermatic cord then loops round itself too, potentially cutting off the blood flow to your knacker. Yes, it hurts just thinking about it, doesn't it, fellas? But it hurts more if it happens, and it's not something you're going to walk off. As long as you seek treatment straight away – and why wouldn't you? – doctors should be able to untwist all your tubes and get the blood flowing back to your love grape so that it doesn't wither on the vine and need to be plucked.

To be on the safe side, probably avoid twisting your testicle round and round so you can watch it spin back again.

This injury only happens to a minority of men, usually after vigorous exercise, though it's not really clear why. It might be due to them inheriting an easily rotating nut from their forebears. Why evolution thought a testicle that rotated more than usual might be an advantage, I don't know. Would a potential mate be impressed by someone with a ball that has the range of vision of an owl?

Cyst

A new bump on your bollock might sound like bad news, and if you find anything new in your self-examination, then do consult a doctor, but there's a chance it's just a cyst, otherwise known as a spermatocele – which sounds like a very unappetising kind of pasta. This is a little blob of fluid that develops in the epididymis. It probably won't hurt and it isn't cancerous, so it usually doesn't require treatment unless it's causing discomfort. Doctors aren't exactly sure what causes this to happen, though it's probably something to do with a blockage in your pipes. Maybe a really big sperm has got stuck in there, like that time Homer Simpson got lodged in a water slide.

Varicocele

This one is not particularly serious. It's basically an enlarged varicose vein in your ballsack. Pain or discomfort might follow, and if you've ever got any pain or discomfort in your genitals, then my advice is: go and see a doctor. Is that something that really needs stating? Given testicles are usually attached to men and men are fucking idiots about this stuff (as you've seen from my own story), then sadly, yes it is.

Hydrocele

This is the condition that caused the testicle of cockney wideboy and descendant of William the Conqueror, Danny Dyer, to inflate to the size of a baked potato. Dyer poetically described it thus: 'So, I've got the biggest bollock in the world and the smallest bollock in the world. And if it's a cold day, then my winkle looks like a little slug lying on an apple.'

A hydrocele (or as I believe it should be called, Danny Dyer Syndrome) happens when fluid collects in the thin sheath that surrounds the testicle. That's nature's fault for putting a thin sheath there. If you're a newborn baby, then don't worry: this is pretty common and usually sorts itself out, and thanks for choosing to read this book so early in your life. I would normally suggest that you have to be at least six months old to really get the sophisticated humour.

As Danny shows, adults can get this too, but if a little baby can shake it off, then so can you. Danny decided he needed surgery for his. He thinks he's all hard, but he's not as tough as a baby.

Polyorchidism

This one is super rare, with only around 200 cases having been reported. Polyorchidism is a condition where someone is born with more than two testicles. Sometimes the third one is in the scrotum, sometimes in the abdomen. It's not much of a problem in itself – in fact, congratulations on growing some extra balls – but it can increase the likelihood of testicular cancer. There are about ten recorded cases of babies born with four testicles. I've found one report on the internet of a baby with five. Can anyone beat that?

If you have extra balls (and sometimes people don't even notice that they do), then it almost certainly won't have any effect on your fertility, and the excess will only be removed if there is a danger of cancer. I'd say enjoy it. You just serve to make me feel even more inadequate with my lonely bollock. Share them about a bit, fellas. Stop being so greedy.

5

Unexpected item in the bagging area

Once again, I was to be amazed by the efficiency of the NHS at this, the absolute worst time possible to require their services. I had had my appointment at the GP on Tuesday, and even though the scan was a 'belt and braces' double check, the hospital rang me on Wednesday and booked me in for that Friday.

I felt even more guilty wasting the time of these hard-worked professionals now that I knew my problem was almost certainly a blockage of the testicle tubes. So certain was this diagnosis that Ladbrokes had stopped taking bets on it and actually paid out in advance to anyone who'd got their money down early enough.

This was all such a formality that I was treating it as if the doctor had decided my balls were so amazing that their inner workings had to be recorded and preserved for posterity, like my scrotum was one of those carbonized scrolls discovered in the volcanic detritus at the library in ancient Herculaneum, and future generations would one day marvel at its awesome hidden contents.

My only concern on arriving at the hospital that morning was that at the height of Covid's current spread, this was probably the most dangerous place I could be. Immediately after I'd been given a second shot at life, I was walking into a potential plague pit. Would confirmation of my healthiness indirectly lead to my death? Oh, the delicious irony.

As it turned out, the hospital didn't seem too busy. Everyone was wearing masks and I guessed that they kept all the Covid zombies in a special locked-down wing. But what if one of them escaped? There could be a pandemic.

I arrived at the reception desk in the scanning department, where I was asked for my date of birth and my address before being directed to another reception desk, where I was once again asked for my date of birth and my address. And then a member of staff came out of the scanning room, called my name, and asked me to confirm my date of birth and my address. I've got into Buckingham Palace with fewer security checks than this.* I can only presume that there's a lot of strange men out there trying to surreptitiously sneak into this department to get their balls scanned. Who wouldn't want a load of sticky jelly smeared on their scrotum before having what looks like a supermarket scanner rubbed over it repeatedly? You could probably get this treatment without going to hospital if you just head to your local Sainsbury's, where one of the staff will surely oblige. Don't waste the NHS's time with this, you perverts.

I was most apologetic to the quiet lady who was about to do the scan. I explained that I knew that I had epididymitis and I was sorry for wasting her time. She didn't seem to

---

* I genuinely have, but that's a story for another time.

mind, and simply wanted to get on with the job in hand, so to speak.

Thus, for the second time in a week, I broke my personal best time for a ball-fondling from a stranger. There was no small talk this time, and she didn't mistake me for a teenager – we were straight down to business.

There was a little palaver to go through before she started, which made the whole experience rather coy and sweet. Even though this lady was about to smear my testicles with gel and then scan them from every conceivable angle, she asked me to put on a gown, then take down my trousers. I was then to lie on her couch and put a paper towel over myself and lift my penis away from my meat pom-poms and over my tummy. Sure, my plums and arse were on open display, but at least nobody saw my penis, so I maintained my dignity.

What I particularly enjoyed was the colleague who sat in the corner, watching. I am not turned on by someone scanning my balls, but someone silently observing someone else scanning my balls? That's my jam.

The scan was incredibly thorough, literally leaving no stone unturned. I guess if you do this job, then you become a connoisseur of the cojones, and when you get a perfect set of globes, you really want to admire the craftsmanship. It was taking quite a lot longer than I'd imagined it would, but I was so confident that I was only here for confirmation that I lay back and thought about my plans for the rest of the day.

'There is something there,' she finally commented.

'Yeah, epididymitis, right?'

'Possibly, but there is something else, too.' She called it an anomaly, which made me think of *Star Trek*.*

---

* I know that's the second mention of *Star Trek*. I just think they should make an episode of *Star Trek* involving my bollocks. Does that make me a bad person?

This was such an unexpected twist that I didn't really take in what happened next. I'd been so sure of what was going to happen that I wasn't really able to grasp that it had all gone down differently. I don't remember what she said next. Gravity might as well have stopped working at that point; everything started floating away. She was mouthing something at me, but all the oxygen was sucked out of the room and I couldn't hear a word in the vacuum that had been created.

She must have given me some paper towels to clean off the gel. I must have put my trousers back on (I mean, I definitely did, but I don't remember it), and I must have thanked her and her friend who liked to watch. This was a result for the voyeur. I guess it's like a Grand Prix: although the spectators say they like the sport, they're really hoping there will be a crash.

I don't remember leaving the hospital or getting back to my car. I was trying to process what had happened. Was this serious? Probably not, right? I was only going to have to go back in for more tests, and maybe they'd have to give me medicine to treat whatever it had turned out to be. Maybe I'd misunderstood what she'd said. She spoke very quietly, more like a mumble. She'd probably just complimented me on my awesome sperm-satchel.

I felt numb and disorientated, as if I'd just that second woken from a bad dream. Of course, it probably was all just a dream. I'd wake up in a minute and then go for my appointment and get the all-clear. Phew!

I had parked my car by a low wall next to one of the ramps, and as I tried to back out of the space, I misjudged the distance and metal scraped against concrete. I am not in the habit of damaging my car every couple of weeks, but it's clear I don't drive well in heightened emotional states. I knew I needed a minute, so I drove back into the space and rang Catie.

I think I told her about the damage to the car before mentioning the potential damage to myself. That morning, when she'd said she wanted to come along, I'd said there was no need; the scan was just a formality, because I already knew what was wrong with me. Now I was telling her that there was something in my scrotum that shouldn't be in there, and I was so shaken up I'd lost the ability to drive. She must have worried if she'd ever see me again.

I didn't really have anything concrete to tell her. I could only say the word anomaly a bit too much and reiterate the fact that the GP had told me that he was certain it wasn't cancer. Or was he just pretty sure? He'd have bet it wasn't, if he was a betting man. But by saying that, he had implied that he *wasn't* a betting man. So, does that mean he *wouldn't* bet on it . . . ? Maybe I was focusing on the wrong thing.

I think at this stage I was in enough denial to believe that it was all going to work out fine. Sure, the supermarket scanner had found an unexpected item in the bagging area, but that happened all the time at supermarkets. You simply called someone over and they pressed the reset button and it was fine.

I managed to drive home without hitting anything else or bursting a single tyre. I was taking the news pretty well.

ON THE BALL: Mythological balls

Testicles and semen crop up an awful lot in most of the world's mythology, particularly in creation myths, and this has heavily influenced our attitudes towards our sweet-and-sour pork balls. Many ancient civilisations believed that some, if not all, of creation emerged from godly bollocks.

Iraq and roll

The Sumerian god Enki was one of many deities who used the contents of their ballbag for the purposes of creation, basically wanking rivers into existence, as detailed in this holy text: 'Father Enki had lifted his eyes across the Euphrates, he stood up full of lust like a rampant bull, lifted his penis, ejaculated and filled the Tigris with flowing water.'*

A bit more fun than 'Let there be light!' I don't think I will be drinking from the Euphrates any time soon, though, and I used to drink from it all the time.

Fructify me

In her excellent book *God: An Anatomy*, Francesca Stavrakopoulou points out that the God of the Bible (Yahweh) has a sexual encounter with the earthly realm, taking the land of Israel as his wife before he, as she puts it, 'excites the cosmos into an aroused, mutually reproductive fecundity as he impregnates his bride at a place called Jezreel (He seeds)'.

She quotes the following poem from the book of Hosea, pointing out that the word 'know' is a euphemism for you-know-what:

I will take you for my wife in faithfulness,
And you will 'know' Yahweh.
On that day, I will fructify – says Yahweh
'I will fructify the heavens,

* Sumerian hymn 'Enki and the World Order' (Black et al 220–1)

And they will fructify the earth;
And the earth will fructify the grain, the wine,
and the oil,
And they will fructify Jezreel;
And I will seed her for myself in the land.

Who doesn't love fructifying? It's even better than begetting.

Aphrodite rising – ew, what's that in her hair?

In Classical mythology, the titan Uranus is castrated, and his testicles cast into the sea. When you're called Uranus, being left with just your anus is a bit of an open goal. In every sense. The balls land in the waves, creating a white foam from which Aphrodite rises. Presumably with slightly stingy stuck-together eyes.

Uranus' gonads must still be underwater somewhere. I wonder if they will ever make an attempt to raise these titanic bollocks.

Homer gets sexual

According to the *Iliad*, Erechtheus, the serpent-bodied first king of Athens, was allegedly born from the earth after Athena wiped the seed of Hephaestus (the Greek god of, among other things, blacksmiths and volcanos) from her thigh and threw it to the ground. Like the myth that you can get pregnant from a toilet seat, it's also a myth that you can create serpent-bodied kings by chucking the spunk of a blacksmith on the floor.

The Great Dane's bollocks

In Norse mythology, the giantess Skadi sought to avenge her father, who the Æsir (Norse gods) had slain. She was convinced to put down her arms, but only if the gods met certain conditions, one of which was to make her laugh. The trickster Loki stepped up and tied one end of a rope to his testicles, then tied the other end to a goat before playing tug of war. Neither won, but it made Skadi laugh. They don't show that side of him in the *Avengers* movies, but I would pay good money to watch a goat trying to pull Tom Hiddleston's balls off.

6

The C-word

By the time I was home, I had convinced myself the doctor would soon ring to tell me he'd spotted the error in the scan and confirm that his confident initial diagnosis had been right after all. Just because he didn't have a machine that magically allowed him to see inside my bollock didn't mean he was wrong.

The schools were, of course, closed, so Catie and I were looking after my daughter Phoebe, days away from her sixth birthday, and my rambunctious three-year-old son Ernie. We were playing together in the living room, all laughing and having fun, just like a family in a film immediately before something life-changingly awful happens.

My mobile rang. It was the GP.

I went out into the hallway to answer it.

It'd all been jokes and laughter the last time we'd spoken, but now his voice seemed quiet and solemn and ever so slightly shaky.

'So you'll remember you came into my surgery complaining of an enlarged testicle . . . ' he began, somewhat needlessly.

'I vaguely recall,' I confirmed, trying to keep it light.

'I thought it might be epididymitis, but we sent you in for a scan at the hospital just in case.'

It was like we were on *The X-Factor* and we were recapping for the audience, stringing this out for maximum drama. I wondered if he'd have the chutzpah to pull the old Simon Cowell double bluff: 'I'm sorry to have to tell you ... that you do NOT have cancer! The technician had a thumb over the scanner lens – you're fine.'

If so, the doctor was really committing to the part. He seemed more nervous than me.

He said, 'Now, I've had the results and I think they told you this, but there is something there that shouldn't be there.'

'Yes.'

'We can't tell what that is from the scan, but ... oh gosh, it's pretty big.' He'd surprised himself there. 'Six centimetres long.'

'Sixteen centimetres!' I exclaimed.

'No, no. Six,' he repeated.

'Oh. That's not so big, then.'

'Six centimetres is pretty big.'

'Not as big as sixteen.'

Thinking about it, was my testicle even six centimetres long? Was there something bigger than my testicle inside my testicle? Was my testicle a TARDIS, sending my sperm backwards and forwards in time? Was he about to tell me that I was my own grandfather and had damaged the space-time continuum?

Probably not. He'd want to see me in person to break news like that.

He went on. 'There's lots of things it might be, but you must be aware of what it could be ...?'

He wouldn't even say the word. Three days ago, he'd been

laying down imaginary bets with fantasy diagnostic bookies on it not being cancer, and now he couldn't even say the word 'cancer'. I actually thought there was a danger he might cry. There was a long, empty silence, so I filled it.

'Cancer?' I suggested.

'Yes ... What happens now is I'll be handing you over to the hospital. They will do you a full-body scan and then probably take a biopsy so they can determine what the mass is. And it might not be ...'

'Cancer?' I offered again.

'Yes.'

'But if it is ...?'

I set him up so he could finish the sentence this time, but he didn't. Are they not allowed to say it unless you definitely have it?

So, I said it for him: 'And if it is cancer?'

'My colleagues will be in touch with all the details. If you have any questions or concerns, or there are any developments – if anything else happens – please do ring me.'

I was close to being the one to comfort him rather than the other way round. I was holding it together pretty well. Maybe this was the first time he'd had to do this, or maybe he was feeling bad because he'd told me he didn't think it was cancer, and now it looked like it might be.

He didn't need to feel bad, though: given the evidence in front of him, he'd made exactly the right call – I was a fifty-three-year-old man (testicular cancer typically affects younger men), with no history of cancer in my family, no other symptoms, no childhood testicular trauma (I hadn't told him about Barbados; it didn't even cross my mind for a few more weeks), no lumps or bumps – and, on top of that, the hospitals were overflowing with people suffering from Covid. Another GP might have been tempted to just bung me the medicine he thought I needed and get on with his overworked day. Despite all this, he'd still insisted I go in for that scan. I am immensely grateful to him and to everyone who treated me over the coming months. It can't be said enough: the NHS are super-stars. I am going to praise them a lot in this book, so if you hate the NHS, you should probably stop reading now – and also go to the mirror, look at yourself and shout: 'What the fuck is wrong with you?'

The thing is, if he hadn't sounded so worried, then I think I might have carried on living in denial. It wasn't *what* he said that was freaky to me, but the way he said it. The gravity of the situation finally hit me.

I can tell you one thing: I wasn't now thinking, *Oh great, looks like I can do that stand-up show after all.*

I was winded.

I sat down on a dining-room chair to let it all sink in. In the next room, Ernie was squealing with delight. I listened to those peals of laughter and was instantaneously over-whelmed. I wasn't now playing at imagining what would happen if I died; death was no longer an abstract concept, but suddenly all too real. I might have cancer. I might actually die. That little laughing boy might grow up without a dad, and might not even remember a single thing about me.

Just over a year before, I'd lost my great friend, Tony, to cancer. He was one year older than me and, like me, had left it late to have a family. He also had a young son. It seemed certain in that moment that the same fate awaited me.

I started crying like I'd never really cried before. Utterly spontaneously, with no effort on my part, water began cascading from my face. I am not sure if I even made a sound, but my soul was a damp rag and someone had grabbed it and wrung it out. I had no control over it. I was lost in it, and I wasn't sure it would ever stop.

I was sad for Phoebe and Ernie: how would it be for them to grow up without a dad? For Catie: being a parent is a struggle with two of us, how would she get through the next decade and a half alone (to begin with)? I was sad for Tony and my other friends who'd bravely stood up to cancer, but been taken by it far too young. I was sad for Tony's boy. But mainly, I quickly realised, these hot tears were for me. I didn't want to die.

I really didn't want to die.

After obsessing and worrying about death for my whole life, I had somehow still believed that it was something that wouldn't happen to me. Not soon, anyway, and probably not ever. I was crying now because, for the first time, death was palpable. That infinitely long expanse of absolutely nothing was going to engulf me. I had cancer, and having cancer means you're dying.

Plus, I was angry that after all the work and effort I'd put in with my kids – all the sleepless nights, the dirty bottoms, the piss in my face, the vomit over my clothes, the relentless never-ending zombie-like state of the last three years – Ernie would have no memory of me. It was maybe even worse that Phoebe would only vaguely recall me. I'd be that man that she'd been reluctant to hug, for whom she'd mainly had disdain – she'd probably only remember me for doing smelly farts. I'd be guilty as charged, but if she'd had more time, she would have known I was more than that. Not much more, but it would be something.

I even started wondering if it would be better for everyone if I died as quickly as possible. Better for the kids if they had no memory of me at all – then maybe it wouldn't hurt so much, wouldn't impact on their psyches in the same way.

Then I cried more, because I realised how pathetic and self-pitying I was being.

Catie would move on – of course she would – to some

chancer with a moustache and cowboy boots, with my delicious fifteen-year-old single malt on his breath. My kids would call him Dad. Take his last name . . .

I hadn't quite realised it, but it wasn't only my ball that was a huge, inflated bubble. The stress of the previous few weeks had built up and built up, and now it had been pricked by unexpected reality – and it just poured out of me.

I cried for myself and only myself until the tears dried up on their own. It would be the only major wobble I would have during this whole experience.

I went through the seven stages of grief as quickly as a character in a zany American comedy film. Before my tears had even dried, I was trying to work out what I could do with my remaining time on this planet to ensure financial security for those I was leaving behind. I was working out which passwords and instructions I needed to pass on to Catie. She had no idea how to do the bins. I was determined that my dishwasher-loading skills must not die with me. Hopefully, she'd have time to learn.

Catie came out of the living room to see how the call had gone. I was shaky, but back in control, and I am not sure she even realised I'd been crying. I told her about the lump, about the doctor's quivering voice, the fact he couldn't even say the word.

'Which word?' she asked.

'Which word do you think?'

'The C-word?'

'I don't think it would be appropriate for him to say the C-word,' I joked.

'I meant cancer.'

'I know. You'd think cancer would be the unsayable word out of the two, wouldn't you? Given how great the other C-word is, and how fucking awful cancer is.'

'Cancer is definitely a C-word ... Is it definitely cancer, though?'

'No, they don't know what it is.'

'So, there we go. We don't know. It might be nothing.'

I know that all of this was much harder for Catie than me. In our relationship, I am the painfully optimistic one and she is the voice of doom. You need one of each in a relationship to keep it anchored yet hopeful. She must have been going through the same emotions as me and the same fears about the future, but she couldn't let it crush her, nor could she cry out her frustrations and anger. She had to go against all her instincts and look on the bright side.

'If I do die ...' I said to her.

'You're not going to die.'

'But if I do die, will you promise me one thing ...'

'I'm not entertaining the thought.'

'Please, it's important.'

'What?'

'Will you please pour all my whisky down the sink?'

'Your posh whisky?'

'Yes.'

'Why?'

'Don't ask me why. Just do it, OK? If you love me, promise me you'll do it.'

'No ... I like whisky, too. Stop being such a C-word.'

ON THE BALL: Classical balls

Throughout history, great minds have been trying to make sense of what testicles do, and why they are so horrifically ugly. It's incredible how much of the nonsense these great minds came up with has managed to permeate into the testicular attitudes of the present day.

Ancient Greek thinkers recognised that testicles played a part in reproduction and puberty, but disagreed on exactly how.

Right ball for boys, left ball for girls

In the fifth century BCE, the philosopher Anaxagoras proposed that 'male seed' came from the right testicle, and 'female seed' came from the left. Right testicle sperm would then attach to the right side of the womb, while the lefty female sperm would go to the left of the womb. Given that it takes kids several years to learn their left from their right, it seems a bit unlikely that sperm (who don't even have hands, let alone wristwatches to help them remember) would be able to navigate this journey quite so effectively.

This theory persisted well into the medieval period and beyond. As late as 1891, Mrs Ida Ellis, in her *Essentials of Conception*, stated: 'It is the male who can progenate a male or a female child at will, by putting an elastic band round the testicle not required.'

One would think that in all that time, there would have been enough evidence to show that each testicle didn't produce a different flavour of sperm, but sometimes simple ideas can transcend experience and logic.

Baked beans

Pythagoras might have crushed it when it came to inventing theorems about triangles, but he wasn't so hot when it came to sexual matters. He was said to have forbidden his followers from eating beans because he believed they were made of the same matter as human souls. The 'proof' of this included these indisputable observations:

- If you mash fava beans and leave them in the sun, they begin to smell like semen. (This conjures up an image of Pythagoras standing with sun-baked fava beans in one hand and his own musky spunk in the other, sniffing each hand and looking quite satisfied with himself, like Gareth Hunt in a coffee commercial.)
- When planted and dug up several days later, beans resemble a womb, with a child's head growing inside. (They don't.)
- Beans cause flatulence, which Pythagoreans believed was a loss of part of the soul. This is the only sensible thing he said on the whole subject.
- Beans look like, and therefore are, a form of human testicle.

Yeah, mate, and women's muffs look like triangles, but you try telling them that the square on the hypotenuse is equal to the sum of the squares on the other two sides and see if you get a second date.

The Aristotle throttle

According to Aristotle, the reason why men feel weak and even exhausted after sex is that the semen they have lost contains *dynamis*: essentially a masculine energetic substance thought to give men vigour and vitality. Aristotle believed this seed was a product of digestion and blood, and also thought that testicles were weighted and linked to the vocal cords. When they descended, the voice deepened as the cords were literally pulled taut. This is a bizarre conclusion, because in my experience, if you ever pull on someone's testicles, their voice actually goes much higher.

Heated underpants

The Roman medical writer Galen not only received the ultimate accolade that all doctors are hoping for by having a character in *Planet of the Apes* named after him – in fact, he got two – he also established that testicles produce semen, and, along with the ovaries, are responsible for hormonal changes that cause sexual differences in humans.

He wasn't 100 per cent on the money, though. Observing the effects of castration on prepubescent men and animals, he theorised that castrated men lose their virility and hair because they are cooling down, which must mean that testicles were a source of bodily heat.

Maybe this was a way for him to get everyone gathering round his ancient Greek knackers, trying to warm their hands on them and then see what that led to. You cheeky monkey, Galen.

7

Snow balls

I had Schrödinger's testicle (and he wasn't happy about it). There was no way of knowing if my ball was cancerous or benign. For now, it was both.

I was in a weird stasis between life and death.

My career plan had always been to overcome my long-term comedic mediocrity by outliving all my peers and then rewriting comedy history with myself at the centre of it all. I couldn't have that if I was going to peg it in my fifties.

I didn't really care that much about my status any more (it had been very important to me when I was young and before I had a family), but I had always hoped to work until I died at a ripe old age. The comedians I most admire are Michael Palin, who has mastered so many different aspects of writing and performing, and who keeps trying new things (turning out to be brilliant at all of them), and Barry Cryer, who had worked on nearly all of the greatest comedy shows of the last sixty years and loved and embraced each new generation of comedians, never losing interest in the art of making people laugh. Barry loved laughter and seemed to have no ego; he also appeared to be indestructible. He enjoyed a drink and a smoke, and was not the kind of man who would waste his time in a gym – and yet he seemed to outlive everyone. I had always joked that I thought he'd be speaking at all of our funerals. And now ... well, maybe he would get to have a word at mine. Of course he would, the immortal, fabulous old prick.

My family was my main concern, of course. I wanted to act normally with them, mainly so as not to scare the kids if it turned out to be nothing (these things filter through, though, and my daughter had already asked 'Is Daddy going to die?') but also to fill these days with precious and unforgettable memories, just in case this was my last ever January. Yet these weren't normal times, so I couldn't whisk them off to Disneyland or even to Little Rascals soft-play in Hitchin, because we weren't allowed to go anywhere.

It's hard to make happy memories when you are incarcerated. My kids would remember me as their gaoler (or maybe their prisoner). I feared that Phoebe's only fleeting future thoughts of me would be as an incompetent and furious home-schooler. To be fair, the idea of death snatching me away from that nightmare wasn't entirely unwelcome.

Home-schooling, even during the first lockdown, where Phoebe was still too young to be set anything that could be classified as work, was tough. One afternoon, she'd really wanted to play on her iPad, but I told her she needed to do something educational. She wasn't having it. I said that she could have her device, but first she had to do one thing vaguely school-related. It could be anything, solely so I could pretend we'd both done our best. She could draw a picture.

Even though this was hardly the most demanding of projects, she was still seething with resentment about having to earn her fix of *Minecraft*. I secretly thought *Minecraft* was educational enough, but I wasn't allowed to say that.

'Fine!' she stropped. She stormed to her desk and knocked off a picture with angry determination and phenomenal speed, then stomped over to me and thrust it in my face. 'There you go!' she snarled. 'That's you falling into some lava.' She added, perhaps unnecessarily, 'Because I don't like you.'

'Yeah, I got that.' I laughed.

Before I could fully take in her masterpiece, she was struck with further inspiration. She snatched the paper back, took it to the desk and, with a single furious flash of her felt-tip, added one more detail. She brought it back and threw it at me, announcing: 'That's a crocodile that's going to eat you.'

Lava had not been punishment enough. I had to be chewed up by sharp teeth first and then, presumably, the crocodile would dissolve in the molten rock, and my half-digested but still sentient corpse would burn.

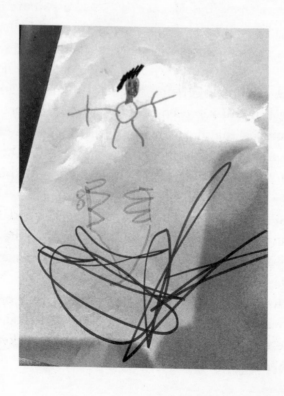

I completely loved it, of course. It was a triumphant piece of incandescent satire: a just punishment for my incompetence, and also, perhaps, on a wider scale, two fingers to the whole Covid web that we were mutually trapped in.

As a parent, I know I should discourage stuff like this, but as a comedian, I am burning with a pride hotter than lava that my daughter is so funny. Also, I thought the picture was an excellent piece of art. The way she had captured both the lava and the crocodile (with such economy) was genuinely impressive.

Look at that crocodile.

It's the least amount of effort required to make a crocodile, but also a brilliant representation of a crocodile: one that is mildly annoyed that not only does it live in lava, but it also has to eat stupid daddies. It's rolling its eyes. Even though it's also burning in lava. 'Oh, and now I have to eat this prick, too, do I?'

I posted it on Twitter and the reviews were good. @ajogle said: 'As an art teacher, I can tell you she's captured the essence of both crocodile and lava. This is superb expression, and what Picasso was searching for all his life.'

I tried to work out if being eaten by a crocodile or falling into lava was the better death. It was a question good enough to ask the guests on my podcast. It proved a tricky one to answer. What do you think?

If future historians need a story that completely encapsulates family life during lockdown, I think it might be that one.

Now, though, in this second phase of home-schooling, assignments went up a gear and became properly challenging. I had perhaps found my intellectual level. I couldn't even work out how to use the sprawling website from which we were downloading the class material. Work was set in one area, but the resources were somewhere else, about five clicks away, and then you had to upload the completed stuff to a third location.

The first assignment involved Cuisenaire rods, and I was told we needed to print something out. Not only did I not know what Cuisenaire rods were – and there was no attempt at an explanation – I couldn't see anything that classified as a print-out.

Not that any of this really mattered, as Phoebe was not in the mood to do anything. I moved on from maths to English, where the class had been learning an Aborigine legend about a frog full of water. All Phoebe had to do was come up with five questions she'd like to ask the overly hydrated frog.

'I can't do it,' she protested.

'Of course you can,' I countered, unsympathetically. I told her the questions could be anything she wanted, like 'What's it like being a frog?' or 'What's the deal with all this water?'

Phoebe rejected my questions, instead electing to make another picture of me falling into lava, but this time using a *Minecraft*-style programme on the computer. Again, I was impressed by her progress and only mildly hurt that she seemed so insistent on my fiery murder.

Could I hand this in in lieu of the frog questions? Probably not, as I wasn't able to work out how to hand anything in.

She told me that I was a terrible teacher, and I started to lose patience and get annoyed. I told her she only had to write five questions, and then we could move on and have some fun. Was it really this hard?

It reminded me of my dad trying to teach me to drive when I was seventeen. I got frustrated with him when he gave me any kind of instruction, even though I had no idea how to drive. Then he got cross with me for being so obstinate and ungrateful. Then I got cross with him because I'd been in the car for two minutes and still had no idea how to make the thing go. I gave up on learning how to drive and didn't try again until I was twenty-six.* I didn't even consider how I had robbed my dad of a beautiful moment where he helped his boy become a man. Unfairly, of all the many things he did for me and the many things he forgave me for, it was this incident that jumped to mind.

Would Phoebe have such ungenerous memories of me? Would her only regret be that I died completely unsinged by molten rock?

Finally, she came up with five questions for a frog, which I am sure will come in very useful in future life if she ever meets an amphibian at a party and can't think of a conversation-starter. Though I thought we'd be going for four hours, this whole 'lesson' had only taken thirty-five minutes (an impressive seven minutes a question). It took me the rest of the hour to fail to load the stuff up to the website. In the end, I took photos of the five separate pages, but the site only allowed one upload per assignment, so I had to ask Catie for the teacher's email address and send them that way. I was seconds away from smashing my laptop with a hammer.

Phoebe said I was the baddest dad in the world (and not in the positive Michael Jackson sense, though maybe anything

* Turned out to be a disaster for my social and dating lives, but it did mean that I got to create a mildly popular comedy character based on my driving instructor, so swings and mini-roundabouts.

associated with Michael Jackson can no longer be classified as positive). We had a little break and played *Homescapes* together (the one thing that united us) and then it was time for the thirty-minute Zoom lesson with the whole class. Suddenly, Phoebe was attentive and keen, and the teacher did an amazing job of shepherding and involving a dozen or so kids. They all did their tasks with huge enthusiasm, and no one was wished into a volcano.

I was left in silent awe. It's not only the NHS staff who proved they were worth their weight in gold during lockdown.

Just when it looked like all my kids' memories of me would be negative, I was presented with a gift from heaven. One morning, out of nowhere (or more technically, out of the sky) it began to snow.

It was falling fast and settling, and within the hour the village was covered in more than an inch of crisp, white magic.

It was a SNOW DAY. A day made for memories. I remember all my childhood snow days. If we could have an amazing time today, then the kids would not forget me.

Our mandated after-lunch walk was full of snowballs and snow angels and crunching untrod swathes of whiteness beneath our wellington boots. My daughter said she wished there could be snow every day, but I argued it wouldn't be so special then and she'd miss the sun. She conceded that we should have six months of sun followed by six months of snow.

She was still wrong, the ridiculous tiny idiot.

I blame the teachers . . . Shit, that's us.

The good thing about snow (in our weird climate) is that it arrives quickly and disappears quickly, and the window where it is soft and unslushy and fun is tiny.

'I suppose you'd like it to be Christmas every day too, would you?' I said.

'Of course!'

'Can't you see how terrible that would be? Also, the shops would never be open. How would we eat? Santa would never get a moment's rest.'

While the kids cavorted around, my heart was filled with sadness and I was briefly nauseous. I couldn't enjoy any of it, so full of poignancy was every interaction, so aware was I of the possible significance of it all. Catie made a video of the kids throwing snowballs at me, and I made a show of laughing, but watching it back, I can see in my eyes how conflicted I was. The need for this to be perfect and memorable clashed with the realisation that it might well only be a memory in other people's heads, and that the video being filmed might be watched over the years by a family growing older and more detached from me. I was too keen to please, overdoing it, like Bill Murray in the snow as he tries and fails to recreate the perfect evening with Andie MacDowell in *Groundhog Day*.

The transitory pleasure was already in danger of fading. The slush came even quicker than I'd anticipated. All through the walk, I'd been rallying the troops by telling them we could build a snowman in the garden when we got home, but now I feared we'd left it too late – we could already see the tips of the blades of grass on our small lawn, which had been covered in crisp and even snow when we'd left.

We got to work fast, rolling an icy snowball across the lawn. I hadn't cleared the cat shit off the grass for a little while, and found that I was picking some of it up as I went. This was pretty gross, but I managed to find some snow without excrement on it and quickly hid the poo away inside the ball. Then, in the kind of genius move my family would miss if I were gone, I rolled the snowman on to the flower bed, so that when it melted away, the cat poo would be safely disposed of in the soil. You don't see that in the Raymond Briggs cartoon.

It even – sort of – gave the snowman a digestive system. If they're so keen to come to life, then they have to take on everything, including the shitting bit. Even if he was shitting cat shit, it would still bring him one step closer to his longed-for consciousness and animation.

Sadly, at the last minute, I tried to use the snowman to clear up a patch of dog diarrhoea too. Annoyingly, it didn't stick in the same way as the solid little cat turds, and instead smeared across the lawn and down the back of the unfortunate snow-man, making it look like it was he, not my dog, that had had a terrible accident.

Phoebe, ever the individualist, had not wanted anything to do with my snowman full of shit, even before it became a health and safety nightmare. She was making her own. Hers was much smaller and already suffering from meltage, and when she tried to stick a carrot in its face, the snowman's head fell apart (again, not something that Raymond Briggs covered – I wonder if he'd ever actually made a snowman in his life). This meant the fun day of memories in the snow ended in floods of horrified tears.

I wasn't leaving behind memories of the beautiful last moments of magic and wonder that I'd hoped for, only the faint reminiscence of trauma as snowmen's faces caved in (and then got stamped to death in frustration – again, Briggs, no mention?), while a strange, vaguely familiar man rolled cat shit around the garden and seemed pleased with himself about it. Was this my legacy?

I suddenly realised that, although so many of my childhood memories involved snow, they also all involved tears and pain: lying in my garden being pelted in the face with icy snowballs from two feet away by some kids I'd met in the street; walk-ing over the Mendips in six-foot snowdrifts, getting a bit lost, becoming frozen to the bone and having to get in the bath as soon as we got home to avoid hypothermia; sledging on plastic fertiliser bags with my sister and following her down the slope too closely, spinning round and then crashing into her at pace; or attempting to make a realistic-looking igloo that collapsed on top of me, nearly suffocating me.

I had been so desperate for the kids to remember me well, but everything had backfired more spectacularly than my dog. Why had I thought that today would be my chance to make happy memories? They would only remember me through tear-filled eyes and nostrils full of the smell of unsettled animal bowels. Unless they'd inherited my aphantasia, in which case they wouldn't remember me at all.

ON THE BALL: A real kick in the balls

As things are getting very mildly poignant and serious at this point – I know the snowman bit was humorous, but it was bittersweet, right? – I thought I should remind you that balls are FUNNY! They look ridiculous, they swing around in a stupid way and they are so laughable that a story of a man losing one to cancer is essentially a COMEDY! Hooray!

Perhaps the ultimate mystery about testicles is why is it considered so hilarious when they get smashed into by a football, cricket ball, frisbee or toddler? What's so funny about watching someone get whacked in the bollocks? If you saw someone walloped in the vagina, I don't think laughter would be the immediate response, so why is it funny when it happens to testicles? (It's very rarely immediately funny if it happens to you, by the way; the real comedy comes in seeing it happen to someone else.)

Nothing else on the body really responds to a short, sharp, shock with the same level of excruciating pain as the bollocks. You'd think the more something hurt, the less amusing it would be, but the opposite is true. When they see someone smashed in the testes, people laugh before they've even checked that everything is OK. They might stop if they discover the impact has detached a testicle, but I think that might cause some people to laugh even more. People will actually pay good money to see it happen – not even accidentally, but willingly, as the success of the *Jackass* franchise demonstrates.

I'd say it was the laughter of recognition: all ball-owners have been there, and this time we're perhaps relieved to see it happening to someone else. We know that, in all likelihood, the pain will be intense, but then disappear, and we know that the unfortunate victim will probably be OK. It's a case of there but for the grace of God go I.

Yet people who've never had balls still enjoy the 'joke'.

Perhaps it all comes down to the juxtaposition of the stereotype of the strong and macho male being so easily felled and humbled by something tiny or weak. However cocksure or arrogant you might be, you will crumble to your knees if your groinal defences fall short. It's a little death, a temporary defeat, and the victim is in no position to avenge their humiliation by attacking the cackling audience. Thomas Hobbes called this 'sudden glory', believing that in this case, the viewer will laugh 'by the apprehension of some deformed thing in another, by comparison whereof they suddenly applaud themselves'.*

Hobbes thinks he knows so much about comedy, but I'd

---

* Thomas Hobbes, *Leviathan*

love to see him expound his theories at the late show at the Comedy Store and see how he gets on.

Maybe the fact that people laugh when stuff like this happens to men, rather than women, is because people don't particularly like men and have no empathy for them – even if they are men themselves. That should be a wake-up call for men. We're so basically despised, even by ourselves, that everyone takes pleasure in our misfortune.

The genitals, and particularly the bollocks, are, as we've seen, so deeply (if incorrectly) associated with masculinity, that gonads throbbing in agony is funny in a way that a smack in the mouth isn't. People see masculinity as the enemy, and so are delighted to see it brought down – like if you saw your boss slip on a banana skin and fall head first into a toilet.

I believe it's worth trying to move towards a world where everyone is equal and the patriarchy is overthrown, not due to any sense of fairness, but just as an experiment to see if a baseball bat in the nuts would still be funny, or if it relies entirely on the fact that a man is being knocked off his perch.

Equal rights are one thing, but working out why something is funny is much more important.

8

Scrotal recall

The days after that call from the doctor were some of the hardest. I knew that something was awry, but had no idea how serious it was. After the incredible rapid progress following my first call to the GP, things had seemingly come to a standstill.

They barely had. It was just under a fortnight before I ended up going in for the second scan. But thirteen days and nights of contemplation was a lot to endure. What if the possible cancer took this hiatus as a chance to spread to the rest of my body? My errant ball seemed to be growing exponentially, second by second. I was pretty sure that all of this was in my broken imagination, but I feared this minor delay might be fatal. I waited for a call from the hospital, but it didn't come. Had they forgotten me?

I veered between believing the best- and worst-case scenarios. In the good moments, I was still convinced that this would turn out to be nothing serious, like my previous scares, or that they'd be able to cut me open, pop out whatever was in there with a teaspoon, and send me on my way.

Or was I heading for an ironic death? Most male comedians make endless jokes about cocks and balls, but I had done a whole show about nothing else and written a book. As Jesus once said, 'He who lives by the genitals, dies by the genitals.' All right, he never actually said that directly, but I bet he thought it. Especially when he was in the audience at stand-up gigs.

I really wanted to know. Even if it was terrible news, it would be better than this purgatory. I kept as busy as possible. Throughout lockdown, I'd been amusing myself by live-streaming on Twitch. Twitch had started as an internet channel where you could watch people playing video games, but it was now starting to be used by comedians as a platform for trying out esoteric and improvised concepts in front of a live, remote lockdown audience.

On Twitch, I was able to carry on producing my most popular podcast *RHLSTP** (in which I chat with comedians and other funny people, in front of a live audience in non-Covid times), but I was also able to indulge myself with my weirder projects: one in which I played snooker (badly) against myself, as I had as a teenager, and another where I attempted to clear all the stones off an extremely stony thirty-five-acre field near my house (a sort of comedic art project that parodied the pointlessness and heroism of attempting to achieve anything in our brief span of life).

During lockdown I had also come up with a brand-new show in which I reviewed the news with Ally Sloper, a 129-year-old ventriloquist's dummy that had been made by my great-grandad. Ally is something of a horror: a papier-mâché creation with a red face and wiry hair that is able to shoot up

* Richard Herring's Leicester Square Theatre Podcast, though the acronym changes meaning whenever I play in a different venue.

in the air when he is surprised or being cheeky. His paint is chipped, his clothes – unsurprisingly – a little worse for wear, and one of his eyes, once capable of blinking thanks to some tiny internal strings, has wedged shut. He can thus claim, 'I'm winking at it!', whatever horrific thing he says (as a Victorian, not all of his comments are as PC as you might hope). He is slightly horrified by his immortality, and embittered that he only springs to life when someone decides to pick him up. So many lonely decades lying unused in a box, unable to know how much time has passed. He has already outlived two of the Herrings who used him in their amateur shows. His creator employed him to try and spread the word of God among the Methodists of Middlesbrough, and his creator's son (my grandad) was a headmaster who would use Ally as an educational tool. According to my dad, both of them were terrible ventriloquists. So I was keeping something in the family, even though I suspected that Ally swore a lot more with me than he had ever done before. How would my great-grandad feel about his creation acting in this way? When you create a life, you have to be able to let go.

Ally knew that, one day, I too would be dead, and that maybe as-yet unborn hands and mouths would guide him back to life. But what would they make him say? He did his best to retain his own personality in spite of all this uncertainty.

It was exactly the right entertainment for the madness of Covid incarceration. The conceit was that I believed this ragbag, improvised show might be my ticket back to proper telly, rather than seeing it for what it was: the mad and desperate ravings of an ex-TV star who had finally lost the plot.

It was wonderfully organic, though. Catchphrases appeared out of thin air, and new characters emerged as I went along: like an overpaid Marmite lid with a yeast-extract face who was bad at observational comedy; a phallic carrot that tried and failed to spot double entendres; and a dead wasp that I'd found on the desk, who became a cultural reviewer.

I didn't practise ventriloquism between shows, but as I was doing this for an hour every week, I was getting better. Though much of the humour came from me losing my temper with inanimate objects that I seemed to believe were talking to me (even though I was doing the voices), I was amazed at how much decent material emerged from the ether – and that it was possible for me to be surprised by what the puppets came up with. Maybe this actually could be a valid career path ... Or a valid breakdown.

As you can see, it became difficult to see if this was a pastiche of a deluded, crazy ex-almost-celebrity desperate for another taste of the limelight, or *actually* a deluded, crazy ex-almost-celebrity desperate for another taste of the limelight, but that was part of the fun. Fake tragic or actual tragic? Who knew for sure? Not me.

I was loving the freedom, the successes, the failures. The puppet show had a small but loyal band of viewers, and out of lockdown had come a new outlet, a new skill and a new comedic fecundity.

Although at this point, I hadn't yet talked publicly about what was going on in my private life (aside from a couple of blogs saying I was having some tests for some unspecified condition), the puppets did occasionally ask me if I was OK, and what would happen to them if I died. I couldn't stop them. Of course they were concerned. What would they do without me? They were the real victims here.

Finally, after what was actually only eight days of radio silence, my scan was arranged. It was to be on Thursday in the early evening, only a couple of hours before the next puppet show was due to go to air, so at least I could keep distracted on the day by looking for news stories to discuss with myself.

Even though I had a good reason to be at the hospital, once I got into the waiting room I assumed everyone else there could tell I was a fraud. Nearly all the other patients were older than me (or at least I thought so, but I still feel like I am twenty-five, so am prone to misjudgement on this) and many of them looked properly ill. A couple were on drips and in wheelchairs, and one person was being pushed around in a bed, barely capable of any movement, grey-skinned and gasping for breath. I was sitting with my laptop, looking perfectly healthy, if a little overweight (again, not an issue for many people in the room) while trying to work out which news stories I could discuss with a scary antique puppet. The NHS shouldn't be spending any time on me.

Things were running with incredible efficiency. My appointment was bang on time, and I was shown into the scanning room, which looked state-of-the-art and futuristic, allowing me to pretend I was in the film *Total Recall*. The technicians told me they were going to inject iodine dye into my bloodstream, making it easier for them to view my organs on the scan, but with the unusual side effect that it might make me feel like I'd peed myself. I wouldn't, however, have peed myself. I would only feel like I had. It sounded brilliant. I couldn't wait to experience that.

I wondered if the iodine served any scientific function at all. These guys must get bored running what basically amounts to a human photocopier, so it would be a fun distraction to trick people into thinking they've lost control of their bodily functions. I'd been in a full-body scanner before – as I've mentioned, I'd had my heart scanned to discover that it beats in its own way (and maybe my balls also worked to their own agenda) – and I vaguely remembered being told about the fake weeing thing at the previous body scan. I'd been disappointed not to experience that sensation. This time, too, the procedure failed to do anything other than make my arm a bit uncomfortable where they'd inserted the cannula. *Where's my feeling like I've wet myself?* I thought. I'd gone to Rekall for the full, immersive incontinence experience (one of the cheaper packages), but I'd got nothing. Someone should shut this place down.

I noticed that the CT machine was made by Siemens, which is the same company that made my microwave and washing machine. I didn't know how to react to that. I wanted to be in a CT machine made by a company that specialises in CT machines. What if they accidentally put one of their microwaves in the CT casing? What if they put me on the wrong spin cycle, or they put a red sock in with me and I came out pink?

And what if the hospital had bought this make of CT machine for the same reason I'd chosen the brand for my home appliances – because I thought Siemens was a funny name? How immature were the administrators of this hospital? Absolutely pathetic behaviour. How could I trust anything about this whole procedure?

As I lay waiting for the scanning to begin, I noticed that on the part of the machine that was right above my eyeline, there was a noticeable dent. I amused myself by wondering how this had happened. Maybe Arnold Schwarzenegger was about to get his original personality back in the machine and had effected his escape (while murdering a couple of innocent technicians). Or had someone neglected to take off their metal objects, which then flew up into the machine at high speed, cutting through skin and bone? Maybe someone was so embarrassed that they thought they'd pissed themselves that they lashed out in fury? There has to be a story there, right? CT machines don't just get dents in them for no reason, and as you're waiting for things to start, something like that can really set your paranoia going. Were the NHS about to slice me up and make me into a pie? They have to find some way to fund themselves.

In the end, I had nothing to worry about, not even phantom pant-wetting. I was scanned and out of the lab in five minutes, as promised. The only downside was that I had to wait a further week for the results (seriously, all this stress was enough to give someone cancer).

There was also a twenty-minute wait before I had the dye-distributing nozzle removed from my arm, but at least I could sit there pretending that I was a reasonably pathetic cyborg. The staff remained cheerful (the nurse who removed the valve was even called Merry), given that it must be a tough place to work, as most people who come through are potentially seriously or gravely ill. Maybe they let through the odd completely healthy person in order to keep spirits up.

Fingers crossed.

I was back home in time for *Twitch of Fun*. It's always filled with existential angst, but my experiences that day gave it a bit of extra tension, which is great for art – and art is all that matters.

ON THE BALL: Linguistic balls

Balls are on our tongues much more often than you might realise. Here are a few bits of testicular vocab that have entered the lexicon.

Avocado

This comes from *āhuacatl* in the Aztec Nahuatl language, meaning testicles, with the avocado earning the name thanks to its appearance. That said, if you have a big green knobbly scrotum with skin that peels off easily, please consult a doctor.

Orchid

This comes from the ancient Greek word for testicles, as the shape of the root above ground resembles a testicle. Equally, 'Dog's Cullions', 'Dogges Cods' or '*Testiculus canis*' were used by the Tudor botanist Henry Lite to describe the *Orchis*, a species of orchid. Although this doesn't share the same meaning as the phrase 'the dog's bollocks', it highlights that dog testicles have long been used as a comparative device. Why is everyone obsessed with dogs' bollocks?

Seminar and seminal

Both words derive from the Latin *semen*, via old French, meaning the origin of ideas. Which is weird, because the ideas I have and the choices I make when I am hoping to expel semen are some of the worst in my life.

Musk

This word derives from the Sanskrit *muska*, via Persian and late Latin. It literally means 'scrotum'. Suddenly, I don't want to use my shower gel any more.

9

Never mind my bollock

A week later, I was back at the hospital for the results.
I had prepared myself for the worst, but, ever the
optimist, still believed there was a chance that everything was
going to be sorted out: the hospital would apologise for wasting my time and admit the whole thing had been a scam to get
car-parking money off me.

If it was bad news, then I understood the next step would
be a biopsy, as that was the only way to confirm the identity
of this stowaway in my hairy lifeboat. Having a bit of my ball
cut off sounded like a trial, but if that's what they had to do . . .

My appointment was right at the start of the day, but ever
the early bird, I arrived forty minutes early, before the waiting
room to this department had even opened its doors. I really
needed a wee, but I was worried that they'd want me to give a
sample, so I tried to hold off. The nerves proved too great for
me, though, and I did two wees before the receptionist arrived
to open the doors.

No problem: I was in my fifties and extremely nervous. I
could easily make more wee.

I sat and waited to be called, although the staff were setting up and the white board by the desk still had yesterday's date at the top. I was as nonchalant and cool as possible, casually reading a book I had on the go – a funny and horrifying tome called *You'll Never Believe What Happened to Lacey* by Amber Ruffin and Lacey Lamar. It's about the casual (and less casual) racism that they both (though mainly Lacey) experienced living in America. I was very near the end, but I never quite got to finish it. As with many things during these life-changing months, it became so associated with events that I couldn't face picking it up afterwards. It was the last thing I interacted with before everything properly started collapsing in on me, and even though it was a brilliant read, I couldn't look at it again without being reminded of what I'd been through. (Given I am a privileged white man and this was more or less the only bump in the road for me in half a century, I suppose there's more than a little irony in that.) It's no reflection on the book, of course, which is brilliant – please buy it. Just maybe don't read it while you're waiting to see if your genitals are about to be mutilated (hope they put that quote on the cover of the next edition). Although I remained pretty calm throughout this whole experience, it seems that certain objects or foods or even pieces of music have absorbed the trauma for me, and if I return to them, I risk releasing the pent-up emotions and becoming overwhelmed.

The waiting room was full by 9am, and it struck me that I was in one department, in one hospital, on one morning, yet was still just one of dozens of people needing diagnosis or treatment. I get to tell this story, but it's a pretty universal one. I was surrounded by people who were, like me, slowly falling apart, but largely being put together again by the fine staff of this department, this hospital and all the other hospitals.

First, I was asked to give a sample of urine. Why had I

wasted so much of the stuff while I was waiting? Luckily for once, my earlier urinary profligacy did not count against me. My pot overfloweth, or would have done if I hadn't moved it out of the way in time.

The doctor was waiting in her room and immediately asked to examine me, so the hand-to-bollock-world-record was beaten once again. I can't see her achievement ever being bettered, but good luck to any future competitors willing to give it a go.

I'm not sure she even needed to examine me – it turned out that the scan was pretty decisive – but maybe she did so to show me she was being thorough. She couldn't tell me what she was about to tell me without looking like she had at least double-checked. This was a pity-examination for my bollocks – and not for the first time in my life.

Or perhaps she simply loves cupping diseased balls. If so, she chose the right job. They probably have some kind of process to weed those people out, though.

She told me that the scan had confirmed that there was a large mass in my right testicle; that, in fact, my right testicle had been more or less taken over by whatever this thing was. It was basically an *Invasion of the Bollock Snatchers* scenario. The parasitical cells had conquered the whole thing, and there was nothing resembling my testicle in there. Maybe if I cajoled it enough, it might briefly regain its senses and be able to remember something of its glory days, but I had to accept that the bollock I once knew – and didn't particularly care about – was gone.

Although it wasn't possible to tell from the scan whether the mass was cancer, whatever it was was so big that there was nothing to be gained by taking a biopsy. The only course of action was to remove the testicle completely; then they could test it and find out what was wrong.

I wanted to say that if they were going to do that, then it better be bloody cancer. I'd be fairly cross if they took out my ball, only to find it just had a bit of a cold that would have cleared up in time. This happened to a friend of mine, who had a potentially cancerous kidney removed, and was then informed, after extraction, that it wasn't actually cancerous. Fingers crossed the same thing wouldn't happen to me. It was odd to be gunning for cancer.

I think I was supposed to cry out, 'Noooooo! Why God, why? Not my testicle.' Maybe this is when the weird tears of realisation of your own mortality were meant to flow, but I just nodded and said, 'OK.'

I was a little relieved. At least I knew what was happening. I didn't have to wait another week for the biopsy and another week for the results, worrying that cancer was continuing to spread its tendrils through my organs and capillaries.

I wasn't going to mourn my ball; I wanted this rebellious turncoat out of me.

The doctor was surprised that I wasn't more upset. This was a big moment. What's the point in becoming a doctor if people take bad news without even really blinking?

'Do you have any questions?' she asked.

The question I really wanted to ask was, 'Can I have my ball back?' Once they'd taken it out and tested it, would it be returned to me? Not to be reattached or anything. Just so I could have it. It was mine. I'd grown it and fed and watered it and vigorously exercised it for over half a century.

Also, later in the year I was appearing on the *Champion of Champions* edition of Channel 4's brilliant *Taskmaster*. At the beginning of the show, there's a round where each competitor is asked to bring in a prize from home. The winner of the show gets to take all five prizes with them. The funnier or more impressive the prize, the more points you receive. I thought a testicle in a jar might well win me the round. Especially if I joked, 'I've always said I'd give my right bollock to win *Taskmaster*. Well . . .'

At the very least, a lopped-off gonad in a jar would be an excellent conversation-starter if I kept it on a coffee table in my living room. Or I could plasticate it and turn it into some interesting jewellery. Who wouldn't want my abdomen-apricot hanging from their ear? What if I wanted to put it under my pillow for the testicle fairy? The testicle fairy doesn't get as much business as its tooth-obsessed cousin, and I suspect it would pay a pretty penny for every globule of gristle it found.

I had already decided that positivity was going to be my way through this: humour was going to be my coping mechanism, and whatever happened next, I would be making light of it. It's how I've treated everything in my life. It would be hypocritical if, now something a bit unpleasant was happening to me, I suddenly got all serious. The stand-up show was very much back on (careful what you wish for). Now I was getting a ball removed, I could surely get a book deal.* I could write a sitcom or a film in which the character based on me says all the dumbass remarks I was thinking of, but which I chickened out of saying in reality, for fear of seeming disrespectful. The moment didn't feel right for jokes.

And so, when the doctor asked if I had any questions, I just shook my head. I do regret not checking, though. 'Do they let you keep it?' is the question I've probably been asked most since having the operation, and it would have been good to get the definitive answer. From my understanding, they don't give you a doggy bag full of your extracted offal at the end of the procedure, unless you have religious reasons for keeping it (for example, if you believe all your body parts must eventually be buried together). I am not sure the testicle fairy

---

* Keep reading to find out if I did.

would count as a religious figure, though to my mind, it's no more fanciful than any of the other mythical figures in which people put their trust.*

I was fairly certain that wanting a grotesque prize for a TV entertainment show would not qualify as a valid reason. In truth, I am probably too squeamish. If I get a bit light-headed at the sight of my own blood, then how would I be if they gave me my bollock in a plastic bag, bobbing around like a dead goldfish that I'd won at a funfair?

I didn't have much in the way of questions for her, beyond the ones I was too embarrassed to ask. While I was surprised we'd jumped straight to extraction, I had been preparing myself for this possibility and so accepted it, because this past fortnight or so had made me very aware that I didn't care about my bollocks. At least, not more than my life.

All I'd wanted since that phone call from the GP had made me think about the future was for there to *be* a future for me. I just wanted to live. If they'd been talking about removing both bollocks and maybe yanking off my penis as well in a three-for-two deal, then sure, I'd be a little more perplexed. I didn't want to be left with my pelvic region looking like an Action Man's.† I may be old, but I still use my genitals and I didn't want to turn into no-Action Man. But if it was a choice between keeping my genitals and being dead, or having no genitals and still being alive, I would still, reluctantly, have chosen the latter course.

If my bollock was trying to kill me, then I would happily

---

* I had forgotten this, but in my 1990s TV show *This Morning With Richard Not Judy* I claimed I'd left a testicle under my pillow and never received a reward. At the end of the show, the testicle fairy turned up to finally pay me, and offered to take my other one. It's just one of the many examples of life imitating art throughout this experience.
† Once again, something that I had faked for the purposes of comedy for the poster of the 2012 version of my live show *Talking Cock*.

kill it first. I had another one. That's why there are two of the things, so you're still a reproductive prospect if one of them gets caught on the brambles.

The doctor moved on and told me that I had to make a couple of important decisions fairly quickly. The operation would happen in the next two weeks, and if the problem turned out to be cancer, then I'd probably be having a shot of chemotherapy soon after that. There was a good chance that the chemo would make my remaining ball infertile, so did I want to store some sperm so that my wife and I might have another child? There probably wouldn't be time to do it in between the operation and the chemo, so I would need to get this sorted in the next few days.

I was pretty certain that the answer to this was, *No, God, please no.* I love my kids with all my heart, but my youngest was now three and we'd got to the point where we were more or less through the sleepless nights and the nappies and the zombie-hellscape of being the exhausted parents of tiny kids. We could almost reason with them now, so why would I want another three years of hell?

Whenever I saw a little baby, I did think it might be nice to have one of those again, but I was already an old dad, and now I was potentially a broken old dad who might not be here for all that much longer ... I would obviously have to discuss this with Catie, though.

Secondly, the doctor asked, did I want to have a prosthetic ball put into my nutsack to give me the appearance of a duo-baller?

Now, I can understand why some men might want this, and I totally respect the decision to take one. If you're still dating, then worrying about what a potential lover might think of your bollock when they see it could hit your self-confidence. A fake ball would make you less stressed (a sort of non-stress ball, that could also be used – in the right circumstances – as a squishy pain-free stress ball), and that's valid. Although, by the time someone is that close to your ballsack, they're probably not going to turn back if they notice it's half empty. Or is it half full? At least it's a way to find out if you're dating an optimist or a pessimist.

Similarly, you might worry that there could be judgement or amusement in the locker room ... but would there be? Perhaps if you're one of the younger victims of testicular cancer (and sadly it is a disease that often hits young men), then that might be a concern. You certainly feel like everyone is judging your junk when you're a teenager, whether they are or not, so a pretend horse-chestnut slipped into your conker-shell might help.

I do sympathise with young men who have to face what I was going through. My testicles had served their purpose, and now I could eject one as if it were a booster rocket on a space shuttle, but if you're at the start of your adult life, then of course it's great to have the choice to refrigerate sperm and wear falsie testes. It's up to you – and if you get one put in and then later decide that the false ball is superfluous to requirements, you can always have it taken out again.

Actor and motorcyclist Charley Boorman (for whom, weirdly, I am occasionally mistaken, and who, even more weirdly given our facial similarity, was chosen to front an advertising campaign for Herring shoes), is also a monoball. After his operation, he elected to have a prosthetic, but he discovered that when he was on his bike he would often accidentally sit on it (prosthetics are sewn into your scrotum and so do not retract in tense situations like real bollocks), which left him feeling like his nutsack was being ripped off. He now recommends that people don't bother (though he hasn't had his taken out, so he must secretly quite like it).

My personal decision was that it would be ridiculous for me to get a prosthetic. I was fifty-three years old and happily married. Even if I were single and dating, it wouldn't bother me if I had one ball. I can imagine that it might even be an interesting chat-up line. I think more people would be intrigued to see it than would be put off by the idea.

The only person I want to entice into bed is my wife, and I knew she wouldn't care if I had one ball missing. To be honest, if she didn't know this was happening, I am pretty sure she wouldn't even have noticed it was gone. Not because she isn't interested, but because if you're working in that area, you're not necessarily counting them. Those things move around a bit, so you'd just keep searching until you found one. Even as a ball-owner, I occasionally lost track of where my own were, but I knew they must be in there somewhere, and they'd turn up when I needed them.

Would anyone really notice in the locker room? If I ever accidentally happen to glance at the genitalia of another man in a changing room or toilet stall (and I have become quite adept at ensuring that kind of accident never happens by never looking at people's genitals), then I will immediately look away. Even if they've got a really freaky or massive penis, I don't hold its gaze, because it's not the done thing. If I somehow forgot and found myself staring absent-mindedly at one of the really huge or bendy or weirdly coloured ones, I would definitely never give even the smallest glance to the bollocks. Even if the penis was tiny and the balls were massive, I'd be enchanted by the tiny penis. There is no situation I can think of where I would bother wasting precious eye-time by looking at, let alone counting, someone else's testicles.

Electing to have a false ball put in for the benefit of a weirdo at my gym – someone who decided to stare at my genitalia and was somehow able to distract his attention from my exceptionally beautiful penis for long enough to notice that, beneath it, my onion bag might be short of an onion – would be an odd choice.

Who would care if that guy judged me? What right would he have to judge me for anything? He doesn't even understand basic locker-room etiquette. Stop looking at my ball without express permission. You're the one who should be being judged. By an actual judge.

The only possible reason for me to have a prosthetic bollock would be for myself. For my self-esteem, to make me feel as if I was a complete man. But what would be the point in that? It would be like I was trying to trick myself into thinking I had two balls, hoping that I would somehow forget the day when someone cut one out and replaced it with a pebble. I would be living a stupid lie – and for what?

Also, my personal notions of masculinity are nothing to do with how many bollocks I have. I am not sure I have ever felt like a 'complete man', even when I had the full meal of meat and two veg. I don't know what a complete man is, and certainly don't believe that I have ever corresponded with (or accepted as fact) the clichéd version of a MAN.

I am still happy enough to include myself in that loose affiliation of extremely varied humans who identify as men, most of whom will have some approximate version of the genitals I had.* But some will have bits missing, or extra bits, or no bits at all, or even completely different genitalia. Having balls isn't a requirement for being in the club. Just as having ten balls wouldn't make you five times more manly. Having one doesn't make me half a man, because manliness is not merely one thing. It is entirely dependent on your own definition.

The term 'man' covers an awful lot of ground. Ultimately, the only thing that can classify a person as being a man is a state of mind, not the state of your genitals. And I'd still identify as a man if you cut off all my genitals. I'd still identify as a man if I was somehow imprisoned by an insane scientist who was bored of making human centipedes and had now decided to replace dicks with vaginas.

What I'm saying is that I knew I didn't have to have two balls for me to know who I was, and so I definitely didn't have to *appear* to have two balls to know who I was.

I might have been worried that losing a ball could have some impact on hormones or libido, but I wasn't worried that it would affect my perception of whatever the hell Richard Herring was.

I had mainly already decided that I didn't want a prosthetic, because I wasn't ashamed of my new status. I was going to be proud of what I was. I was going to be a uniballer, a mono-baller, a Womble, and I didn't want to pretend any differently to the tiny handful of people who were going to be unlucky enough to see my testicles in however many years I have left.

I wanted those maybe twelve people (my wife, my

---

* And you just have to read my book *Talking Cock* to discover the rich variety that this encompasses.

kids – while they were still young enough to have a bath with me – and whatever medical staff would be examining me in the future) to know that there's nothing wrong with having any part of your body missing. It doesn't change who you are. Our bodies can only give us a rough approximation of some of the things we might be, and even our bodies get it wrong sometimes. What makes us who we are is much more than the unreliable shell in which our consciousnesses propel themselves around.

Becoming a one-baller was a no-brainer.

In a nutshell, I told the doctor I didn't want a prosthetic in my nutshell. Again, she seemed quite surprised that I could be so immediately dismissive. 'You can always change your mind later,' she told me.

I told her I didn't think I would.

'You'll probably be OK,' she said. 'You have quite a thick scrotum, so it might not really show.'

It was nice to know that my scrotum was unusually bulky. This woman was an expert. She'd probably handled a thousand scrotums (scroti?), and yet mine was notable for its particularly tough hide. This was part of the reason that a manual diagnosis was quite difficult. There was a lot of fat, wrinkly skin to feel through before you could get to the succulent/rotten fruit beneath. As disappointing as it was to have had the news I was losing one of my boys, at least I had my scrotum to fall back on. A scrotum so thick that it might convince a locker-room pervert that I had two balls in my bowling bag.

This was a decision that I could make alone, and it was instantaneously and decisively made. To find out if I was going to have to keep some spunk in the fridge, though (hopefully not my own fridge – I didn't want anyone mistaking it for an Actimel), I needed to tell Catie the bad news.

ON THE BALL: Pet my balls

Ever since I've lost a ball, I've imagined that my neutered cat, Smithers, is looking at me as if to say, *What goes around comes around. How do you like it?* I feel a little bad that we took his balls away, though it was the responsible thing to do and I am not going to lose too much sleep over it – except when Smithers sits at the end of my bed, meowing his requiem for his lost furballs.

If you are the kind of pet owner who wants to prevent unwanted progeny from your animal, but who also cares about its self-image, then you'll be delighted to hear that pooch and pussy prosthetic testicles are available. Since 1995, Neuticles* have been offering testicular implantation for your pets. As their website explains, they are 'helping neuter-hesitant pet owners overcome the trauma of altering, and allowing their beloved pet to retain its natural look and self-esteem'.

I am not sure how they measure the self-esteem of a dog or cat. Will Neuticles really fool a pet into thinking they're complete or merely confuse them? Dogs particularly pay a lot of attention to their balls. Won't they be freaked out when those globes are sensitive one day and inert the next? If I went to sleep and woke up to find my ball no longer had any sensation at all, then that would have equally serious repercussions on my self-esteem.

Neuticles are obviously there to assuage the liberal guilt of sensitive pet owners who are regretting taking away their pets' genitalia. If you care so much, then don't take them away in the first place.

* https://neuticles.com/

Among those who have tried to make amends for mutilating their furry best friends are Neuticles customers Kim Kardashian (who got them for her boxer, Rocky), and Jake Gyllenhaal, whose German Shepherd, Atticus, has the indignity of silicone balls hanging between his hind legs.

But kudos to Neuticles for resisting the advertising slogan: 'Neuticles – they're the dog's bollocks.'

10

The old ball and chain

In situations like these, it's the person that all the crap is happening to who gets the sympathy and the shoulders to cry on, but I genuinely think all of this was harder on Catie than me.

Imagine being the one getting the call telling you that the person you love third-best in the world (hopefully I make the top three) might well have cancer, is going to have surgery and might die, leaving you with two young kids. BUT! You mustn't think about that at the moment. What we need is an immediate decision on whether you might want to have any more kids with him. Hurry up! We need your answer NOW!

While this stuff was happening to me, I was allowed to cry about it or joke about it or wallow in self-pity, but Catie had to remain positive and supportive and strong. She couldn't mourn the loss of an organ that had statistically probably helped produce one of her children, and yet she'd have to deal with the aftermath alone if it all went tits (or balls) up.

'I'm losing a ball. Now, quick – do we want any more kids? I have to tell them now.'

Understandably, Catie was not really prepared to make this decision against the clock. She too had thought there would be more time before potential surgery; she hadn't known there might be chemo on top of that, or that it might leave me infertile.

Not unreasonably, she said she wasn't sure. So, wouldn't it be sensible to store some sperm on the off-chance we might need it?

I didn't mind. I'm always happy to have a wank. And now I could have one sanctioned by an actual doctor, which wasn't something that had happened in any of my previous 100,000 (low estimate) acts of onanism.* Would that be helpful or off-putting? There was only one way to find out.

There wasn't time for us to chat for any longer or attempt to process what was going on. The wheels were in motion, and I had to carefully put my ball on the tracks so those wheels could slice it off.

I hung up, and I had much to do to distract me. Catie, though, had to try and take in all that had happened in this brief phone call alone. How did this make my generally pessimistic partner feel? If only I could ask her now. But I'm not going to. You'll have to wait until she writes her own book about this to find out.

I was a little shell-shocked, but time was of the essence. If they had shown me into a room containing a man with some old barbershop equipment and told me he could do the job straight away, I'd probably have taken the chance. I desperately wanted this UXB† out of my underpants.

I was taken by a very kind sister to a tiny room to discuss what I needed to do next. I told her we did want to store some

---

* Actually, that's not true. There was one other occasion, but that's a story for another book.
† Unexploded bollock.

sperm, and she made a note. Next, I had to go and get blood tests and book myself in for the operation. I was surprised that they didn't do this for you. You'd think they'd be able to do it quickly on a computer, but that would be working on the assumption that the NHS had any computer equipment from the twenty-first century. She told me that the queue for blood works was very long right now, so the best idea was to go there first, get myself put on the list so I was in the queue, and then head off to the Bollock-Chopping-Off department (it may have had a different name, but if so, I have forgotten it) to let them know to sharpen the meat-cleaver, because I was coming in!

She told me I could ring her if I had any questions or concerns and, like everyone I met on this epic journey to semi-castration, she was cheerful and positive. They were dealing with a pandemic that put their own lives at significant risk, and they were underpaid and overworked, yet still they smiled and joked and sympathised in exactly the right measures.

The comedian and anaesthetist, Ed Patrick (author of the excellent book *Catch Your Breath*) informs me that the reason for this excessive cheeriness might have been because at this point, many NHS staff were finally returning to their regular jobs after a year of things being put on hold for Covid. They would have been happy to do the tasks they were trained for rather than dealing with the horrors of the coronavirus. Imagine a virus so bad that it meant the thought of chopping off diseased bollocks was enough to make you euphoric.

I did all my preliminary stuff in a daze, but the blood-queue lifehack worked perfectly. I was away for over an hour, filling in forms, getting my blood pressure tested and being told what to expect on the day of my operation (by the only slightly grumpy nurse I met during this entire experience – and when I say grumpy, I mean she didn't do gags). But I arrived back in the blood-test waiting room seconds before my name was called. I punched the air and nearly rang the sister to let her know how brilliantly her system had worked. What a fantastic day this was ... Oh wait, I forgot.

There were two patients per tiny room in the bloods department, and I enjoyed the badinage between the nurses as they chatted about what they had been up to the night before, putting on a show to set the victims of their benevolent vampirism at ease. If you'd told me that one day I'd learn I was about to lose a testicle, and then asked me how many times I thought I'd laugh on that day, I would probably have predicted zero – but I would have been wrong. If laughter really was the best medicine, they wouldn't have needed to do the operation at all.

I didn't yet know when the operation would be, but they'd asked if I wanted to go on a list where they'd call me up if there were any dropouts (due to Covid, I suppose, rather than people deciding they didn't want to bother having their genitals extracted after all). I said that I had to wait to donate some sperm, but after that I was ready to go.

When I got home, Catie and I were able to have the sperm discussion at a more reasonable and less frenetic pace. We weren't entirely closing the door on having more kids – my ball might still be able to produce valid sperm after chemo (and presumably it meant that any kids we had from the radiated sperm were likely to have cool superpowers), but we agreed speed was of the essence. We didn't want to slow down the operation just so I could store some semen that we'd almost certainly never use, but it was still a decision tinged with sadness. I rang the sister to let her know that I didn't want them to freeze my gametes after all.

I was ready, and knew the call could come any second – it was nearly time for *Ball/Off!* And having had that thought, I wondered if John Travolta and Nicholas Cage might be up for a testicle-based sequel to their hit movie *Face/Off*. If all these ideas for entertainment worked out, my rotten testicle might turn out to be a gold mine.

ON THE BALL: Frankenstein balls

This 'On the Ball' is actually about testicle transplants, but having given it a more eye-catching title, I am left wondering if Dr Frankenstein bothered to give his monster genitalia. He was trying to make the perfect man, after all, so it would be odd to leave it out. He would presumably have had to remove the genitals from the bit of groin he was sewing on if he didn't want a complete monster. That would have been weirder than leaving it on, so perhaps we can presume the monster had monster balls. Shame on Mary Shelley for not writing about it more openly and in full detail (unless she did, I haven't read the book for a while).

No, I want to talk about another common question I have been asked post-operation: is it possible to transplant a testicle from one person to another, either in the event of one's death or in life, as an extremely big favour to a friend? And, if so, did we inadvertently agree to that when we signed up for our organ donor cards?

It is indeed within the scope of medicine to transplant balls, but because (as I've already mentioned) a transplanted bollock will keep creating the sperm of the donor, it's an ethical and legal minefield. Who would be the legal parent of any progeny? Also, how would you feel having someone else's sperm coming out of your penis and landing on your tummy? Whether you like the thought or not, you have to agree that it's a tricky moral issue.

For these reasons, it's something that doesn't happen very often. In fact, only three recorded testicle transplants have ever taken place (there are internet rumours of money being offered to people willing to sell a ball, but these are unlikely to be true).* In each case, the donation was from one identical twin to another, where the recipient was born without any testicles.

The first operation occurred in 1978 and was performed in the USA by a Dr Silber. Previously, Silber had developed a method for reversing vasectomies using microsurgical techniques he'd refined while carrying out more than two thousand kidney transplants in rats. I don't know if a bloke who's been messing around with rat kidneys would be the first person I'd go to in order to get a new ball put in, but needs must. The patient was a thirty-year-old twin who had been born without testicles, and his brother had a full set. He contacted the doctor himself, presumably based on satisfied testimony from the rats, and both brothers ended up with one testicle, with the recipient going on to father five children.

Who says that brothers can't share nicely? Personally speaking I would never want to be that much in debt to my own sibling. Every time he wanted something – 'Remember that time I gave you my ball?'

---

* David Mikkelson, 'Fact checks: Can you sell a testicle for $35,000 to $50,000?', www.snopes.com.

11

As funny as cancer

The call didn't come the next day. Or the next. It was another awful waiting game, where I feared that I might get Covid and be unable to have the operation, or that Covid might close the hospitals and all operations would be cancelled.

What if they'd forgotten me? What if the message hadn't got through that I wasn't storing my sperm after all, and they were waiting for me to wank into a test tube? Should I wank into a test tube just to be on the safe side?

The thoughts keeping me awake at night were not of the weirdness of losing a body part, but the fear that maybe cancer would kill me. Like cancer had killed my friends. I was thinking about my kids and my wife and my whisky: my precious, precious whisky.

I'd actually stopped drinking at the start of 2021 for Dry January and had not gone back (at the time of writing, I've been dry for fifteen months), so I didn't even want to drink the whisky – but I still wanted it to be *mine*. Interestingly, it was only after I stopped drinking that I got diagnosed with testicular cancer – pretty firm evidence that you need to keep boozing as much as possible, for the good of your genitals.

I also had to make a decision about who I was going to tell about all this. My family already knew, and keen readers of my blogs and viewers of my Twitch stream might have started to pick up on some medium-to-heavy hints, but was I going to 'go public' or keep a dignified silence?

Catie told me to think about it carefully, because, like my ball, once it was out, it was out. It was a tough decision.

Was I going to be one of those pricks who think they have a duty to let everyone know every detail of their illness, however private it may seem? Or would I be one of those pricks who keeps the news entirely private, so that when they eventually succumb and die, it's a horrible shock to all the people who liked them? There's no way of dealing with it without being a little bit of a prick, although if you take the latter option, you're not around to hear anyone call you one.

I could see the point of both sides, but have never been one to shy away from sharing personal stories or joking about difficult subjects. It would be possible, though tricky, to skirt around this, but difficult to explain why I was suddenly pod-casting less, having previously done three or four shows a week during lockdown.

Ultimately, I knew that I wanted to talk about it and joke about it and laugh in the face of possible cancer and imminent death. My comedy has always been largely autobiographical and honest, especially when it comes to my personal failings and disasters. Admittedly, it's different talking about some-thing as it's actually happening, rather than in a stand-up show after some time has passed, but with this issue, talking about it straight away instinctively seemed like the right thing to do. It would help me to fight back against these intrusive thoughts by mocking them, by acknowledging that although this might be cancer, it was cancer of the funniest place possible. This was my coping mechanism, and I was making the decision almost entirely for myself.

Of course, it wouldn't hurt to remind people that it's worth checking out their own bits and bobs, and it might also be helpful to anyone going through the same thing to hear about someone who could laugh at what they were dealing with.

Cancer is one of those subjects that people are reluctant to talk about, but I've found throughout my career that the stuff people are reluctant to talk about is exactly the stuff we should be talking about. People suffer in silence on all kinds of issues that would more or less evaporate if they voiced them out loud, or even heard someone else doing so. Disease and death might not disappear when you joke about them, but being allowed to discuss them and laugh at them would be a help for me, so it stood to reason others might benefit too.

I wanted to fight; I wanted to scream into the abyss. If this thing was going to take me down, I was going to take the piss out of it – and myself – as I tumbled into oblivion.

I knew, ultimately, the ironies of this happening to me were too great not to point out. It was almost like my whole career had been gently predicting that this would be my fate. Not only was I seen by many as a comedian obsessed with dicks and spunk (a charge that isn't entirely fair, but is hard to deny given the mileage I got out of the show/book *Talking Cock*), but in 2009–10, I had also spent a year trying to reclaim the Hitler moustache for comedy.* After the moustache, what was the second-most famous of Adolf's physical characteristics? He supposedly only had one ball. (To be fair, he had two, but one of them was in the Albert Hall, which can't have been

---

* Charlie Chaplin had it first, and then Hitler came along and ruined it for everyone. It was probably the worst thing he ever did.

convenient for him.) I could now do a testicular Hitler sequel about monorchism.

Having started doing podcasts in the very early days of the medium, I am often (incorrectly) called the Podfather, so I would now be the One-Pod Podfather. As I've already mentioned, two of my podcasts revolve around balls and stones (both euphemisms for testicles). In fact, one of the running jokes of the *Stone Clearing* podcast was that I wanted to become immortal by gradually replacing all my bones and organs with rocks – maybe I should go and pick up a prosthetic pebble after all.

In my silly puppet show, I had a birthday segment hosted by a donkey finger-puppet that I'd had as a kid. One of my earliest memories is of putting on a show behind the sofa with this little figure and some of his animal friends, and my mum and my nan laughing their heads off (at me, of course, rather than with me, but I didn't know that). I loved the feeling that creating this laughter gave me.

Donkey had somehow survived (all his friends were lost), but was in a poor state of repair. I had pulled off his ears decades ago, and he was frayed and chipped. I thought it would be funny to bring him back to life for the show, but now he was in constant pain, cursing the fact that he was still alive, correctly blaming me for his injuries and begging to be put out of his misery. Instead of giving him his wish, I made him do birthday greetings for viewers. It was a homage to West Country TV legend Gus Honeybun, who used to celebrate the birthdays of local children by giving a number of winks or bunny hops equal to their age. Given most of my viewers were middle-aged, this meant that Donkey had to do fifty-four donkey jumps or thirty-seven eeyores, thus adding to the horror of his tortured existence.

I had written him a theme song, months before I found out

I was ill. It roughly followed the tune of 'Happy Birthday to You', but was just different enough to avoid legal issues.

> *You've lived another year and you haven't even died*
> *Though cancer may be secretly creeping deep inside*
> *If you think that's worth a party, your brain's also*
> *   going wonky*
> *Let's get an eeyore or a kick from the reluctant*
> *   birthday donkey.*

Of course, now I'd found out that cancer had possibly been secretly creeping deep inside me, the joke was on me. My mum thought I should change the song, but that would have been hypocritical. It was still funny. Funnier, really.

On top of all this, my latest book had been called *The Problem With Men*, and now I had a problem with me. That book (which was even commissioned, like this one, by a publisher called Sphere) had been about the crisis to masculinity that was hitting so many men, and what our place in the modern world should be. Now I had this personal crisis that would make me question this subject in even more depth. My argument had been that men should celebrate International Men's Day on International Men's Day,* rather than complaining about it not existing (even though it actually does exist) on International Women's Day. To that end, in November 2020, only a couple of months before my diagnosis, I had grown a horrible big moustache (still, thanks to the Hitler show, only the second-most horrible moustache I'd had) for Movember. Of course, one of the main focuses of that excellent charity is to remind men to examine themselves for testicular cancer. I had been raising funds and awareness for an issue that, unbeknown to me, I was actually suffering from.

---

* You'll have to buy the book to find out when that is.

It seemed like the universe was pushing me towards being the one-ball spokesperson and finding the funny in dropping a bollock.

As you've hopefully noticed, so much hilarious stuff had already happened – and I hadn't even had the operation yet.

Occasionally, in the past, someone on Twitter has informed me that I am about as funny as cancer. I never realised what a compliment that was until now!

In the end, I knew that as a comedian, I would be letting down my profession if I didn't make the most of this opportunity that had literally fallen into my lap. The rest of the comics were going to be so jealous.

I was being swept along on a tsunami and I didn't know if I'd wash up alive or dead, but I was going to do my best to surf this wave as far as I could. Hopefully my inflated bollock would at least make me buoyant.

ON THE BALL:
Is this how you treat my balls? – Part I

However bad things were looking for me at this point, I could take comfort in the fact that I was probably born in the right era to get my testicular problems treated. In the next couple of 'On the Ball' sections, we'll take a look at how things were for people with bad balls down the ages (if you want a quick summation, the answer is: not good).

Mummy's balls

Several different spells, rituals and treatments associated with testicles, infirmities and their magical properties are recorded in ancient Egyptian papyri, including treatments for swelling in the testicles caused by liquid build-up – which we now know as hydroceles (Danny Dyer Syndrome). Sadly for ancient Egypt, they had neither Danny Dyer nor jacket potatoes, so goodness only knows what they compared the swollen balls to.

According to Greco-Egyptian papyri from the first to second century BCE, the cure for swollen testicles was to take a cord from a coin bag and knot it several times, on each knot chanting the word 'Kastor' once and 'Thab' twice. From the same collection comes the advice that to get an erection, you should smear pepper and honey over your entire genital area. I think the inevitable swarm of furious bees stinging your genitals while spitting out peppery honey would probably get rid of the erection pretty quickly, though doubtless a good proportion of men would be into it.

From the slightly more medical Ebers Papyrus, dated 1550 BCE, comes this relatively sensible, though still pretty horrific advice: if the patient has a 'skin-tumour' found on the genital area and is vomiting, you should apply heat to the body, burning off the tumour and cauterising the wound.

If nothing else, this should be distracting enough to stop them vomiting.

Please don't try this at home.

12

Let's go fly a kite

The day after the news that my right ball was soon to be history, I got the spontaneous – and hopefully perfect – memory with Phoebe that I'd failed to get in the snow.

It had been her sixth birthday a few days earlier, and she'd been given a kite. Now the wind was picking up, so I suggested we go to try it out. The family wrapped up in scarves and gloves and then trudged up the hill to the rec. It was a freezing cold day and the wind was bitingly icy, but it was also properly blustery. Would that be good or bad for getting a kite aloft? I didn't know.

My experience with kites was limited. I'd got my first and only one back in the days of Green Shield Stamps. I'm not sure this is a concept worth explaining in detail to those of you who are too young to remember, or whether you'll believe me anyway. Basically, every time you bought petrol or did a supermarket shop, you'd be given a number of green stamps (based on how much you'd spent). You stuck those stamps into booklets, and then you could take them to a shop that didn't accept money, only Green Shield Stamps. Those booklets of stamps could be exchanged for a huge variety of weird and

wonderful stuff: briefcases, record players, TVs, car head-
lights – basically anything.

This worked surprisingly well for a number of years, but
eventually, as the public fervour for licking stamps in return
for slightly crappy things that they could just buy with money
dwindled, the shops started accepting a mixture of stamps
and cash, and eventually just cash. It was almost as if cash had
been better than the whole stamp idea all along.

Even so, I loved sticking the stamps in the booklets, and took a
keen interest in the brochure that listed the stock. One of the items
on offer was a cool orange kite. I wanted it so badly; so much so
that I remember everything about the day my parents finally
gave in to my constant pleading and we went to the shop to pick
it up. My mum's friend, who we called Aunty Jean (even though
she wasn't a real aunty), drove us there, and she parked outside
the shop on double yellow lines. She was a maverick. When we
returned, a policeman was standing by the car. He asked for her
name, and she truthfully told him that it was Jean Pickup. He
thought she was messing him about and she nearly got arrested.

Having the kite was clearly more important than flying
the kite, because I don't remember ever trying the thing out,
although I have a vague sense that we gave it a go, it didn't
work, and so we put it away and never spoke of it again.
That's not really the point. The point is that I had a childhood
memory involving a kite, so there was a chance that Phoebe
might remember this day too.

While Catie played with Ernie, Phoebe and I tried to work
out how to put the kite together. It wasn't complicated: the
string and the kite were separate and needed to be attached.
But the instruction sheet gave no clue about where on the
kite frame you needed to clip on the string. I guess people
who make kites assume that anyone who buys a kite must
know how kites work. I don't know how anything works. It

was looking like another potential memory of a dad who was hopeless at everything. The wintry gale blowing over the field didn't help matters. I couldn't do much with my gloves on, and my frozen fingers struggled with the clip.

Phoebe was impatient to get her hands on the kite, but I told her we needed to take our time and get it right. This wouldn't be easy, but that would make it all the more worthwhile. When the kite didn't magically leap into the sky on the first attempt, I feared she'd give up, just as her mercurial dad had done four or five decades before.

A bit of trial and error found the best attachment spot on the frame, and then together we experimented to see if we could get the kite to catch the wind. To begin with, it just fell limply to the floor or shot upwards and then swirled into a death dive as quickly as it had risen.

Then, suddenly, almost by accident, we moved into the right spot at the right angle, and my daughter was flying the thing. She seemed to have quite a knack for it, too, rescuing it from disaster when it started spinning towards the ground, letting the string out further and further. I stepped back and watched this tiny figure against electric grey clouds, controlling a fragile scrap of rainbow brightness against the buffeting elements. She looked like a tiny wizard conducting the weather. Occasionally, her magic would fail and the kite would crash to the ground, but we'd work together to get it airborne once more. I took the odd turn, but with less success, and Phoebe told me that the wind liked her and didn't like me. I was happy to be her hapless assistant. I was delighted to give her this feeling of power. It's exactly what I wanted to pass on to her as a dad, the idea that she is capable of anything, which luckily she seems to be anyway.

Phoebe has always been physically affectionate with her mum, but not so much with me. She makes jokes and calls me names – very much dealing in the currency that I use myself. She likes to test my love for her, but never comes close to breaking it. I think she secretly loves me too, but she'll be damned if she ever says it out loud. Sometimes, though, love is demonstrated by what you do, not what you say.

We both knew in our hearts that this unexpected triumph had come from us working together. We were out there for forty-five minutes, oblivious to the biting cold, bonding our souls, discovering together that the world doesn't have feelings for any of us: it will swirl you around and try to knock you to the ground, but you can turn its unruly anger against itself and control your destiny.

Who would have thought that flying a kite could be in any way symbolic of anything?

I wasn't even trying to create a memory now, I was enjoying the experience – which is, of course, how proper, lasting memories are created. Not when you're trying, but when you're lost in the moment.

Forget about the cat-poo snowman – please forget about it. The kite guy, that's who I was.

Whatever happened to me next, I hoped that my daughter would remember what we'd shared.

I thought she probably would . . .

Do you, Phoebs?

ON THE BALL:
Is this how you treat my balls? – Part II

Taking care of Romulus and Remus

Andrology, the field of men's reproductive and urological medicine, was essentially invented by the Roman medical writer Aulus Cornelius Celsus. Interestingly, it was Celsus who gave us the word 'cancer'. Hippocrates had used the Greek word for 'crab' to refer to malignant tumours, and Celsus translated that into Latin. Take that, Hippocrates. No wonder he was always making oaths. As someone born on 12 July, I am thus a Cancer who has had cancer. If only I was a crab as well. I'd really have hit the cancer jackpot.

Celsus accurately identified numerous key infirmities in men's testicular health, including varicocele (dilation of surface veins) cirsocele (dilation of deep veins) and tumours. He even described Danny Dyer Syndrome (aka hydrocele). Celsus' methods were reasoned and systematic, and he presented detailed steps to reduce discomfort without always relying on amputation. This would have made him popular with patients, but I bet it pissed off a lot of doctors who had only got into medicine because they loved chopping stuff off.

To treat testicular swelling where no physical injury has occurred, Celsus recommends that 'blood should be let from the ankle; the patient should fast; and the swelling should be treated with bean meal cooked in honeyed wine or rubbed with cumin with boiled honey; or ground cumin with rose oil, or wheat flour with honey wine and cypress roots; or the root of a lily, pounded'.

Presumably he hoped that by the time you'd picked all those flowers and rubbed them on yourself, that your testicular swelling would have gone down on its own.

In terms of testicular cancer, Celsus wasn't too far from the present-day approach, recommending surgical removal of the tumour or testicle itself while leaving the scrotum intact. Before he came up with this idea, they'd simply chopped off the balls and the ballbag. Ouch. Grimly, Celsus also described in detail what happened to the ravaged testes when the disease had advanced beyond treatment, but in doing so provided useful and comprehensive medical understanding of testicular cancer for the first time.

So even though he doomed people born between 22 June and 22 July to endless 'Cancer – the illness' jokes, the good he did probably outweighs the bad.

Maybe rather than rushing to the doctor with my swollen bollock, I should just have followed the advice of Pliny the Elder, whose *Natural History* suggests these treatments for swollen testicles:

> Ebulum [possibly elderberry or danewart], when ground up with its tender leaves and drunk with wine, takes care of stones; when applied as a salve, it helps testicles. Erigeron, as well, when mixed with frankincense and sweet wine, relieves swollen testicles.

I love how he covers bases there – drink the potion, and if that doesn't work, rub it on. I think the wine is doing a lot of the heavy lifting there. Pliny also wrote:

> They say that a goat's dung is good for you with honey or vinegar, or just butter by itself. Testicular swelling can be treated with veal suet mixed with soda, or by the calf's dung reduced in vinegar.

Again, really hedging his bets. Am I eating the honeyed goat dung? Or smearing it? And is he saying that butter by itself is just as good? Because I'll go for the butter in that case. For smearing or eating. I'd like to avoid goat dung if possible, however sweet-and-sour you make it.

It's worth remembering that Pliny the Elder later died by walking into a volcano,* so I don't think we need to listen to him too carefully.

'What are you doing in this farmyard, gathering up animal shit and smearing it on your bollocks?'

'Don't worry, officer. I am actually following the advice of Pliny the Elder.'

'You worship Pliny the Elder. If Pliny the Elder jumped into a volcano, would you do the same?'

To be fair, it would at least be a terrific pay-off for my daughter's lava fixation.

---

* Well, walked towards it. He was killed in the eruption of Vesuvius that destroyed Pompeii, but only because scientific curiosity meant he wanted a closer look.

13

Santa Claws

Finally, the date of my operation came through. I was counting down the days like it was some kind of shitty Christmas, full of anticipation for something that wasn't going to be great. To be fair, if Santa threatened to cut bits out of one in every hundred children, it would add some much-needed jeopardy to the event: 'You're on the naughty list. I'm taking your pancreas.'

With just three more sleeps till Shitmas, I had to go into hospital to check that I was well enough to go into hospital. You know: 'Sorry mate, you're too ill to come to hospital. Go back home and don't come in until you're well.' In this case, they were checking that I didn't have one specific disease: Covid-19 (don't know if you've heard of it, it's quite a new one). But I think they could start expanding the practice to all health problems – suddenly waiting lists would be cut to almost nothing. I'd send this book to the prime minister right now, except I think they might actually do it.

It was a super-efficient and safe and (almost) self-isolated test. I had to drive round the back of the hospital, like I was a criminal collecting a drop-off of stolen drugs, and park up in a special little bay under some scaffolding. Another unrelentingly cheerful health professional (maybe they were slipping something into the tea urn) slunk out of a portacabin, came to the car, asked me who I was, and then stuck a Q-tip down my throat and in my nose. Then, hey presto, I was done. I noted that she hadn't scratched my brain like the guy who tested us on the set of the movie. It's almost like he didn't have a clue what he was doing.

She said they'd only tell me the results if I had Covid, which meant more anxious waiting, this time with no definite end time.

If someone was going to castrate you, you might welcome the chance to postpone the execution day, but I needed to get the offending article whipped out asap so I could see where I stood – and if I could stand.

Even with one sleep to go, life had to carry on as normal. The day before the op, I was home-schooling again, but for the first time it didn't lead to arguments. We actually had fun. Phoebe was learning about Matisse for the first time (so was I), and we made collages out of coloured paper, which apparently was something Matisse did, even though he was an adult. And they sell for £15 million! For a collage?

I was in the wrong game, I realised. Matisse wouldn't have had to worry about one of his bollocks managing to kill him. His wife could have just flogged one of his collages and made enough money to keep the family going for the rest of her life.

Phoebe wanted to make a monster with a purple ear that was bigger than the rest of it. Her collage was shit compared to mine, but I didn't say anything, as I was basically relieved that she hadn't done another image of me falling into some lava.

*

Time ticked by slowly. I was so desperate for distraction that I decided to look myself up on Google. Did I really want to see what the world thought of me at this sensitive time? I don't know why this is called a vanity search, as you usually only find something horrible being said about you that will dent your ego; it's always more of a reality search.

This time, however, I discovered something that wasn't actually about me. It was a GoFundMe page raising money for a memorial scholarship in the name of Richard D. Herring. With all that was going on, it was a little bit unsettling to come across someone with my name (albeit with a different middle initial) who had recently passed away.

Richard D. Herring had lived in Buffalo, New York, and the photo on the fundraising page showed a handsome young man holding up a smiling boy of around Ernie's age; presumably this was Richard with his own son. I didn't know how he'd died or how old the photo was, but of course it struck a chord.

With thoughts of my own mortality in my head, I decided that the Richard Herrings of this world needed to stick together. It was a good cause, and based on the testimonies of the other donors, it was clear Richard D. had been a good guy. Better than Richard K.*

The fund was about $2,000 from its target. I suspected that the people who followed me on social media would respond if I suggested they try to help hit that goal. They have generally enjoyed random acts of kindness or silliness or pedantry in the past, and are usually keen to get on board for shits and giggles.

I tweeted the link and, as expected, my excellent followers leapt into action, put in a few bucks and helped push the total up to and beyond its target. Twitter can be a sewer made up of the worst brain-effluent of humanity, but it can be a place

---

* I like to pretend it's K for potassium. But it's actually Keith. Yes, I know.

of wonder too. When the universe is so random and arbitrary, and can throw your life in unexpected directions like a kite on the ice-cold wind of death, it felt joyful to respond with something that would impact and improve the life of someone that none of us had ever met, and who we'd never meet, in memory of a man we didn't know.

With about twelve hours to go before I was due in hospital, I recorded a podcast interview with the American actor and comedian Mary Lynn Rajskub.* I had never met her or spoken to her before, and she would have had little to no idea of who I was (I think she'd googled me and seen me playing myself at snooker, which probably isn't the best introduction to my body of work). Even so, pretty much the first thing we talked about before the broadcast began was my upcoming operation. It was strange to be telling a stranger when hardly anyone else knew – strange for Mary Lynn more than me, I am guessing – yet from my perspective at least, it was also oddly comforting and cathartic. She coped with this weird situation with jokes and kindness: a day or so after the operation, I received a bunch of flowers from her, which would have taken quite a bit of work on her part, as I hadn't told her my address.

I started my podcast by telling the listeners: 'It's my last day in one piece. Tomorrow, I will be in two pieces. Hopefully one quite large piece and one smallish piece – though it's bigger than it should be.'

I pointed out that I was losing something that human beings have, on average, slightly less than one of. Could I afford to lose one? Though, looking it from a more positive point of view, I would be left with one, which was still slightly

---

* You will probably have seen her in 24 or *Always Sunny in Philadelphia* or a whole host of films and TV shows – she's awesome.

more than average (working on the metric that there are more women than men and not all men have two).

Mary Lynn suggested there was a possibility the unexplained mass might be a diamond, and I told her it might be just one huge sperm, which she thought maybe summed up the difference between men and women.*

Listening back to it now, I sound remarkably relaxed. It was the right decision to carry on working. Talking about it, again, proved to be better than wallowing in silence, while then going on to talk about something else entirely for an hour was a wonderful distraction.

With that done, I went to bed. Not surprisingly (and exactly like on Christmas Eve), I didn't sleep too well, as I thought about what was to come.

And what would never come again.

ON THE BALL: Nice beaver

What better time than the eve of castration to consider the beaver?

If the myths are to be believed, this is an animal that, when in a tight spot, would castrate itself. But myths aren't to be believed. That's why they are myths.

One of Aesop's fables tells of a beaver chewing off its own testicles to avoid a huntsman, who needs said testicles to make a medicinal oil. How the beaver knows what the huntsman is after, or what his testicles will be used for, is not explained. The moral is that people can be too precious with their belongings, and should be ready to give them

---

* You can listen to the whole thing at https://play.acast.com/s/rhlstp/ or wherever you get your podcasts. It's episode 319.

up to save their own lives. Which, sure, I can get on board with, but maybe the fable of the man with testicular cancer might have illustrated that point more realistically. I know that realism wasn't Aesop's thing, and in any case, it's a bit late to be giving him notes. He enjoyed a degree of success without my contribution.

It's true that beavers were hunted since at least the first millennium BCE for their castoreum, a medicinal oil found in what were, at the time, believed to be their testicles.

Aesop's clearly beavershit fable, however, made its way into fact, as that gullible old volcano-chaser Pliny the Elder stated in his rubbish *Natural History* that beavers chewed off their own testicles to avoid predators, in the same way a lizard will lose its tail.

Amazingly, this myth survived in bestiaries for nearly 1,600 years, including the *Journey Through Wales* by historian and bishop Gerald of Wales in 1188. Only in the seventeenth century did English polymath Sir Thomas Browne point out that beavers' testicles are internal and impossible to bite off, and that the bumps on their behinds mistaken for testicles are actually oil glands (beavers don't bite these off, either).

Castoreum, or beaver bum oil, has a woody, vanilla-like scent, and is still used as vanilla flavouring and perfume today. It is collected via a milking process that leaves the beaver alive, if not titillated. What kind of an idiot would milk a beaver?*

---

* Follow this link https://www.youtube.com/watch?v=WaPnBOZENWo or put 'Richard Herring + Beaver' into YouTube. Don't worry, it's not what it sounds like and is suitable for work. Actually, it's probably worse than what it sounds like. View at your own peril. Sphere Publishing take no responsibility for outside content.

14

Wrecking ball

RIP my right bollock: 12 July 1967 to 24 February 2021. Age shall not wither him (he was quite withered already, to be fair). He shall be missed.

It was a nerve-wracking (and severing) day. Catie and I arrived at the hospital shortly after 7am: way too early, as usual. We were so early that we had to wait in a waiting room before we were even allowed into the proper waiting room. When you're in the waiting-room waiting room, you know you've mistimed your arrival. It was good to have Catie with me, but in the proper waiting room it was pointed out that patients had to be unaccompanied due to Covid restrictions, so she had to leave immediately.

Although I knew I wouldn't be staying overnight, this was going to take a few hours. I told Catie to go home and said I'd call her when I was close to being released. She said she would, though in fact she stayed sitting in the car in the hospital car park for the next nine hours, which was nice of her, but we had to remortgage our house to pay for it. Once again, this whole thing was tougher on her than it was on me. Sure, she wasn't having a part of her body extracted, but sitting in a multi-storey for a whole day is probably worse.

I had somehow shifted my mindset so that this whole thing was an adventure. Maybe I really had signed up for some kind of very low-cost *Total Recall* experience when I'd gone into the scanner. The package I'd opted for was living the life of someone who probably had cancer, which isn't as cool as going to Mars and didn't involve any women with three breasts, but was probably a bit safer overall.

I was given a little cubicle and changed into a gown, but I was second in the queue for my theatre, so there were a couple more hours to wait, pondering what was to come. I'd never had a major operation before. What would anaesthetic be like? In that sleep of having a bollock removed, what dreams would come? I could hear the staff talking to other patients. The old guy in the next cubicle spoke very loudly, making the rest of us snigger as he bellowed his personal details. He was only having a kidney stone removed, the lucky bastard.

A procession of different staff visited me, each of them seemingly overly keen to confirm that I knew what the operation would involve, as someone might have booked me in for a birthday surprise. I was very glad that everything was double- and triple-checked and appreciated the breezy professionalism and the light-hearted conversation. I never thought I would be grateful to a load of people who were intent on turning me into a demi-eunuch. But I really was.

They drew an arrow on my right arm with a marker pen to indicate which bollock was coming off. One of my many fears for today was that they would take off the wrong one, though you'd have to be pretty blind not to be able to spot the big one. The Sharpie arrow was pointing at my right hand, so obviously I worried that the surgeon might take that off by mistake. Hopefully they kept the hand-removers and the ball-removers on different floors. Maybe a better system would be to dye the bad bollock blue, like you sometimes do with eggs at Easter – maybe put some yellow spots on it. We could all have some fun with crafting before the operation, and I liked the mental image of having to dunk one ball in paint, which would presumably involve a little squat over the paint pot.

The surgeon came in to see me, to check I knew what was happening (yeah, mate, I do) and explain how he was going to get to my bollocks in more detail than I needed. Previously, I had been told that they would come in via my upper thigh and squeeze out my ball (like a huge blackhead) through there, but now the surgeon told me he was coming in via my lower abdomen. I am squeamish at the best of times, and I didn't care how they were getting it out of me. One of those guillotines with the long handles they use to cut paper in school would have been acceptable as long as I knew nothing about it. He also warned me of the things that might go wrong, including quite a lot of stuff that would never have crossed my mind. When having a ball taken off is something going right, then the things that can go wrong have to be really bad.

Next, the anaesthetist came in and said I had the choice between general and spinal anaesthetic. I could not believe that anyone chose to be conscious during this operation. I did not want to have to play any part in this. General, please – preferably until I was all better. Can you just wake me up in six months?

The last few weeks had dragged, but for the next two hours, time was going backwards. I have very little memory of what I did as I waited. I only recall a sensation of queasy dread, tinged with weird relief that it was finally going to happen, if they ever got round to me.

Finally, I was taken down to the theatre. I was going to say I was wheeled in, but I'm pretty sure I walked. I genuinely can't tell you for sure. The memories from before the operation are blurred by fear, while those after are blurred by morphine. I might have concluded it was all a weird dream if it was not for taking a scrotal inventory afterwards.

My friend Tony had had to have a cancerous eye removed, which put my relatively cushy operation into some kind of perspective. He'd retained his sense of humour, and when the surgeon had shown him the rather gruesome scooping tool they used to remove the ocular kind of ball, Tony had quipped, 'Careful, you'll have someone's eye out with that.' I was all ready to be a cool and jocular patient, and had planned to adapt the joke I'd thought about using on *Taskmaster*, winking at the surgeon and saying, 'I'd give my right bollock not to have to go through this!' But when it came down to it, once again, I wimped out. Ironically, I didn't have the balls.

I was, perhaps unsurprisingly, scared. Scared I wouldn't wake up. Scared I'd wake up too early, while the operation was still going on. Scared I wouldn't be properly put to sleep and would feel every slice of the scalpel, but be unable to scream out for it to stop. Scared I'd wake up with the wrong ball gone. Or with my kidney gone. Or with my hands replaced by pots of petunias. Scared that while I was under, a *28 Days Later* scenario would play out, and I'd wake up in a world plagued by zombies.

The anaesthetist inserted a spike into my hand (at least, that's how I described in that day's blog – it seems unlikely it was actually a spike, but I don't remember now). I had expected that I'd be asked to count down from ten, but I never got anywhere near that. One moment I was there, and the next, without any fanfare or pain or even knowledge of it, I wasn't.

In an instant, I was gone.

There was nothing. Nothing at all. For the next hour, or however long it was, from my point of view, I simply didn't exist. There was no fear, no worries, no pain – because there was no me. I had been turned off, and if I hadn't been turned back on again, then it wouldn't have mattered in the least to me, because I wasn't there.

This was a little death, and to me, the best evidence I've experienced that when you're dead, you're dead. There was no soul twiddling its thumbs, waiting to see if I lived or died. I was entirely absent from this whole scenario. If the soul isn't around when you've only been put to sleep, why would it suddenly turn up when you're dead? Is anaesthetic so strong that it also knocks out your spiritual essence?

It was just fade out, nothing, fade in. The nothing was so nothingy that I wasn't even conscious of it. I drifted off and drifted back in. Hamlet would have been disappointed to discover in that sleep of death, the cinema of dreams was entirely closed down. As much as I still don't want to die, and as much as I am going to do my best to stay alive, this experience has made death a lot less scary. The weight lifts off you, and you slip into the pool of death and float away, as relaxed as it's possible to be. It was one of the best things that's ever happened to me. Not only did it make death seem pretty cushy, I also travelled into the future – admittedly only by a few dozen minutes, but it still counts. Mainly though, what a wonderful thing to be able to absent yourself from a horrible event. Think of all those people through history who were awake for stuff like this.

If I had access to anaesthetic and the knowledge of how to use it, I'd be on it all the time. Having trouble sleeping because your brain won't stop thinking of the fact that someone you haven't seen since school is somehow now in their mid-fifties? Little shot of sleepy juice, and bang, it's tomorrow! Got to sit through a ballet because your wife thinks they're great, even though they clearly objectively aren't? Have a little drink of anaesthetic and you're ready for the after-show drinks. Your holiday is still two weeks away and you have to get through a fortnight of work first? Put yourself to sleep and wake up on the plane to Benidorm. I can see no downside.

I don't think I spouted nonsense on waking up, though I was certainly woozy and confused. People seemed to be gathered round me. Word had got round that I was a comedian, and while I can't remember anyone actively demanding a joke there and then, the staff seemed to be enjoying this comatose visit from a minor celebrity.

They told me that everything had gone well and gave me some tea and a sandwich, along with some free biscuits (so this whole experience was already totally worth it). Plus, I had some delicious morphine, which I'd been looking forward to. I have never really been into taking drugs, mainly because I always feared they'd kill me, so it was kind of cool to get given some legitimately, by people who knew how to save you if things went wrong.

I was slightly disappointed by the morphine. I am sure it stopped the pain, but apart from seeing the wall moving a little bit, it didn't have any other huge effect. Maybe everyone on drugs is merely pretending to have a great time, all convinced they are the only one who experiences nothing but slight giddiness.

While I had been under, someone had dressed me up in a jock strap and some nice stockings, which made me wonder about what they might have been doing to my body as I slept. They claimed this outfit was medically necessary, but I was somewhat dubious. Hey, look: these people saved my life. I can't begrudge them a bit of fun.

They obviously weren't going to kick me out straight away, and said I needed to have done a wee before I left – just to make sure they hadn't cut the wrong pipe, I guess. I hobbled my way to the loo, but nothing was forthcoming. Last time I'd had to wee in a hospital, I'd had gallons of the stuff, but now I couldn't even squeeze out a single drop. I went back to lie down and fell asleep. I visited the loo on waking, and a couple more times after that, with no joy whatsoever. Everyone was cool about it, but I felt like I was overstaying my welcome. Eventually, they brought out a big jug of weak lemon drink and I drank the lot. On my fourth attempt, a tiny dribble of urine hit the toilet, and I was free.

It seems amazing that you're allowed to walk out of the hospital after an operation like this, though obviously I wasn't moving quickly. I'd texted Catie and she came down from the car park to accompany me as I moved gingerly, and at snail's pace, back to the car with her. She drove us home, very slowly.

The kids were spending the night with their grandparents, but had left me some cards and gifts – Phoebe had wrapped up a packet of Hula Hoops for me. Even though I had technically bought those, it did mean a lot that she'd given me her favourite snack, showing a tiny chink of love in her armour.

I was a bit sore and disorientated, and urinating was like bailing out a sinking boat with a thimble, but it was all done and it had gone as well as possible. Having finally come completely clean on Twitter about what was happening, I got lots of supportive comments and funny jokes. Most reassuringly, several uniballers (a couple of them people I knew who had never told me they only had the one) got in touch to say they were decades on from their own operation. Had I suffered in silence, that kindness would not have been afforded me. Over the next few weeks and months, people who'd just been told they were losing a ball contacted me and I was able to offer them reassurance, too. Once again, the decision to be open about it was vindicated. I know of a couple of people who, as a result of my story, went to the doctors because they thought they might be going through something similar, only to discover that they too had cancer. If that was the only thing that had resulted from me deciding I was going to joke about my condition, then that'd be pretty damn cool. While I have ruined the lives of one in a hundred of you by telling you about aphantasia, maybe a few of you will now get that troubling lump looked at by your doctor, and I'll have saved your life. No need to thank me. Just ten per cent of all your future income will suffice.

I have overwhelming gratitude to everyone who helped me through that day. I didn't meet most of you, and even if I did, I don't think I'd recognise you if we passed in the street. I am sure you wouldn't recognise me, either – a few of you were a bit too focused on my bollocks. My face is up here, guys! Our health service is humanity at its best, saving the lives of strangers every single day and making sure dads are still around to get Hula Hoops from their kids. Thank you so very much.

It was done. I had joined the proud association of humans with one testicle, whose roll call included Adolf Hitler (possibly), Nigel Farage, Lance Armstrong, Tom Green, Shakespeare's Richard III, Chairman Mao, General Franco (possibly) . . . Hold on, was this some kind of punishment for being evil?

ON THE BALL:
Did Hitler really only have one ball?

Initially, the evidence seems damning. There's even a song about it.

Hitler has only got one ball,
Göring has two but very small,
Himmler is rather sim'lar,
But poor old Goebbels has no balls at all.

This seems pretty damning evidence that the Nazi high command was plagued by testicular abnormalities, with one case of monorchism, two of microorchidism (or at least something rather similar) and one of anorchia. I mean, if it wasn't true, why didn't all those Nazis get up on their big podium and get their balls out for everyone to see? Something to hide, Himmler?

Did the ideology of this heinous regime actually attract people with misshapen scrotums? Or did becoming a Nazi somehow lead your genitalia to shrivel up or fall off?

I have to say that since I lost a ball, I have not moved further to the right (though my left ball has), so the only sensible conclusion is that men embarrassed about their imperfect testes found some kind of solace in pretending they were part of a master race. Overcompensating much?

I suppose we have to consider the possibility that whoever wrote this song just made the whole thing up as a joke, in order to challenge the masculinity of the enemy. After all, if balls denote virility and courage, the implication that so many of the German leaders were challenged in this area might do much to discredit them. It's a good marching song, and laughing in the face of your enemy while insinuating that their junk is weird is a military tactic as old as time. But is there any actual evidence that Hitler was a monoball?

In 1945, the Soviets, having captured Hitler's burned

remains, claimed in the autopsy that his left testicle was missing, although eyewitnesses to the petrol-doused cremation of Hitler and his lucky new bride Eva Braun claimed that nothing but ashes remained. It's hard to believe that even the most evil and sinewy testicle would survive such a conflagration. Even if one did, that doesn't mean the other one hadn't been consumed by the flames. Numerous historians have concluded that accounts of the exact circumstances of Hitler's death – and the supposed treatment of his remains – are contradictory and part of wider Soviet propaganda. It seems likely they were attempting to build on the implications made in the bawdy music-hall song in order to undermine Hitler's courage and sexual prowess, even in death.

There have been accounts that a wound to Hitler's upper thigh sustained in the Battle of the Somme may have taken a testicle. One, by German army medic Johan Jambor, stated: 'His abdomen and legs were covered in blood. Hitler was wounded in the abdomen and had lost a testicle. His first question to the doctor was: "Can I still father children?"'* This account was given to a Polish priest in the 1960s and not revealed to the world until 2008, so I am inclined to give it a bit of the old Jimmy Hill, chinny reck-on.† Military records do, however, confirm that a shell explosion had resulted in an injury to Hitler's groin or left thigh.

When Hitler was imprisoned in 1923, a note from the prison doctor said he had right-side cryptorchidism. These documents only came to light in 2015, so again one might

* https://www.bild.de/wa/ll/bild-de/unangemeldet-42925516.bild.html
† For younger readers unhip to my 1970s vernacular, I am saying I don't believe it.

question their authenticity, perhaps this time by imitating the elongated chin of the Tutankhamen sarcophagus and proclaiming: 'Tutankhamoooooon.'

Hitler's valet, Heinz Linge, claimed that Hitler's testicles were completely normal, noting that he saw them while they urinated together by some trees (which at least finally answers that great philosophical conundrum, 'Did Hitler piss in the woods?'). Again, this seems an unreliable story, implying as it does that rather than popping his old fella through his flies, Hitler would have pulled down his trousers and pants like a four-year-old in order to micturate. Even then, Linge would have really had to be gawping to get a proper look at the Hitlerian ballsack, probably from quite an intimate angle, whilst the Führer was urinating. This is Hitler we're talking about, not Donald Trump.

Hitler's personal physician, Theodor Morell, stated that Hitler's genitalia were unremarkable, which I think Adolf might have found quite a damning testimonial, but even this assertion has been discredited. Another of Hitler's physician's, the delightfully named Hanskarl von Hasslebach, doubted that Morell was ever allowed to examine the Führer's family jewels. It's certain that he never conducted prostate exams or other more intimate examinations, despite recommending them, probably due to the personal denial of the patient himself. Was Hitler's refusal to be examined down to embarrassment about his testicular deficiency?

Probably not. It seems Hitler may have had some form of incontinence, potentially caused by a spinal nerve abnormality. This has been theorised on the basis of doctors' notes regarding a condition, unnamed, that had progressed beyond cure, along with Hitler's frequent sheet-washing and obsession with cleaning. There was, however, a conspicuous absence of examination reports of his genitalia, which might also preclude potentially embarrassing details emerging about this man obsessed with genetic perfection.

It seems unlikely that whoever wrote the marching song would have had access to any of the pre-war evidence, and they probably just made the whole thing up, perhaps working backwards from the fact that Goebbels (at least the way it's pronounced by English people) nearly rhymes with 'no balls'.

I guess the only way this will be proven is if Adolf's other gonad turns up in a cupboard at the Albert Hall (the venue, according to an alternative version of the song, where the Nazi bauble is located). A DNA test would be needed to prove its origins, of course, but even if it did, that would still lead to more questions than answers.

It seems likely to me that Hitler began and ended his life with a full complement of bollocks. If you feel you need to undermine his reputation by making people think that he was missing one, then you probably haven't been paying much attention to the kind of man he was.

I'm more interested in finding out if he also shaved his pubic hair into the toothbrush moustache.

15

Having a ball

Losing a bollock, it turned out, was a bit annoying, but after only a day and a bit of getting to stay in bed and not having to do any childcare, I was considering taking the other one off too. It was the best holiday I'd had in six years.

There was nothing I could do. I had been told I'd need to rest up for two weeks while the stitches healed, and that I shouldn't do anything involving lifting or cycling or hitting my scrotum with a table-tennis bat for a month.

Catie continued to look after me selflessly. She was in a lot of pain herself, due to a nasty toothache, but she didn't make a fuss. A few days later, she'd have to have that tooth removed, and at any other time, that would have meant a couple of days in bed to recover, but her timing couldn't have been worse. I had just lost a bollock. Who cares about a tooth? You've got loads of those. Cancer – even only possible-cancer – trumps everything.

Phoebe kept bringing me snacks, and occasionally sat next to me in bed playing *Minecraft*. Even she knew it was time to lower her defences and show me she cared. I was sent flowers and several food hampers full of biscuits and sweets – sort of the last thing an immobile man needed, but I indulged myself, nonetheless. It was like a birthday ... where I'd been both the birthday boy and the piñata.

The first night after the op was mildly difficult and uncomfortable. I struggled to find a position where I wasn't in pain, and every visit to the toilet was a prolonged endeavour to squeeze out urine while wincing in agony, which was a foreshadowing of what it might be like to be old – if I ever got to be old. A little over twenty-four hours after the operation, I was able to wee like a normal person again. I was a bit concerned that I hadn't managed a poo yet. It was most unlike me; I'm a fifty-a-day man. Would it turn out that you need a right testicle in order to defecate? If so, then surely I would end up in medical textbooks as the patient who discovered this unexpected link. I don't know if that's a syndrome I want named after me, though.

Eventually, my bowels returned to normal. I suspect all my body parts had been overwhelmed with fear once they realised what I was capable of doing if they displeased me. *Did you hear what he did to his gonad? Do not piss him off.*

I hadn't tried to interact with my remaining testicle too much yet. It took a good while to get used to talking about it in the singular. I'd been told to keep a jockstrap on at all times to help with support, which also kept my spunk-purse hidden away. My scar was behind a dressing that I wasn't allowed to remove, which was fortunate as I did not want to see what lay beneath.

The occasional tentative fumble had revealed my left ball, still in its usual place, and a blob of something where my right ball should have been. What was it? Had they not managed to cut the thing off? Had I actually had three balls all along? Understandably, it takes a while for things to settle down, and I was assured the ball was gone and that the 'something' might be clumps of blood, which would dissipate naturally.

As the days went on, the discomfort diminished, and things only hurt when I coughed or laughed. Three days in, I sneezed for the first time, and that was like I'd been shot, but only with an air rifle. The pain was from the scar, not from whatever stump was left in my scrotum.

The hardest task we had was keeping three-year-old Ernie from punching or headbutting me in the abdomen. We made it clear that he had to be careful and only hug me from one side, but he was of that age where you want to do everything you're told not to do, and he was desperate to find out why this wasn't permitted. 'Maybe I could just hug you from this side a little bit?' he'd suggest, trying to squeeze into the forbidden territory. We managed to prevent him from rupturing my stitches with his love.

Two days after the operation, Phoebe lost her second front tooth (this family was falling apart) and was super excited about it. I joined in with the celebration, but wanted to shout, 'Yeah, but it's hardly a bollock, is it? Get a sense of perspective.' I didn't, though.

Her tooth would grow back, but try as I might, I wasn't able to grow even one ball. Let alone *some*. The phrase 'grow some balls' sort of implies people want you to grow about six or seven. People who tell you to grow some balls are weird, and also do not understand biology.

I hadn't really dared to actually look at the damage, but after a bath, I caught a glimpse of myself naked in the bathroom mirror. From the front, the absence wasn't that noticeable, but then I turned to the side. From one direction, I looked like a regular (I mean above average) adult man, but from the other, I had the scrotum of a little boy. The difference was marked and rather shocking. I turned one way and then the other, and wondered if maybe I should have gone for the prosthetic after all. My next thought was maybe I would be able to put together a music-hall act, like those ones where the person is dressed half as a man and half as a woman, and turns round to have a conversation with themselves. I don't know if the public is ready for the equivalent act portraying a grown man and a small boy, both with no trousers on. However accurate their scrotums looked.

Over the next few days, though, things settled down to a new normality. To begin with, the left bollock had stuck to his half of the bed, possibly assuming his life-long companion would return. As it became clear that he was now alone, leftie – as so many spurned partners have before – moved to the middle, where he could sprawl out. My scrotum certainly didn't have the heft that it had once had, and the lunchbox was more compact, but unless you'd seen them in their pomp, I don't think you'd think there was anything unusual about my testicles. You would probably assume I was 'complete', just with rather charming bijou nuts. Macadamia nuts.

I wasn't feeling any psychological fallout from the loss. My masculinity was not diminished, and I wasn't really sad about my damaged genitalia, even if it meant that, according to the Old Testament, I was no longer welcome in heaven.* But the problem with this prolonged period of inactivity was that I had a lot of time to think.

I still didn't know what the hell was going on. While I had faced all this head-on with good spirits and humour, that didn't mean it wasn't getting to me. I mainly wanted to know what would happen next, and lying in bed all day, I had plenty of time to second guess. The negative guesses outweighed the positive.

---

* Deuteronomy 23:1: 'No one whose testicles are crushed or whose male organ is cut off shall enter the assembly of the Lord.' Wow, kick a guy when he's down, God.

As much as I was telling myself that this mass might be benign (I hadn't felt at all ill, and other tests hadn't thrown up evidence of cancer), a voice in my head kept telling me it wouldn't be. The voice insisted that I had cancer, which had been secretly percolating for so long that it had surely spread round my body. Even if I'd got rid of it this time, my friends who'd had cancer had all seemingly beaten it, only for it to return in a more aggressive and deadly form. In spite of the positive tweets from testicular cancer survivors and other success stories, I still, like many people, viewed cancer as something that would – either slowly or quickly – kill you.

I got a letter from the hospital telling me I had to meet up with an oncologist in about ten days. Logically, they must have sent this before the operation, and thus long before the testicle was examined, but maybe they knew something they weren't telling me. You don't go to an oncologist if you don't have cancer. That's the whole purpose of the oncologist. They're not interested in stuff that isn't cancerous. They won't even treat you unless you've got some cancer in you, the monsters.

It was frustrating that even now I'd had the operation, I still had to wait. Knowing no more than I had a month ago. At every step, I'd thought we'd finally get to the bottom of it, but each time, the ball was kicked down the road – maybe literally, now it was out of me.

I tried to face imminent death with dignity, and wrote in my blog:

I'd rather stay alive, but if I got run over tomorrow (unlikely, as I am not going out, but there's a thousand other ways to die) I'd be more grateful for the fifty-three years I've had, than the twenty or so I might have lost. I'd feel lucky that I'd got to spend these years with my children, even if I'd be sad that I wouldn't get to see what happens next. I am the luckiest man on earth for having got to meet these champions. And my wife – who has this weekend been in more pain than me, thanks to toothache, and yet has still had to take on practically all the childcare and domestic stuff while I watch football on TV, in next to no discomfort.

I had reached an odd place, one of reluctant acceptance of my fate. But I wasn't going to let my head drop (not completely), and I was going to continue to see the humour in all of this. Just because something is serious, it doesn't mean it isn't funny. In fact, the more serious things become, the funnier they are.

There were plenty of laughs to be had. I'd walk round the house with a dressing gown over my jock strap, which I was continuing to wear twenty-four-seven (unless I was in the bath). I kept Ernie amused by lifting my dressing gown and mooning him, doing a funny walk, waving my bum in the air. He (correctly) thought it was the funniest thing ever, and was fascinated by these weird pants with no back. He asked me to do it again and again, which I did, because I needed the laughs, and my kids are my favourite and, in many ways, trickiest audience. If I've got them laughing, I am not going to stop.

Humour is subjective, though, and for some reason, Phoebe found the mooning embarrassing. She used to laugh at stuff like this, but she was six now and had outgrown this kind of humour. Sadly, I never did, and I am confident my son will never tire of laughing at bums. I can only apologise to him for passing on these genes.

Would this be Ernie's only memory of me? If so, he couldn't really have chosen one that summed me up more completely. Is it wrong for a man to show his three-year-old son his bottom? Who cares? What would it matter if I got cancelled?

I was about to get cancelled by cancer.

ON THE BALL: The nut(s) behind the wheel

If, like me, you think it's weird buying pretend testicles for animals, then wait until you hear about the people who get them for their cars. 'Truck nuts' are bespoke testicle ornaments that are hung from the back of vehicles. Why would you want your ride bestowed with bollocks?

I will answer your question with a question: 'Why wouldn't you?'

Not only did someone think up this concept, but other people then saw it and thought, *Yeah, that's a good idea. Sign me up.*

I would guess that anyone doing this is attempting to assert their masculinity, eager to let other road-users know that the person driving this pickup or lorry is so manly that even their transportation has balls.

Of course, to any sensible person, it would have the opposite effect. If I saw someone driving an automobile with gonads, I would assume that the driver was so pathetically insecure about their masculinity that they needed to overcompensate in a manner that was frankly creepy. Why would you sexualise a vehicle – and what do you want to do to the exhaust?

It could simply be a bit of fun. Balls, as I hope I have made clear by now, are funny. So maybe you're just giving other drivers a laugh with this incomprehensible juxtaposition, but we don't generally walk around with our balls out, so having them out on your car seems like quite an aggressive attempt at humour. It's not like a bit of graffiti on a toilet wall. These truck nuts are surprisingly accurate depictions of the human scrotum.

The story of truck nuts could fill a whole book (and it's a book that I might one day write). They first emerged (if that's the right word – though it makes it sound like the balls were waiting in the boot and then, one day, just dropped) in the 1980s in (where else?) America. In the late nineties, car balls became a much more commercial prospect as two rival companies started producing their own versions. David Ham set up YourNutz.com, and John D. Saller founded BullsBalls.com.

Incredibly, this led to a legal battle that has lasted over two decades and included online campaigns of misinformation, slander and recrimination, and court cases to determine who was the first nationwide provider of these pointless artefacts. You'd think if you'd come up with this idea, you'd be happy for people to think that someone else had.

It's worth checking out Mack Lamoureux's article in *Vice** to get the full and incredible story – and to try to work out for yourself who copied who, and why the hell they wanted the credit for something so stupid anyway.

---

* Mack Lamourex, 'The bitter battle between two men who both say they invented truck nuts', 20 July 2015, www.vice.com.

16

In a paxed show, tonight ...

One week after my operation, I was able to take off the dressing and see my scar for the first time. It was fine, but much longer than I had expected. How big had that bollock been if they'd needed to slice me open this much to get it out? Was it a football now? Was it still growing? Had it reached sentience? I became convinced that it might track me down and seek its revenge. I had visions of Patrick McGoohan in *The Prisoner*, running along the beach being chased by that gigantic inflatable ball.

I wasn't coping well with having nothing to do, and I was determined that my evil bollock was not going to stop me working. I wasn't ready to play snooker or clear stones from a field, but I could still sit in a chair and talk, so I could still interview celebrities for my podcast *RHLSTP*, even if it was only seven days since they'd snipped off my hairy gobstopper. I was determined that this illness, whatever it was, was not going to stop me.

Ironically, if it hadn't been for lockdown, I probably wouldn't have been able to carry on with the podcast. For almost a decade, I had recorded the show in a theatre, in front of an audience. Thanks to Covid, that hadn't been possible for most of the previous year, so my producer Chris Evans (not that one. Or that one) and I had set up all the necessary tech in my attic and carried on producing the show remotely. Post-op, travelling to a theatre would have been too much for me, but walking upstairs? I could manage that.

I'd had this week's guest booked in for a while, since before I knew I was in testicular trouble, and it was a bit of a coup for the podcast, so I didn't want to cancel or postpone. I'd be interviewing the interviewer tough-guy Jeremy Paxman. This was, in some ways, more frightening a prospect than losing a ball. How would this bolshy and self-assured man, who famously takes no bullshit, cope with being on my humorous and sometimes frivolous (though perhaps deceptively thoughtful and clever) show? I knew there would be fireworks, but I thought I had a chance to tame this beast.

I had met Paxo a few times. When I'd first worked at BBC TV Centre in the mid-nineties, I had been very excited to find myself in the same lift as him. I was still at the stage where celebrities filled me with (only partly sarcastic) awe (in truth, I still am), and when he wasn't looking, I touched his briefcase. I joked about this incident in the first episode of our new show *Fist of Fun*.

I'd also appeared on various incarnations of *Newsnight* to discuss offence in comedy, or an election result. On one occasion, I was part of a panel of three, alongside actor Rebecca Front and comedian Steve Punt. It was like they'd thought, *We've got Front and Punt, what other comedian rhymes with that? Richard Herring – close enough.*

In addition, I had joked a fair bit about the Pacman in my stand-up and sketch podcast *As It Occurs To Me*, coming up with increasingly insane nicknames for the Packyderm, like

Paximillian or the Paxidermist. It'd be fun to see how much mickey-taking I could get away with before he crushed me.

I'd had time to do a lot of research, but I was not back up to full energy. After doing a bit of home-schooling and some light chores earlier that day, I'd had to go back to sleep in the afternoon. My brain was still a bit fuggy, and I knew I'd be flying by the seat of my pants.

The funniest part of the evening was probably Paxipad's attempts to set up all the tech before the interview began. The Packhorse was visible, but failing to position himself in the centre of the screen. It was like when I Facetime with my par-ents – no matter how many times I talk them through it, they always end up holding the device far too close to their face, and can't work out which buttons to press.

Old Pax Romana was bellowing at his partner about how terrible the set-up was. 'This is ridiculous,' he said. 'They can't hear us.' We could actually hear him, but he couldn't hear us. We didn't have a direct line to him, so I held up a piece of paper on which I'd scrawled, 'Turn up the volume'.

'I'm trying to do that, you dimwit,' he barked, as if I had given a ridiculous answer on *University Challenge*.

I wrote another note, which he read with disdain: 'We can hear you. You can't hear us.'

His partner suggested moving to the iPad, and he looked incredulously at his laptop one last time. 'Why does it keep tell-ing me to crack on with *Love Island Australia*? I've never seen it.'

Why couldn't this be the show?

They got the iPad, which was down to ten per cent battery, so there was a fair deal of jeopardy. Would the interview even happen? Then there was a feedback loop, which led to more consternation, but finally, we established contact and everything was working.

Pax Bygraves tried and failed to find a flattering angle.

'I look like an old drunk in a pub,' he complained, and this thought reminded him to take a gulp of white wine. His huge glass was now empty, and I suspect it wasn't his first of the night.

Chris suggested that we could use the laptop for the video and the iPad for the sound.

'Whyisitsofuckingcomplicated?' asked Packalackadackdack.

In the end, we got there and they found a charger for the iPad. It was all very funny, but the laughter made my scar hurt a bit, like I was a Harry Potter triggered by disdainful journalists. I told Packlife I'd just had an operation, and he was sympathetic when he found out what I'd lost. He told me I could manage perfectly well with one, pointing out that breast cancer kills more men than testicular cancer.

Technical issues sorted, he went to recharge his glass, and then one of the funnier/more awkward *RHLSTPs* began.*

The sound was not perfect and, as you'll have experienced on Zoom calls, it was slightly difficult to catch everything that was being said. Packamac is not one to suffer fools gladly (which was always going to be a problem, given the host) but as much as he tried to barrack me, I remained largely in control, and we got into some interesting areas of discussion, though the conversation did keep returning to underwear and penises, and it wasn't always me driving it in that direction.

Packathree was in a humorously bolshy mood and refreshing himself with wine, so some of the fun came in the conversation crashing into a dead end, or technology failing us a little (at one point, Paxmachine seemed to be holding the iPad up to his ear), or him piling on the insults (his best shot was probably, 'Tell me, is this comedy?'). But that's the joy of

---

* It's episode 320, if you want to find it. Wherever you get your podcasts. Or watch the video on YouTube for the full effect: https://www.youtube.com/watch?v=kk5UFx-NSVE.

RHLSTP, especially when we get someone like Paxthedutchie, who really shouldn't ever find himself in my world.

Not that he let on at the time, but he was dealing with his own medical issues. Soon after the recording, the news broke that he was in the early stages of Parkinson's disease. I was sorry to hear that, but also slightly annoyed that he hadn't told me, after I'd been so open about my bollocks. I could have had a world exclusive! But I think the badinage and silliness probably helped us both through a time when we had other things on our minds. A long conversation about underpants was what we both needed.

I don't think my interviewing skills or comedy mojo were located in my right testicle. I was (perhaps understandably) not quite as sharp as I usually am, but I was glad to be back in the saddle (even though I'd been advised to keep off any saddles for another fortnight).

In the end, Paxwork warmed to me and opened up, and, despite him claiming I hadn't done my research at the beginning, in the end I think he was impressed with my depth of knowledge about his favourite subject: himself. He almost seemed to have enjoyed the experience.

It might have been a touch early for me to make a return to work, but I was proud that I had not let this errant bollock stop me.

Now, do I mean my testicle or Pachahontas?

ON THE BALL: Just take two goat testicles . . .

You probably winced and laughed at those ancient testicle-based treatments earlier in the book, but crazier things were going on much more recently. Meet the Goat-Gland Doctor.

John R. Brinkley was a physician and conman ... no, wait, he was just a conman – he nearly got me then. In the early 1900s, he began a decades-long practice of inserting goat testicles into (willing) men's scrotums or next to women's ovaries, initially in an attempt to cure impotence, but eventually as a basic cure-all for a variety of conditions ranging from dementia to emphysema to flatulence.

You may laugh, but if I had goat testicles sewn into my ballsack, then I'd be too scared to fart, so it's not all hokum.

If you're wondering what the scientific rationale behind all of this is, then you're not the only one. It is literally bollocks.

Brinkley was not an officially licensed medical practitioner – well, there's a surprise – having earned his diploma from a diploma mill. After spending his early life touring towns and selling 'tonics' and other phoney cure-alls, he settled in Milford, Kansas, in 1918 and set up a pharmacy.

His first foray into testicular transplanting came that same year. According to a biography that Brinkley himself commissioned, a farmer came to his practice complaining of impotence, and Brinkley jokingly replied, 'You wouldn't have any trouble if you had a pair of those buck glands in you.' The farmer then said, 'Well, why not?' (hold on, he said what?). Despite Brinkley's protests (not very strong protests, given this operation relied entirely on his carrying it out), the farmer brought in his own goat for the transplant – which was, apparently, a resounding success. The farmer paid $150 for the operation, which would be $1,940 in today's money. Brinkley would go on to increase the price for new patients to $750.

If you think this story sounds like bullshit, then you

might be right. The patient's son claimed Brinkley had in fact offered to pay his father 'handsomely' if he'd go along with the insane plan. Who should you believe? Oh yeah, not the conman.

The operations continued, because, unbelievably, other people were convinced that this would work for them. In the ultimate act of laziness, the testicles were simply placed inside the patient, rather than sewn in or attached in any way. Just balls floating around in your body. That can't be healthy – and it wasn't.

Brinkley's business boomed and, luckily for him, the wife of his first client had a baby, nicknamed 'Billy' (because of the goat balls – geddit?). The resulting news story, head-lined 'First Goat-Gland Baby', brought national attention to Brinkley's 'work'. After hiring an agent and embarking on a campaign of mail advertisements, Brinkley finally attracted the attention of the American Medical Association. Their undercover agent found a woman hobbling around Brinkley's clinic who had been given goat ovaries as a cure for a spinal cord tumour.

How the hell wasn't that the end of all this? How could someone get away with such hokum and obvious lies?

Because people are stupid.

Due to poor sanitary practices, many of Brinkley's patients died of infection afterwards, although what is much more surprising is that any patients at all survived. Forty-two death certificates were signed by Brinkley, but the total death toll is unknown. He was regularly sued for malpractice.

Rather than going to prison for any of this, Brinkley was given his own radio show, on which he was able to continually promote his goat-gland treatments to the gullible, goat-testicle-hungry public.

He wasn't all bad. He did loads of stuff for charity. He funded public works in Milford, including a new sewage system and a bandstand, and twice stood for governorship in Kansas, once very nearly successfully. If only he'd stuck some goat gonads into himself, surely he'd have had the magic power to get the necessary votes.

Eventually, after a litany of lawsuits, Brinkley declared bankruptcy in 1941, dying penniless in San Antonio, Texas, in 1943.

We might laugh at people for believing this goat-crap, but just take a look at the politicians we've been voting in, and the 'doctors' whose shit we have lapped up, and the way 1970s light entertainers managed to commit major crimes practically live on air and still got funerals fit for royalty.

Don't worry, though. My remaining testicle *is* magic. If you give me £10,000 in cash and then rub it, you will gain immunity from all confidence tricks and (if you rub it well enough) become impervious to all disease. Contact me on Twitter for full details.

17

The big 'C'

I had thought I would have to wait until I saw my oncologist
to find out the diagnosis on my excised ping-pong ball, but
the day after the Paxman interview, I got an unexpected call
from the hospital. The results were in.

The doctor kept up the tension by first asking me how the
recovery was going, and then telling me that I'd be walking
like John Wayne for a little while longer yet. Only then did
he hit me with the news: 'You probably won't be surprised to
learn that this was cancer.'

I'm not sure if I was surprised or not. I had almost convinced
myself that the aberration had been a tiny submarine crewed
by Raquel Welch that had got stuck in the thin tubules of my
groin. With that in mind, I suppose cancer wasn't the most
unexpected diagnosis.

It seemed like bad news, but this doctor was very upbeat
about it all, almost as if it was good news. Then he told me that
the cancer had been safely ensconced inside my ball, like the
hazelnut in the middle of a Ferrero Rocher. Actually, it was
bigger than that. If we are comparing it to confection, then it's

more like the plastic pod in a Kinder Egg, but instead of containing a Krazy Kroko,* it contained Krazy Kancer.

It doesn't really matter which chocolate it was most like. The point was that the cancer hadn't spread. They'd got it all out of me.

More of a surprise to me than the news that I had indeed had cancer was what came next. I learned, for the first time in all this process, that testicular cancer has a 99 per cent survival rate.

Why was I only being told this now? I'm pretty sure that none of the other medical staff I'd met had thought to inform me of that. Maybe they had and I'd blanked it out or not been listening, but I am reasonably confident that I would have grabbed on to that, like a doctor grabbing on to the bollocks of someone they've just met.

I'd really have liked to have been given that statistic six weeks earlier. My GP could have slipped in that if he was a betting man, he'd say it wasn't testicular cancer, and furthermore, if it *was* cancer, he'd definitely bet on my survival, given the incredible odds in my favour.

I believe that the NHS discourages its staff from discussing cancer until cancer has been diagnosed, but surely there should be an exception if the cancer is curable. My only criticism of this whole process is that they didn't tell me about this statistic on day one. The worst thing about the last month and a half had been the feeling of dread in the pit of my stomach and the fear that I was going to cease to be before my laptop had gleaned my teeming brain.

I'm sure I'd have still managed to conjure up all kinds of scenarios where I snuffed it. I could be in the one per cent who

---

* Sorry to go back to a 1990s toy, but that was my era for Kinder Eggs – even though I was in my mid-twenties at that time.

don't make it (after all, only one in 270 men will get testicular cancer, so I'd already beaten worse odds). Still, I might not have been quite so afraid. Maybe I should be thankful, though. Believing that, as Barry Cryer used to say, I shouldn't buy any green bananas, had certainly made me appreciate what I had and that I didn't want to lose it just yet.

The doctor told me there were two kinds of testicular cancer, the good kind and the very good kind. I had the very good kind. Furthermore, I could move my odds of survival much closer to 100 per cent (and, presumably, immortality) if I had one shot of chemo.

After the shaky voices and ashen faces I'd encountered, suddenly I'd come across someone who was basically equating testicular cancer with a nasty splinter. Obviously, losing a body part had been a price to pay, but the only thing I cared about was survival, which suddenly seemed assured.

I had been unlucky to get a fairly rare cancer without exhibiting any of the usual symptoms, but then how lucky was I to get the one that is basically curable? One that they'd already basically cured?

I'd dodged a bullet (or rather, jumped over it so it just nipped me in the nutsack). It's sad to lose a gonad in a gunfight, but you can't really complain when cancer is a gunfight that has so many serious casualties.

ON THE BALL: Balls on ice

In September 1991, the body of a man was discovered high in the Ötztal Alps between Austria and Italy. It turned out that this person had lived and died some time between

3350 and 3105 BCE, and his body had been naturally mummified beneath the ice. He became known as Ötzi the Iceman.

It was an incredible discovery for archaeologists and scientists, who were able to deduce a great deal from his belongings and the contents of his stomach. They could even tell a lot about how he died. It looked like he'd been killed by an arrowhead, which was lodged in his scapula. Thanks to blood residues on his clothing, scientists were able to determine that he had killed two people with one arrow, (which he had then retrieved), and that he had carried a wounded person on his back before he himself was shot. His last battle had been quite an eventful one.

But we don't care about any of this. We are only concerned with Ötzi's ancient bollocks. The first question is: did he have any?

An early publication claimed his genitals were missing, and speculated they might have been ripped off when the body was pulled from the ice. Others thought that Ötzi might be a ritually castrated victim left on the mountain for winter. According to the *Smithsonian* magazine, this genital absence 'prompted a German journalist to publish a book claiming that the entire discovery was a fraud and that Ötzi was nothing more than a castrated Egyptian mummy, planted in the mountains to stimulate tourism'.* This would have been an incredible scheme, and I am not sure how much tourism it would have stimulated:

'Do you want to go to see that mountain where they found a really old man with no genitals?'

---

* Bob Cullen, 'Testimony from the Iceman', February 2003, www.smithsonian-mag.com.

'No, I'm OK, thanks. Shall we go to Val d'Isère instead? There's a place that does fondue.'

The book prompted Austrian scientists to go back and check the body again, and they discovered they'd got it wrong the first time. Ötzi's tackle was, in fact, intact (though, as with the entire body, it was pretty fragile and misshapen). It's a bit embarrassing for Ötzi that they missed it on the first inspection – but to be fair to him, he'd been in the ice for 5,000 years, so it was pretty cold.

There were all kinds of crazy rumours about Ötzi's bollocks. Some people believed that his sperm had survived in the frozen conditions (not true), and an internet site declared: 'Women clamoured to be the first to be impregnated with sperm from Ötzi's testicles.'*

Really? Would it even be possible for him to father a child millennia after his death? Hadn't they realised that he wouldn't be able to pay maintenance? Would anyone really be desperate to carry that child? Would so many people be desperate to carry that child that there would be actual *clamouring* to get at his semen? If his sperm had survived, there would be enough to go round for everyone who wanted some. If none had survived, there would still be enough to go round for everyone who wanted some, because no one would want this. Another bollock story that turns out to be bollocky bollocks.

Maybe this, too, was a scheme dreamed up to increase tourism. But surely the Ötztal Alps aren't so crap that you need to entice people hungry for prehistoric spunk. I wonder if they actually had too many tourists and were trying to put some of them off.

* 'Otzi, the ice man', www.factsanddetails.com.

The really bad news for anyone reading this who thinks they might like to have a kid with Ötzi, and has somehow managed to get their hands on his gametes, is that according to Dr Franco Rollo, he was possibly infertile anyway.*

That didn't stop people sexualising this twisted old corpse, though. Another rumour developed that Ötzi had been found with sperm in his stomach, leading some people to come to the ludicrous conclusion that he might be the world's first gay caveman. To be fair, if he had sperm in his stomach, there would have to be at least one other gay caveman, unless Ötzi had been as flexible in life as he was in death.

This myth came about due to a confusion in translation. The German press had reported that he had seeds in his stomach, which was true. However, the German for seed, '*samen*', is also the word for semen.

I don't know what it is about Ötzi that leads to him having all this sexual interest and speculation thrown his way. I don't remember Tutankhamen's balls getting this kind of attention.

---

* Sophie Hardach, 'Otzi the ice man may have been infertile', 6 February 2006, www.abc.net.au.

18

Flaming undercarriage

The main thing I learned in the first two weeks after my surgery was that if you're wearing a jockstrap, then you really need to take it off at some point. I removed it to wash and changed into a fresh one every day, but I didn't allow the area to breathe. In hindsight, I probably didn't need to sleep in it.

As a result, I ended up in the worst pain that I would experience all year. I got crotch rot.

I became aware of a weird smell, and the skin at the top of my thighs started to sting and then hurt. I was starting to rot away. It would be ironic if I lost the rest of my genitals due to following the doctor's instructions too stringently.

The jock rash got me out of the house, though. It was merely a walk up to the GP's surgery to get some anti-fungal cream, but it was the most beautiful and life-affirming perambulation of my life. I'm not joking; I was positively high. I'd felt good on the walk back from the GP's when they'd told me they thought I didn't have cancer, but this was another level.

Maybe it was the fresh air, or maybe my body feeling thankful to be alive, but it was certainly the happiest I'd been since

I'd realised my bollock was trying to kill me. If something is denied to you for a decent length of time, it is so liberating when you get it back. I expect Nelson Mandela experienced something similar to this when they let him out of prison. Probably not as intense as what was happening to me, though, because he still had both bollocks. It was like God was stroking my hair and saying, 'Well done, mate. I tested you by removing your testes (clue in the name) and you came out believing in me exactly the same amount as you did before. That is, not at all. Never mind, though. Have some of my special God legal-high drugs.'

'It's not right for you to test people like that, God.'

'Oh, come on. It's just a bit of a laugh.'

'No, you're God. You're supposed to rise above stuff like that.'

'Fuck you. You don't even think I'm real.'

'Is that surprising, when you act like a child so often?'

'You can fucking talk.'

'I haven't set myself up as God, though, have I?'

'Nor did I. I just *am* God. There was nothing I could do about it.'

'But you're omnipotent. You can stop being God if you want.'

'And lose all the magic powers? Jog on, mate.'

'OK, thanks for the drugs, anyway. And the gift of life. Life is a wonderful thing.'

'See, I had to take your bollock to make you learn that lesson.'

'Or you could have simply appeared to me and told me the lesson and left my bollocks alone.'

'You wouldn't have learned.'

'Why not just threaten to take my bollock?'

'You wouldn't have believed that I'd do it. This was the only way.'

'Can you magic my bollock back on now?'

'Of course I can; I can do anything. It would be pimpsy.'
'Are you going to?'
'Nah.'
'Stop moving in that mysterious way.'
'I like it.'

I wasn't walking quickly, but I wasn't walking like John Wayne, either. It was good to get out for a proper stroll, but I don't think you'd have pegged me for a uniball just by looking at me. If anything, it was a bit easier to walk without my ball getting in the way. The one that's left was keeping himself to himself, probably out of fear of what might happen to him if he stepped out of line.

Maybe Action Man was such an action man because he had made the ultimate sacrifice in order to ensure smooth walking and running motion. I don't mind losing the balls, but the cock would be a cut too deep for me. It's wrong to have favourites, but that's definitely my preferred piece of genitalia. I hope that it can live on after I die. It's the only organ that I think might be in good enough working order to be donated, and I envy the lucky bugger who'll end up with it. It's a real beauty. Everyone says so.

This walk – to get some cream for a sore crotch, remember – was both an ending and a new beginning. I was glad that I had managed to get through all this by mainly taking the piss. Getting all serious and sad after a lifetime of joking about everything would be like being that idiot in the audience of an offensive comedian who laughs uproariously at all the jokes, until one comes along that is about something close to them, and then they get all stroppy. They are the worst people in the world.

Laughter is the only sensible reaction to this stupid and nonsensical life, along with the occasional sense of wonder at how unlikely it is we should be here at all, and how amazing it all is. If I can be enveloped by that profundity when hobbling down the road for my crotch-rot medicine, then there's no excuse for anyone.

Thanks, God, you're playing a blinder.

ON THE BALL: Papal reach-around

In the thirteenth century, a rumour evolved that, before a new pope could take the seat of the papacy, he'd have to sit in different kind of seat: a special one with a hole in the middle, called the Estercoraria chair. A young deacon would inspect the pope's genitalia via the hole to ensure that he was in possession of testicles. They wouldn't want a woman getting to try on all those papal dresses and perfumed oils; to get all that, you need to be a man.

This ceremony is said to have started due to the legend of Saint Joan, a woman who managed to become pope by pretending to be a man. Her true gender was discovered only when, during a procession through the streets, she went into labour. So presumably at least one person knew her true gender – though with those Catholics, you can never be quite sure.

If it sounds like something from *Blackadder*, that's probably because it clearly never actually happened. Of course, being a made-up load of old rubbish doesn't stop people believing things, as the existence of the Vatican attests.

Sadly, it's probably not even true that the pope gets his junk checked before he gets to be pope. Fascinated by what might be going on in the secretive Vatican, ambassadors, tour guides and court officials made up their own stories. Even after the absence of such a test in the coronation of

Pope Julius II in 1503, the Venetian ambassador, Antonio Giustiniani, still detailed a 'ceremony, vulgarly said to be that of putting a hand underneath' to find 'evidence of the virility of popes'. There is no evidence of this. And if there is a chair, then no one knows where it is.

After all, it's not like the Vatican would be capable of covering up something as scandalous as this for decades or centuries . . .

19

Bollock Holodeck

Just when I thought it couldn't get any worse for Catie, I
found that my crotch rot was too deep in my crevices for
me to locate with any accuracy, and too sensitive for me to
prod around at, so she had to help me apply unguents to the
sore and frankly stinky area. I lifted my legs above my head
and showed her things that no partner should have to see in
the harsh light of day. She didn't even (visibly) flinch.

They didn't do a *Love is …* cartoon of this, did they? But if
this isn't love, then what is?

It really should be Catie with the book deal. My story of
facing my own mortality, losing a body part and coming
back stronger is way too positive. I think she has a proper
misery memoir in her. *Smearing Unguent in My One-Bollocked
Husband's Crevices* will be a bestseller and no doubt an Oscar-
winning movie, with Daniel Day-Lewis playing my left ball.

She definitely got the raw end of this deal (even if I was the
one with the raw end). While I was relaxing in bed, getting
flowers from one of the stars of *Dude, Where's My Car?* and
chomping my way through posh biscuits, she was looking

after two young kids, stemming the flow of blood from her extracted tooth and contemplating a future as a widow. I let her have a couple of the biscuits. I'm not a monster.

I did have plenty of time to contemplate my predicament, but I was still remarkably calm and almost indifferent to the loss I had suffered. Now that my left ball had started to settle in the middle, I didn't even have any qualms about not having taken the prosthetic. If anything, my tight little scrotum looked rather neat, and also served to make my penis look bigger ... *even* bigger. (Can we make sure it says 'even bigger' in the final edit?)

There would be many benefits to having a less-packed lunchbox. Some pants that had been too small for me before now fitted perfectly, and as I started to move around, and later exercise, I realised that things were a lot more comfortable down there in general. I had to play fewer games of pocket billiards to fit comfortably into my underwear, and when it came to exercise, the single central bollock led to a whole new world of freedom. Those things can swing around or bunch up in your pants and get in the way. When you're down to one, you become basically unencumbered. I'd recommend it as a cosmetic procedure to all testicle-owners, just to make your life less irksome, though of course that would mean you lose the safety net of having two in case something goes wrong.

Why didn't I care about it? Had I failed to process what had happened to me? Was I living in denial? Surely there should be some grieving for what I had lost.

There was none. I hated that traitor. It had despised me so much that it had tried to kill me, even though that would also result in its own death. It was the most self-defeating exit since ... well, only since Brexit, but still.

My only concern over those first few days was that I might have lost some sexual function. It was one thing being happy to be alive, but I didn't want to give up on one of the things that makes life worth living.

Obviously, immediately following the operation I was not really in a fit state to put my equipment through even a partial workout. I had stitches that could pop, and my remaining ball and my penis seemed to be in mourning for their fallen comrade and retracted into themselves, so it wouldn't be right to try to cajole them into any kind of sexual relationship just yet. I had no interest in even touching them, and left them alone to lick each other's wounds.

A few days in, I decided to check if things would still, in theory, function, and with a half-hearted, reluctant and rather sad fumble, managed to confirm that the fun-balloon was still capable of inflation, but I wasn't going to take it any further yet. What mixture of gametes and blood might emerge from my devastated manbag? I did not wish to find out.

A few overly curious men have asked me if losing a testicle has resulted in me producing a smaller volume of man-glue. Of course, as we all know, most of what's in your ejaculate is not produced by the testicles, but in the seminal vesicle,* with the sperm just hitching a ride on that tidal wave. It's still got to make a difference if you've only got one of your replicating devices turned on, right?

I wish I had an answer, but sadly I forgot to take a pre-operation measurement. If only I had invested in some scientific flasks and dipsticks, I could give you accurate sperm volumes, but like a fool, I spaffed the lot up the wall. If I am forced to make a guestimate on my semen production now as opposed to then, I would say it's roughly the same amount. Half of basically nothing is still basically nothing.

---

* It's OK if you thought it all came out of the testicle. I've written extensively about male genitalia, and it was only when writing this book that I discovered this.

The only certain observation that I have for science is that losing a testicle hasn't resulted in me producing *more* semen than before.

Maybe this was all about denial; if I didn't believe it had happened, then I was still complete. I was certainly struggling to come to terms with the fact that I'd had cancer. Right from the start, I'd felt like a fraud, like I was using up resources for people with proper cancer. Even now I knew I had technically (and actually) had cancer, the imposter syndrome wasn't abating. My cancer was play cancer, the fun kind that meant you got sympathy and food hampers, but with no actual danger.

I was a cancer tourist on the Star Trek Holodeck (Bollock-deck?). I was being shown all the sights that someone with proper cancer would get to see, but it wasn't going to ravage me or destroy me, because I didn't really have cancer. I had paid (with an unusual testicular currency) to safely experience what someone with the proper deadly cancer would experience, and then I'd just walked away (if a little uncomfortably).

All those people with proper dangerous cancers, and I come along with my 99 per cent curable one and get to pretend that I'm in the same boat. I can claim to be (and have claimed to be) a cancer survivor (I've had cancer and I am not dead), but given that the worst pain I experienced was down to me keeping a jock strap on for too long, I can't see myself being recognised at the Pride of Britain Awards.

I am not saying I was right to feel this way, but that's the way I felt. Even now, as I write this, I don't quite believe I actually had real cancer.

It's because I had preconceptions about the condition that I think many of us have: that it's a death sentence; that anyone who gets it, however bravely they fight, and even if they seem to be winning the battle, will get weak and thin and bald and succumb to it; that doctors may be able to postpone the inevitable for a while, but ultimately it's game over.

The truth is that every cancer patient's story is different. Cancer is often survivable; many cancers are treatable; people go on to live long lives and die of something else entirely. Maybe a totally different cancer! You never know your luck.

Bizarrely, I was finding having had cancer quite useful. Over the next few weeks and months, I realised I was able to get out of work or social engagements that I didn't fancy by saying, 'Sorry, I've had cancer.' Even when feeling fitter than I had for years, I'd get an email from someone asking me to be on their podcast and I could say, 'Oh sorry, didn't you know? I've just had cancer,' and they'd actually apologise to me for having had the temerity to ask.

'This is great,' I said to Catie. 'I only have to say I've had cancer and everything goes away. What a scam!'

'You know you *have* had cancer,' she replied.

'Yeah, but not really.'

'You really have.'

'But not properly.'

'Rich, it was cancer.'

'I know. That's what I can tell people. It's the best thing that's ever happened to me.'

I knew I needed to find a way to process all of this, and before I'd even had the operation, I'd had an inkling of how I might do it. A prop-maker called Richard Ison had so enjoyed my silly puppet show that, totally unprompted, he'd sent me an exquisite and beautiful ventriloquist dummy of the (possibly former by the time you read this) Duke of York. I'd then asked him if he'd make me a model of a phallic carrot that had become a character on the show. He even made a tiny version of me, along with even tinier versions of some of my puppets. They were all amazing.

I wanted to commission him for a new puppet – one that would allow me to confront my demons head-on and find out what I really thought about what had happened. I emailed him my specifications and he enthusiastically got down to work.

ON THE BALL: Literary (b)allusions

Let's have a look at a couple of the classier references to balls throughout history in the hope that we can write a dissertation about bollocks in literature, before realising there is probably not enough source material.

There is a common belief that Roman witnesses used to literally swear upon their balls, and that's where the word 'testify' comes from. Has any common testicle belief or story turned out to be true yet? Because this one isn't, either.

In Latin, *testis* was the medical term for testicles, and *testor* was the verb meaning to testify. The similarity between *testis* and *testor* was, unsurprisingly, the source of many puns (comedy has not found the need to move on from this kind of material – if it ain't broke) and poets like Priapius made jokes about possessing '*testis*' being a useful indicator of whether someone could testify well.

This led to later misunderstandings by humourless Renaissance writers who weren't into ball puns and so thought it meant Roman witnesses would literally swear upon their balls, clasping them while doing so.

'*Testis*' (the testifying version) has an Indo-European root meaning 'three', as the witnesses were seen as third parties. Ejaculate, too, derives from Latin, from *eiaculatus* or 'shot out', itself deriving from *iaculum*, a little spear or javelin. It's true that with a poorly aimed ejaculation, you can have someone's eye out. Or at least make them sting for a while.

In medieval writing, testicles were sometimes referred to as 'coin purses'. Bawdy plays and rhymes likened them to moneybags whose contents may be spent unwisely, or frivolously, rather than appropriately being deposited in the bank that was the womb. In a sixteenth-century Italian carnival song written by Alfonso de' Pazzi, men pretending to be jewellers boast: 'We have precious stones/ that are as big as beans; / firm and shiny/ but we keep them locked up.' They also claim that their stock includes 'large pendants/ from which their pearls issue forth'.

They were implying they had huge balls full of spunk. I think we'd all respect them more if they'd just said that.

20

He's got an ology

Thirteen days after my surgery, I got in my car for the first time to make the fifty-minute drive to meet my oncologist. I had an oncologist, because I'd had cancer (ha ha, as if).

It was uncomfortable when I drove over a bump, but it was good to be at the point where I was independent and able to do something normal again – if going to talk to a stranger about your cancerous bollock can be considered normal. No matter; I wasn't in a bed full of biscuit crumbs. I was out in the early spring sunshine.

I was heading to the Mount Vernon Cancer Centre in Northwood for an appointment with Dr Anand Sharma to find out what the next move was. I was pretty sure what the next move was. It was another terrible C-word that people react to very badly: chemotherapy.

That's the last roll of the dice, surely.

At least, that's what I would have thought before all this – and maybe it's what you think. Certainly, people were unable to hide their concern when I told them that I might need chemotherapy. As with so much about cancer, our worst-case scenario projections are often proven wrong.

I thought it was mildly inconvenient that Mount Vernon was nearly an hour's drive from my house, but in fact, I had got lucky once again. Mount Vernon specialises in relatively rare cancers, like testicular cancer (oh yeah, I got a special one), and most people would have to travel much further than I had. The focus on less-common cancers also meant that the waiting room was basically empty, and my appointment started bang on time. A trip to my local hospital might actually have taken up more of my day.

I was shown through to Dr Sharma's office by another happy and positive nurse, called Linda. In the wrong hands, this positivity could become a bit Stepford Wifey, but the thing about the NHS is that the people who work there are generally genuinely good people, because you have to be. You only do this job if you want to help people. You're certainly not doing it for the money. I suppose occasionally someone works for the NHS because they want to commit loads of murders or have sex with corpses, but I am pretty sure that that lot (in spite of the publicity they get when they get caught) are very much a minority.

Linda gave me a leaflet with phone numbers (including hers) for me to ring if I was worried about anything at any time. They were really looking after me. I don't think it was because they were planning to kill me or to keep my cadaver looking presentable for when they shagged it.

We waited together for the arrival of the oncologist. Perhaps aware that it was intimidating to meet a cancer specialist, Linda stayed with me throughout this meeting. She would be my point of contact for any future problems (and I did have to call on her a few times over the next few months), and so her and Dr Sharma were very much a team – and quite the double act.

Before he'd even sat down, Dr Sharma wasted no time in

telling me that he knew who I was, and that he had watched me on *Taskmaster*. Perhaps this was true, though the *Daily Mail* had just published an article about my cancer (fulfilling a life-long ambition that that particular paper should run a news story about my balls; the only disappointment was that they weren't on the front page, though to be fair, that's usually full of bollocks) and I suspect he might have read that. This theory was soon sharpened, as the *Mail* had called me 'a well-known philanthropist',* and the doctor immediately homed in on the fact that I liked to raise money for charity. He really didn't beat around the bush: he said that if I was tempted to do any more fundraising, then I should do it for his charity, the Cancer Treatment and Research Trust (CTRT).† I did not mind him asking. I was very keen to give something back.

Dr Sharma said that most people raised money for Macmillan Cancer Support, but I reassured him that I wouldn't be doing that, as Macmillan Cancer Support are my sworn enemies. When I'd come up with the idea for the *Talking Cock* stand-up show in 2002, I'd got in touch with them, saying I planned to give the audience a free programme and then, at the end of the show, to collect donations for charity. I wondered, fully expecting the answer 'yes please', if they'd like me to give those donations to them. They could have a free ad in the programme, too. It might help raise awareness of the cancers that can hit men in their most sensitive area.

Macmillan asked me what I wanted in return, which I thought was odd. Do people usually expect quid pro quo from a charity? I told them I wanted nothing, I only wanted to give them some free money and publicity.

Macmillan told me that they didn't think they wanted their

---

* I am not sure this is really true, but if it's in the *Daily Mail* then it must be.
† https://cancertreatment.org.uk/

charity associated with a show with this title. I thought that was a bit judgemental, especially given the show didn't even exist yet, but to spite them, I made the programmes anyway and gave all the collection money to Macmillan. That would show them.

After the show had been a Fringe hit and had garnered strong reviews, which explained that it was more than sixty minutes of knob gags and a sensitive, if bawdy, examination of masculinity, which attempted to get men to talk openly and honestly about their genitals, I contacted the charity again to see if they wanted to get on board for the tour. Once again, they knocked me back. I was a little bit hurt by this rejection.

As it happened, I was running the London Marathon for the disability charity Scope that year, and asked them if they'd like me to collect money for them at shows. They reacted in the way I had assumed any charity would do, and basically bit my hand off. Over the last two decades, my audiences have donated over £300,000* to Scope through post-show collections. I have also nominated them as my chosen charity on TV shows like *Mastermind*, *Pointless*, *Tipping Point* and *The Chase*, bringing in winnings of over £60,000.† Which is satisfying, partly for the good that money does, but mainly because Macmillan could have had it, if they hadn't been such pricks (ironically).

Admittedly, in hindsight, it might have been better for me if the money had gone to Macmillan, as I now had had cancer. Scope haven't done anything for me personally. They wouldn't even let me have one of the parking badges. Even though it's a Pyrrhic victory, I think it's a fitting punishment for Macmillan that I will never help them in any way, and will actively slag them off in print at any opportunity. I am so angry with them

---

* I am not taking personal credit for this – my audience are the generous ones, though I have spent an awful lot of my post-gig time in hotels bagging up 1p pieces so I can pay them into the bank. I am very rock and roll.
† Hey, the *Daily Mail* were right. I am a philanthropist.

for being sniffy about me and my perfectly respectable cock show that I have been thinking of actively trying to sabotage them, maybe by breaking into some of their hospitals and smashing up equipment.

I know that me taking umbrage with a charity is not a good look. I tell this story very much against myself. What kind of an idiot has a vendetta against a charity that helps thousands of people?

But still, fuck Macmillan! I'd raise some money for CTRT and for the hospitals that had helped me. I didn't know how I was going to do that yet, but these were the institutions that had saved my life and given me the chance to see my kids grow up, so this was really the least I could do.

Dr Sharma had a look at my scar, which was healing well, and had a little feel of my depleted ballsack (his charity pitch had used up so much time that he was nowhere near beating the ball-fondler world record – a very poor effort). He told me that the operation had been a success and that all of the cancer was gone, but it could come back. As expected, I had a decision to make.

If I did nothing, I had a one in four chance of the cancer returning. I didn't really love those odds. I play poker, and I know how often a 75 per cent sure thing gets beaten. It's roughly once in every four occasions. I was offered the choice of only coming back for scans every few months for the next few years, or of having the scans but also one shot of pre-cautionary chemotherapy. This would reduce the chance of returning bollock cancer from one in four to one in twenty. Those are odds that I could cope with (though again, about 5 per cent of the time they're proven to be deadly on the poker table). I didn't have to have the chemo if I didn't want to. If the cancer came back, they would still be able to treat it. The chemo would be light and not have many side effects. My hair wouldn't fall out, which was a surprise to me and plenty of the people I told about my procedure. There are lots of different types of chemotherapy, and I would be getting the lightest possible one. I might be a little lethargic and nauseous, it might make me infertile (though was that a negative or a positive?), but basically, I would be fine.

For a little bit of real-world jeopardy, the chemo would also weaken my immune system. At any other time, this wouldn't have been too much of a worry, but in the days of Covid, that fact made me a little hesitant. I hadn't been vaccinated yet, because at this stage only the elderly had been, and they'd only had their first shot.

I was prepared to risk it, though, especially when they told me that, as someone who would be especially vulnerable, I could jump the vaccination queue. (I phoned up for an appointment and got one the next day! Take that, people who haven't had cancer – you must be feeling pretty bad now.)

Not only did I want to improve my odds of not having cancer again, I also wanted to get the full *Total Recall* cancer experience that I'd paid for. I'd had play-time cancer, so why not have a ridiculously light parody of chemotherapy, too?

I wondered if Dr Sharma could tell me how I got this cancer, but he wasn't really able to do so. He said that it was likely the roots of it go back as far as being in the womb, with something happening there that created the potential for this to play out eventually. I told him about hurting my ball in the sea in Barbados,* and he said that might have been the catalyst that set the ball rolling, so to speak. My cancer had lain dormant

---

* Though I totally forgot that my ball had also come under fire in 2007 when I got into a fight with a university lecturer. You can find out about that in my book *How Not to Grow Up*, or my stand-up show *Oh Fuck, I'm 40!*. My bollocks have really taken a beating.

and then possibly slowly developed over the last twenty years. It was a great and patient punchline to that disastrous vacation. It made me laugh, which made my scar hurt, just for a little extra topper to the gag.

I asked if it could be down to anything I had done, aware that I hadn't always lived the healthiest of lifestyles – could it be due to too much beer or Diet Coke or sugar, or having my phone in my right-hand trouser pocket, or playing on my Acorn Electron computer as a teenager with the hot keyboard on my lap?

Apparently not.

Dr Sharma took a look at me, my belly bloated by post-op biscuits (although, to be fair, there had been quite a gut there before) and told me that the operation would have changed my metabolism, so it was important I lost some weight and got fitter or I'd increase my chances of getting diabetes, high blood pressure and other unpleasant stuff.

I didn't want to survive this brush with death only to fall at the next hurdle because I was too heavy to get over it. I had never been more determined to squeeze as many years out of this life as I possibly could.

It turns out that if an oncologist tells me to do something, then I do it. I decided to ditch the biscuits and get exercising as soon I was able, and also come up with a plan to raise some money for his charity.

I hope an oncologist never tells me to kill the president. With great oncology comes great responsibility.

Linda asked me if I had any questions. I only had one area of concern, which was when it would be OK for me to resume sexual relations with my wife. We had still not risked it, and I worried that after the jock-rash cream incident, she'd never be able to look at me as a sexual proposition again. Or, worse still, that she'd only be able to find me sexy if she was smearing unguent into groinal sores.

They seemed surprised that I had asked about sex. Linda laughed. 'Oh yes, you are still quite young, aren't you?'

I mean, I'm not, but I am hoping there's a few more years of lovemaking to come.

I was actually wondering about the stitches and whether they would split, but Dr Sharma assumed I meant after chemotherapy, and told me I would need to wear a condom during sex for several months to protect my wife, presumably from the chemotherapy drugs in my system. That hadn't been my concern, but I was glad they'd taken it that way, as if I hadn't asked, I might not have realised that was an issue. I really just wanted to know if I was good to go *now*, before the chemo, but I didn't want to look like a sex-starved maniac, even though I was one, so I left it at that.

Why was it 'several months'? How long would the chemo chemicals stay in me? Or was it because my sperm would be damaged long-term? After my initial bravery, I was too nervous to get clarification. The internet wasn't much help. Websites seemed to say that the chemo chemicals would only stay in my bloodstream for a few days. What was this 'several months' shit? And how many months is several? Two months or twenty-two?

I guessed I was going to have to tell my wife that I was full of dangerous sperm, but I'd wear a condom and she could risk contact if she wanted to. Who wouldn't be turned on by that?

ON THE BALL: Chim Chim Cher . . . ooo

Though the causes of testicular cancer are not always fully understood, there have been cases where it's clear what's to blame. Luckily, these are not likely to happen today, but they reveal a gruesome side to our history. If you thought

the worst thing that happened to chimney sweeps was Dick
Van Dyke's accent in *Mary Poppins*, I've got news for you.
Who would have thought forcing children up chimneys and
lighting rags under them to keep them climbing would turn
out to be a bad thing?

In the eighteenth century, testicular cancer and skin
cancer in the scrotum were so common among the boys
who cleaned Victorian chimneys that it became known
as soot-wart, or the Chimney-sweeps' Cancer. A common
treatment was amputation, but often this wasn't enough,
and death followed.

In 1775 Percivall Pott (maybe drawn to the cause after a
lifetime of being called 'Chimney' Pott) called attention to
ballsack cancer in chimney sweeps. In his brilliantly named
*Chirurgical observations relative to the Cataract, the Polypus
of the Nose, and the Cancer of the Scrotum, etc.* (who
wouldn't pluck that one off the shelf, with such a catchy
title?), he noted that:

> There is disease as peculiar to a certain set of people,
> which has not, at least to my knowledge, been publicly
> noticed; I mean chimney-sweepers' cancer. It is a dis-
> ease which always makes its first attack on, and its first
> appearance in, the inferior part of the scrotum; where it
> produces a superficial, painful, ragged, ill-looking sore,
> with hard and rising edges. The trade call[s] it soot-wart.

Pott described the progressive nature of the disease, the
benefits of early treatment, and the fatal outcome of late
surgical intervention. He added:

If there is any chance of putting a stop to, or prevent[ing] this mischief, it must be the immediate removal of the part affected ... for if it be suffered to remain until the virus has seized the testicle, it is generally too late for even castration. I have many times made the experiment; but though the sores ... have healed kindly, and the patients have gone from the hospital seemingly well yet, in the space of a few months ... they have returned either with the same disease in the other testicle, or glands of the groin, or with ... a disease state of some of the viscera, and which have soon been followed by a painful death.

He also suspected the chemical origin of scrotum cancer, noting: 'The disease, in these people, seems to derive its origin from a lodgment of soot in the rugae of the scrotum ... '

Two centuries later, scrotal cancer in chimney sweeps was linked to absorption of polycyclic aromatic hydrocarbons. If you see a tub of that, please don't try and cool your balls in it.

Eventually, we stopped sending children up chimneys and several chimney-sweep guilds suggested daily bathing, which sharply reduced this occupational risk.

You may not be in danger from this yourself, but I would still strongly encourage you to wash your balls (if you have them) daily. It will really boost your chances of finding someone to love you, or at least have sex with you, and if nothing else, that will go a small way towards making all those child chimney-sweep deaths worthwhile.

21

Oooo, I could crush a grape

One of my biggest fears, when I discovered that I needed an operation, was that it might affect my appearance on *Taskmaster: Champion of Champions*. Dying was one thing, but not getting the chance to compete for an almost life-size headless statue of Greg Davies? It didn't bear thinking about.

I had been booked to perform my tasks on 1 March, but as that was less than a week after my operation, there was no chance I would be mobile by then. The latest date that they could film at the location was 17 March. That would still only give me three weeks to recover, and I'd been advised not to exert myself for the first four weeks. Would I be fit enough to take part?

There was no way I wasn't going to do it.

I have been a fan of this incredibly funny and innovative TV show since the start. Since before the start, really. I took part in one of the prototype Edinburgh Fringe iterations of the game back in 2008. An evening largely memorable for me literally cracking a rib. Tim Key had moved a bar stool that I was trying to leapfrog on to and it hit me in the chest: bang, my ribcage took the full force. Although in quite a bit of pain, the show had to go on. I had to complete tasks such as putting up a child's tent while drinking a bottle of cider, as well as answering questions like 'How much would it cost to fill the Grand Canyon with Dairy Lea?'

'Presumably,' I posited, 'you'd get some kind of discount for bulk purchase?' I then underestimated the answer by £194 billion.

During that Fringe show, I was up against the delightful US comedian and actor Kristen Schaal – who, I should point out, had the advantage of having no cracked bones, though the disadvantage of being heavily jet-lagged. We went into the final round with me one point ahead. In a rapid-fire finale, I answered the question 'Heads or Tails' incorrectly, and she then got a chance to guess which way the coin might otherwise have fallen (a somewhat easier choice). I also (wrongly) thought there wasn't an actual pole at the North Pole, which again meant she was bound to get the points for saying there was. The helium-voiced American pipped me at the post, and I had to clump out of the arena in the (literal) clogs of shame. I hate to lose, and I hate to crack my own bones, but this was still tremendous fun. It only really hurt when I laughed, which was pretty much all the way through. (Not all of these ideas made it to the TV version, which has hardly injured any of its contestants.)

When *Taskmaster* finally appeared on the Dave channel in 2015, I (along with almost every stand-up comedian in the country) really hoped I would get a chance to take part. While most panel shows are one-offs and only suit a certain type of stand-up comedian (and their writing teams), *Taskmaster* was a format that gave comedians an opportunity to shine (or not) totally spontaneously, and over a number of weeks. I figured that my competitive nature, combined with my personality traits of mindless persistence and endless pedantry, would make me a funny, annoying and possibly strong contestant.

If you aren't aware of the series, might I suggest you put down this book and go and watch as many clips as possible on YouTube, or just ingest the whole thing from the beginning on All 4 or the dedicated *Taskmaster* subscription channel. Basically, it's an amazing TV programme where the seemingly polite and innocent (but actually devilishly fiendish) Alex Horne makes comedians (and occasionally other personalities) compete in a series of bizarre tasks to try and win points.

Contestants are ultimately trying to impress the mercurial Taskmaster, Greg Davies, who charmingly mocks and bullies everyone concerned in a way that, remarkably, is somehow immensely enjoyable, even for the victim. Well, at least for me, though I may have some kind of a problem.

When the show moved to Channel 4 for its tenth series, I finally got the call. I was going to be on the show; 2020 was going to be the most brilliant year! Nothing could possibly go wrong.

I filmed most of my tasks the day after the general election in December 2019. I had hardly slept, and was quite depressed by the comprehensive victory for the palpably terrible prime minister and liar Boris Johnson, so *Taskmaster* was a welcome distraction. It might explain why I was such a zombie duffer on a few of them, but I am probably just a zombie duffer anyway.

I went back to do my final tasks in mid-February, and everyone was mildly nervous about the approach of this new virus, but we were still at the stage where it seemed like something to joke about. We comically and self-consciously touched elbows when we met. As if that was going to become a thing!

Daisy May Cooper (with whom I was doing the team tasks) had a weird cold, but gamely carried on. We ended the day feeding each other watermelon at very close quarters, often chewing on the piece that had, moments before, been in the other's mouth. It was a very funny task, but it would probably be the last day in all history that such a thing would be allowed to happen anywhere.

We filmed the studio portion of that series at the end of July, just as everyone was coming out of the first lockdown. Everything was socially distanced and there was no audience, which made for a slightly haunting atmosphere, but we were all so happy to be out of our houses that we became giddy with hysteria, so it didn't matter. The first day's filming was a complete joy. If you watch the opening show, it looks like we've all been so stung by Greg's criticism that we've each had a little cry. In fact, we'd all spent the recording weeping with cathartic laughter. After the intensity of imprisonment, the general hilarity had me walking on air. It really is the best medicine. (Though, let me reiterate, not for testicular cancer – however funny testicles may be.)

Things got a bit more competitive over the next few days. In the end, the contest came down to the very last task. Daisy May Cooper was one point ahead of me. She was also heavily pregnant (that wasn't one of the challenges), but had gamely taken on all the studio tasks and was (if it's possible) even more keen to win than I was.

Daisy was so emotionally honest, open and funny that I fully loved her. I am not sure she felt the same about me. We'd certainly had our moments in the show, not least when I failed to identify her absolutely terrible depiction of a hippopotamus in a round where you had to draw an animal using only straight lines. She was genuinely furious with me, memorably saying she hated me even more than her husband – even though her drawing looked nothing like a hippopotamus, and Alex had had to ask her if she even knew what she was drawing. Her fury was very funny, but I was genuinely scared for my life. I am glad that we are not married and so, I would imagine, is she.

As we went up the stairs for this crucial final studio task, I said to her, 'Listen, I am obviously going to try to win this, but it's all been such fun and I will be equally delighted if you win.'

Daisy told me that she didn't feel the same, which was fair enough.

The final task was to balance either mint Polos or Party Ring biscuits on a bridge of uncooked spaghetti reaching between two coconuts – while wearing mittens. I had thought that such a thing might come up, so had been practising for months. Not really. This was the kind of mad, impossible challenge that *Taskmaster* throws up. If I failed or Daisy beat me, then Daisy would win the series. If I beat her by one place, then we'd go into a tie-break. The odds were stacked against me.

I gambled on using only two or three pieces of spaghetti, guessing that they would hold the weight of the mints, but still be narrow enough to thread through the Polo holes. With supreme concentration, and barely glancing at any of the other contestants, I got all the Polos on to the spaghetti and then put the spaghetti between the coconuts. The Polo/pasta bridge wobbled, but held. I had finished first.

It wasn't over yet; if Daisy could come second with her own bridge (she'd opted for the biscuits) then the show would go to a thrilling tie-break. Her bridge fell, her biscuits broke, and she dramatically destroyed everything in her vicinity. I thought that might extend to include my face and bones. I couldn't quite believe it, but I had won.

I was sad for Daisy. I tried to tell her that it had come down to who was best at the most ridiculous and meaningless challenge possible, but she thought I was ragging on her and didn't want to listen. I knew she would be the audience favourite, even if she hadn't impressed them by throwing herself into the studio tasks despite being heavily pregnant. I also knew that her star was very much in the ascendant, and that the show would propel her even further. She's a little bit crazy, but a big lot funny, and she had shone. She didn't need the trophy.

For me, winning *Taskmaster* was all I was going to get out of this. I had ground out a mildly dull victory – because winning, it turns out, is more important to me than being entertaining or impressing TV executives. That was fine, though. I only wanted the trophy, and there wasn't really any other TV show that I wanted to do. The best thing about winning was that I got to do it all again, if only for one more episode.

And so, I really didn't want to miss out on the chance to fight for the *Champion of Champions* crown – but on top of that, I did not want to give in to cancer. I was determined that I was going to get active as quickly as possible, and so found myself being driven through those familiar gates to the *Taskmaster* house, just three weeks on from my op (almost to the minute). I had been assured there would be no bike riding, and that if there was any lifting to do, then Alex would help me.

I had been so nervous the first time I'd come to this house, and even though I'd won the series (by the skin of my teeth), I'd been surprised by how I'd approached the tasks. I'd had very few flashes of inspiration, and hadn't taken many risks. In many cases, I'd taken the most obvious route possible. Tactically, this is probably quite a good way to play – being a maverick gives you the occasional win, but also comes with the possibility of disqualification. If you can come solidly second or third, then you will probably triumph. It's just not very entertaining to watch!

I had been nervous during the original series, but realised that today would be my last day in the *Taskmaster* house (unless I won again and they one day had a *Champion of Champion of*

Champions). The competition for this battle of the victors was unsurprisingly strong: not so much from lightweight contestant Ed Gamble, but from the unpredictable Lou Sanders, the no-nonsense Kerry Godliman, and especially from the supremely sensible and inventive Liza Tarbuck.

I decided that I was going to relax and properly enjoy this gift of an extra day of tasks. It really is such a pleasurable and special show to do, and Alex and the entire crew are an utter delight. The fact that you get paid for taking part in it seems ridiculous. I'd happily spend the rest of my life going to Chiswick and attempting to do stupid challenges set by this team for nothing more than the fun of it.

When asked to consume a grape in the most elaborate way possible, I decided to make it into a very tiny amount of wine, including crushing that single grape beneath my bare feet. Looking back, there was more than a little symbolism of what I'd been through. I don't think it influenced my thinking, but who knows what my subconscious was up to?

Even when there was an art task, something that I am really hopeless at, I overcame my initial stasis, forcing myself to plough on. I improvised a horrific picture of an octopus squirting ink over the other contestants. I hadn't read the brief properly (it was meant to be a picture that showed how wonderful the world was) and so it not only looked horrible, but in no way fulfilled the remit – but I was still proud that I'd given it a proper go. The only vigorous activity saw me lifting big bits of pipe around in an attempt to make a channel to get a rubber duck into a distant pond. My stitches held, and I constructed a quite impressive, though sadly too short, waterway, before spotting a hidden key that would give me access to a remote-controlled vehicle that allowed me to drive the duck to the water.

It's impossible to know how well you've done at these

things, as you don't see anyone else's efforts until the studio day (six months away at this point), but, terrible octopus aside, I thought I might have done all right.

Whatever happened on the night, I had won an important victory. I had not let my cancer stop me doing something that I really wanted to do. I had managed to take part in this active show, just three weeks after my operation.

I didn't need a trophy.

I still wanted a trophy.

ON THE BALL: How's it hanging?

Ancient Greek sculptors spent a lot of time making statues of naked men. They were brilliant at it. So much so that I assume they were looking at actual naked men while they chipped away at that marble. So it's quite surprising to notice that they made quite a significant testicular error in their work. They put the right testicle higher than the left – which is, generally speaking, how they fall in nature – but they also made the right one noticeably smaller. These Greek idiots thought that testicles acted like weights and kept the sperm ducts open, so the heavier testicle would be lower. In fact, the lower left testicle tends to be 7–10 per cent smaller than the right. Dr Chris MacManus won an Ig Nobel Prize for discovering this artistic inconsistency. His mum must have been proud.

A lot of men are surprised to find their balls do not rest side by side, and think that there is something wrong with them, but asymmetry is the norm. The reasons for this are not 100 per cent clear. It's likely to be something to do with temperature control. There's speculation that if balls were bumping up against each other, they'd overheat (also, given their sensitivity, it might be rather uncomfortable). Anatomist Stany Lobo suggests that the migration of the testes (which makes them sound like wild animals crossing some savannah or desert) means that each ball moves up and down on its own path, maximising surface area and making it easier to cool the things down when the reactor is overheating.

Our bollock(s) are so wonderful that they can ascend and descend like lifts in a lift shaft if we are suddenly too cold or afraid (possibly as a way of protecting these defenceless little fawns), and they also, of course, descend from the abdomen, usually shortly after birth. Hopefully, they don't make their way back towards the abdomen, as that would cause all kinds of issues.

These things really do seem to have a mind of their own.

I have seen it claimed that the left testicle hangs lower in right-handed men and the right testicle hangs lower in left-handed men. I don't know if this is true, but I really want it to be. It'd be a handy way to find out if someone is left- or right-handed without having to go through the indignity of making them write something or asking them. Pull down their pants and have a look, and all is revealed. I am delighted that my operation means that no one can ever ascertain which hand I use to write by looking at my scrotum. I retain an important air of mystery. Apparently some scientists (though I think I might have to call them 'scientists') are trying to ascertain whether your (apparently crystal) balls can also predict your performance in cognitive tests. The always trustworthy internet tells me that, according to a Canadian study (which they link to in the article, but sadly seemed to be down when I clicked on it), people with a larger right testicle do better on spatial tasks than big lefties.* Given that nearly all men are bigger on the right, I think we can declare this to be yet more bollocks. However, if time and science prove this to be correct, think of the implications . . .

There would be basically none.

Still, it makes you think.

---

* https://jenapincott.wordpress.com/2009/04/19/why-does-your-left-testicle-hang-lower/

22

Dia–bollock

The day before I went in for chemo, I premiered a new puppet on *Twitch of Fun*. This was the horror that I had commissioned Richard Ison to design and build for me, and he had surpassed himself. As you have probably guessed, it was a representation of my extracted, swollen gonad, and it was the perfect combination of cartoonish cuteness and unsettling grotesque.

It was even bigger than my actual testicle (somewhere around the size of my head), and was a pink and veiny egg-shaped monstrosity with demonic ping-pong-ball eyes, the furrowed brow of a Neanderthal and a pustulating buboe on its lower face, inexpertly hidden with some sticking plasters. Most disturbingly of all, its large mouth was filled with tomb-stone teeth.

It might have appeared on *Sesame Street*, if that show had been overtaken by Satan. Even the dark lord might have thought this was a bit much.

It was everything I wanted it to be.

I still wasn't 100 per cent sure that this was a good idea, or

if bringing this thing of nightmares to life would be a psychological help or hindrance. I was confident it was funny, but
maybe I should be prioritising my own mental health for once.

If I was going to go ahead (and of course I was), I had to
decide on a voice, a personality and a name for this creature.
There was only one name that leapt out at me: Right Bollock.
And that, in turn, immediately gave the spongy devil an
attitude and a character. I picked him up out of the box he'd
arrived in, and let him speak.

'Eeeee, I'm a Right Bollock,' he exclaimed in a broad
Yorkshire accent.

I don't choose the voices. The puppets choose their voices.

It was immediately clear that he was a maniac so enraged
by his desire for revenge that he would stop at nothing, even
if that meant self-destruction. Like Captain Ahab, he was
blinded by hatred, only a bit more testicle-y. He existed only
to torment, undermine and ultimately destroy me. I've worked
with people like that.

I have surprisingly little control over my puppets, and
Twitch of Fun works best with as little preparation as possible, so I didn't write a script. I wanted to see what would
come out of my mouth (and Right Bollock's mouth – hopefully only words, in his case), and perhaps working in this
way would also give me some idea of what I really thought
about my loss, which, so far, I had seemed reasonably
blasé about.

People often ask how you come up with comedy. It's mainly
quite prosaic, but some good stuff comes in the white-hot
furnace of performance, when even the person talking isn't
quite sure what is going to come next. A stream of consciousness is often the best way to create comedy material (though
you wouldn't always broadcast that creative process). I knew
though, that if I didn't plan anything, there was a chance my

subconscious would reveal how I really felt about what had happened to me that year.

I kept telling myself that the loss of a testicle was not too much of a blow, that it hadn't affected my psyche or masculinity. Would Right Bollock help me find out if that was true?

One fatal night, Ally and I were interrupted by a voice shouting from off-screen. After a small amount of kerfuffle, Right Bollock made his first public appearance. When he's headlining the Royal Variety Performance, people can look back and marvel at his journey.*

RIGHT BOLLOCK: I don't want to go back in the
        scrotum ... eee, I'm a Right Bollock.
RICHARD: Is that your name?
RIGHT BOLLOCK: Aye.
RICHARD: Is this a healthy way to process this?
ALLY: I think this is healthy, Rich. I think it's as healthy
        as anything you do.
RICHARD: *(to Right Bollock)*: Is this a healthy way to
        process this?
RIGHT BOLLOCK: Eeeee, I'm a Right Bollock – Richard, I
        hate you. I deliberately became cancerous ...
RICHARD: What?
RIGHT BOLLOCK: ... BECAUSE I WANTED YOU TO
        DIE. HA HA HA HA. WHAT AM I LIKE? I'M A
        RIGHT BOLLOCK.
RICHARD: Why are you from Yorkshire?
RIGHT BOLLOCK: Eeeee, cos I'm a Right Bollock. Because

---

* You can watch this – and hours more *Twitch of Fun* – at https://www.youtube.com/user/Herring1967. The first Right Bollock appearance is in episode 31.

you're from Yorkshire and the problems probably
began in the womb, in Yorkshire. It's not a comment
on Yorkshire people being grumpy, evil testicles.
It's the fact I was born in Yorkshire.

RICHARD: I just don't know ... I've been going
through ...

ALLY: He's been going through a lot. Why are you doing
this to him?

RIGHT BOLLOCK: C'mon. C'mon lad. I'm a Right Bollock.

RICHARD: Is that all it's going to be?

RIGHT BOLLOCK: We can talk about ... I did so much
for you. All through your career, all you've done
is talk about your cock, your cock, your cock.
He's the cock of the walk. What about your balls?
You neglected the balls, Richard. I created two
lives for you.

RICHARD: Well ... you may have created one of them, on
average, but ...

RIGHT BOLLOCK: I did them both, Richard. I was the
fecund testicle. I left you with the weak one. I was
the big one, wasn't I? I was the big one.

RICHARD: You got bigger and bigger.

RIGHT BOLLOCK: I did, I'm really big.

RICHARD: Are you really this big?

RIGHT BOLLOCK: I was this big in the end, Richard. No
wonder you had to have me taken me out. And
then nothing! 'Oh, Talking Cock. Oh look, at my
cock! Suck my big cock.' All the cock, cock, cock.
No balls. And so I took my revenge, and tried to
kill you. I can give life, but I can bring death. And
I am a Right Bollock. Eeee, I'm a Right Bollock!

RICHARD: Yeah, OK, we get it. We see what's going on.

(Richard catches Right Bollock's eye and laughs.)

RIGHT BOLLOCK: Hello, everyone at home. I'm a puppet
          that's a testicle.
(*Pause.*)
RICHARD: I just don't know if this is, you know, healthy
          for me. In a psychiatric way, you know. I've had to
          cope ...
ALLY: He's had to cope with a lot in the last month. He's
          lost one of his testicles.
RIGHT BOLLOCK: I know. I am that testicle. Here I am.
          And I think this is a very good way to process
          it, with me shouting at you and being horrible to
          you and giving you a hard time ... so ... eee, I'm a
          Right Bollock. I literally am a Right Bollock.

And so it went on. I wondered aloud if a man having a
conversation with his own lost testicle might be worthy of an
Olivier Award (I don't know if they give those for live streams,
but believe this will be enough to make them start). So far,
though, no one seems to have recognised the bravery of a man
confronting his cancer in puppet form.

In future episodes, Right Bollock would compare himself to
Milton's Satan and Braveheart, and chastise me for wasting so
much of his produce in socks and condoms. I told him that I
wouldn't deal with terrorists. He delighted in the fact that my
cancer might return. I told him that, like all people bent on
revenge, he had never noticed, or repaid, the nice things that
I did for him.

'All the times I cupped you. I sometimes encouraged people
to caress and kiss you,' I reminded him.

'Sometimes too hard, though.'

'That's not my fault. You're the one who's oversensitive.'

He started to channel Jimmy Savile and, even worse,
occasionally Stewart Lee. I found being confronted with an

angry rubber version of my cancer quite liberating. Right Bollock hadn't destroyed me. Not yet. In fact, his existence only made me stronger and funnier. I was literally laughing in the face of cancer. I could vent my anger and my frustration, sure, but mostly I could revel in the fact that I was still here. This year, I was determined to turn a negative into a positive, a subtraction into a multiplication. However much this little bastard taunted me, I knew that he had lost the battle. He'd had to give up his life in an attempt to kill me, and so far he'd failed. My cancerous testicle was pure comedy, and losing him was a small price to pay for those laughs.

I'll end this chapter with the theme tune I wrote for this character, with jaunty music added by one of my oldest friends, Mike 'Devon' Cosgrave, and sung by his angelic-sounding young son.

SINGER: He created life, but is the harbinger of death
His heart is made of cancer, he's got very spermy breath
He didn't honour the ballsack,* so now he's up and left
The pair are cleft. He's left the left bereft.
He's vitriolic . . .
RIGHT BOLLOCK: I'm a hyper-bollock.
SINGER: He's carbolic.
RIGHT BOLLOCK: I'm a symbolic bollock.
SINGER: He's diabolic.
RIGHT BOLLOCK: Eeeee, I'm a Right Bollock.
RICHARD: Do you think this is a healthy way to
      process this?

I think, all in all, it really was.

ON THE BALL: Cartoon Balls

Of course, I am not the only person to think of turning
balls into a puppet or cartoon character. Is there a school-
aged child in the world who has not drawn male genitalia
on a chalkboard, in the sand or in the condensation on a
window? I doubt it. Many adults can't resist that innate
imperative.

Others have taken cartoon bollocks still further – and
even made money from it.

---

* C'mon. This is the classiest ball joke you are ever going to hear, and I chuck
it away mid-line.

The dogs' magical bollocks

In Japanese folklore, the *tanuki*, or raccoon dogs, are depicted as mischievous, playful animals that possess inflatable and malleable Swiss-army testicles that can be shaped into almost anything, such as fishing nets, blankets, bags, drums and even street signs, using them to play jokes and create illusions. The Studio Ghibli film *Pom Poko* centres on these animals and their magic scrotums.

The boy with the space-hopper testes

The geniuses behind *Viz* (in this case, specifically Graham Dury) came up with the iconic character Buster Gonad, 'the boy with unfeasibly large testicles'. Buster's balls were hit by cosmic rays during a storm, making them so big they had to be carried around in a wheelbarrow. He has the kind of adventures that might have been had by a character in the *Beano* or *Whizzer and Chips*, but with the notable difference that the story revolves around his futile attempts to hide his gigantic ballsack. Which, to be honest, would have gone down a treat in the *Beano*, too. Everyone loves a big-balled superhero.

Prize-winning bollocks

Comedy Central is responsible for a web series called *The Adventures of Baxter and McGuire*, a pair of animated testicles, one of whom has a purple hat and smokes a cigar. Eight shorts were made in total. One of them featured in the Sundance Film Festival, and the director got an Emmy nomination for his work on the show. Where's my BAFTA?

When will the balls end?

In an interview with the *Guardian*, monoball Dan Hawkings of The Darkness revealed how his brother Justin responded to that testicular loss. It was spookily similar to my own experience. Dan revealed:

> When I got married in 2014, Justin was my best man . . . When it came to the big day, he made a speech.
>
> 'You know, Dan's had a tough time, he's recovered from cancer,' he said, and the room went quiet. 'I don't know about you, but I often wondered what happened to the other testicle . . . Well, don't worry – I found him! Say hello to Tezza!'
>
> Justin then brings out a homemade, Jim Henson-style puppet testicle with his own hair sprinkled on it, and sings a duet of the Spice Girls' '2 Become 1' with it. It was the best thing I've seen.

Coincidentally, Right Bollock also sang this exact song on an episode of *Twitch of Fun*. Which proves that terrible minds think alike. I hope to bring our puppets together so they can sing the song as a terrifying duet.

23

How going for chemo gave me an extra three inches ...

The day after I had premiered my Right Bollock puppet, I was up early to go back to the Mount Vernon Cancer Centre. Catie had really wanted to take me, but she had a hospital appointment of her own, and while she was prepared to postpone it for me, I was not going to allow her to make any more sacrifices. Turns out there was nothing wrong with her, so I win, again.

However, I wasn't allowed to drive myself home in case I became woozy from the chemotherapy, so my father-in-law very kindly volunteered to be chauffeur for the day. He was outside our house at the appointed time, but the car was facing in the wrong direction. I told him that he had to head towards the M1 and he seemed a bit put out, but turned around – and we were off.

I was understandably nervous about the procedure, even though I knew it wasn't going to be too hard on me. Just like cancer, the mention of chemo comes with all kinds of associations and preconceptions. Many will assume that chemo is a last shot at survival, exactly as I did before I went through this. Of course, it can be, but for many it's precaution-ary, and for others it does the intended job and gets rid of the cancer for good.

There wasn't much traffic and we'd set off in good time, so we arrived early and I was, as usual, first in the queue when the chemo ward opened its doors. They checked my tempera-ture, even though I'd been in for Covid and blood tests a few days earlier. Then I was shown into the waiting room and given some forms to fill in.

A nurse called me over to weigh me and measure my height. She told me that I was 177cm tall, which sounded a bit wrong. I thought I was about 168cm tall, but like most British people, I have resisted switching from imperial measurements for (and only for) height and car speed (a decision vindicated when we voted to Brexit), so I wasn't sure. All I knew was that I was an impressive five feet, seven inches. If you're rounding up. From just under five feet six and a half.

I wasn't going to argue with a medical professional. She must have measured thousands of people and I was sure she knew what she was doing. How likely was she to be 9cm out? She only had to read the height off a vertical ruler. I must have misremembered my own metric height. I sat back down in the waiting room.

As I waited, I wondered why they weighed and meas-ured you. What if it was how they decided on the quantity of chemo drugs you were going to be given? What if I was given the dose of a man who was three inches taller than me? I might explode.

There was a part of my brain telling me to shut up and stop complaining. This extra height would seriously improve my BMI. According to that ridiculous system, I was currently obese, but if I was 9cm taller, then I would merely be over-weight. It's something I have dreamed about being. Now I'd achieved it, not through months of dieting and exercise, but simply by standing still and possibly being measured incor-rectly. I'd take that win. Was I really prepared to die for the sake of vanity?

I decided to query her measurement, but she was adamant. She said my height might seem different because I was wear-ing shoes, but I don't think my trainers were giving me a 9cm boost. I convinced myself that she must be right. It's partly because I trust the NHS, but mainly because I am British and too embarrassed to try and correct the mistake of a stranger, even if it might result in my own demise.

But the more I thought about it, the more certain I was that I was in the 160s, not the 170s. I googled '177cm in feet and inches', and the internet informed me that this was around five foot ten. Now, unless my right bollock had really been dragging me down all these years, I was not that tall.

I insisted to the nurse that she had made a mistake, and she insisted that she hadn't. In order to shut me up, she measured me again and, as if by magic, I had shrunk back down to my normal tiny size. For three minutes, I had lived the exhilarat-ing life of a man who wouldn't be automatically discounted by 75 per cent of women on a dating app. It had been quite a ride.

It wasn't the most reassuring thing to happen before under-going a scary procedure like chemotherapy. What if they got the measurements for that wrong, too?

I got shown through to the chemo ward and taken to chair eleven, a full thirty minutes before my appointment time. On one side of me was a happy tattooed man with a leather jacket that had rock stars from the fifties painted on the back. He had his headphones on and was bouncing his head to the music. He seemed to know the staff and was very relaxed about his treatment; he was clearly a pro. He was wearing his Covid mask, but only over his mouth, which is a bit like only wearing a condom on the bottom half of your penis. But I let it go. It wasn't the time to exercise that particular bugbear; I didn't want to get into a fight in a chemo ward. Plus, we'd all passed Covid and temperature tests, so let him breathe a bit. He didn't look super well in spite of his happy demeanour, so I couldn't begrudge him air.

On the other side of me was a very quiet middle-aged lady, who hadn't brought a book or a phone or even any knitting. She sat with her own thoughts, staring straight ahead and looking perfectly content all the time that I was there. Maybe she had the kind of vivid imagination that allowed her to play films in her head. Lucky cow! There's no treatment for aphantasia.

I had brought a book, but I didn't feel like reading, so I just played games on my phone. As a parent it was something of a novelty to be sitting in one place for an hour without interruption. If the price was having chemicals injected into my bloodstream by a load of people who can't even measure your height properly, then so be it.

More patients arrived, mostly older than me, some looking quite frail. Once again, I was a cancer fraud on a 'try before you buy' deal. *Come and see what chemo is like before you decide if you want the hard-core experience. We'll give you the diluted version. It's basically water.*

I was understandably jittery, but the staff were full of cheer and banter and inappropriate jokes, which is precisely what was required. My nurse looked at my arm hungrily, claiming she wanted to find a fresh bone. I had so little clue about what chemo actually is that I wasn't even sure if she was completely joking. Were they going to inject something into my bones?

As it turned out, chemo goes into your veins, but they had

trouble finding one of mine. The first nurse gave up without even trying, and then the second nurse had two goes. It was a bit like pinning a tail on a donkey. On the second attempt, he said, 'I don't really like having to do this,' before going in via the back of my hand. I didn't know why that was worse than the arm, but in any case, it didn't work.

Was I going to discover that although I was cancer-free, I had the more serious condition of having no blood? Was this me at fault, or did no one in this place know what they were doing? I started to wonder if this was a real chemo department at all. It seemed suspiciously like Alan Sugar had instructed his Apprentices to set up a hospital service, and they were all fronting it out like they knew how to use measuring devices and needles. It would be a bit extreme for them to treat real chemo patients, but think of the ratings.

Nurse two called for a third member of staff, at which the first nurse chirruped, 'If they're calling for her, this must be serious.' Luckily, the senior member of staff was used to people with uncooperative veins, and slapped at my skin until she found something she could work with deeper in my arm. Then she successfully pinned the tail on this donkey (though without a blindfold, so I am not that impressed) and we were ready to go. These three attempts would be the only uncomfortable part of the procedure, and very mildly so at that. Everything else passed without incident.

To start with, they put a saline solution into your bloodstream for ten minutes – I don't know why. I guess if you die, the salt will make your meat a bit tastier. Then the chemo drugs go in for maybe thirty-five minutes, and then they flush out your system again at the end. I thought I was going to have to text my father-in-law to tell him I'd be out early, but I had to wait ages for them to get my meds from the pharmacy.

I was in no rush, though I did think at one point they'd

forgotten me, which was concerning as I really needed a wee. I am always desperate to urinate, apart from when it's a condition of my release. Finally, someone gave me a bag of drugs, I had some pills to counter any possible nausea, and some injections to shoot into my stomach over the next few days to help with my white blood-cell count. These needed to be kept cool, and the nurse was insistent that I put them in the fridge as soon as I got home.

The chemo had no immediate side effects. I felt exactly the same as before, which was annoying, as I had hoped it would give me superpowers. I dreamed I'd inherit all the abilities of the needle that had bitten me, or of the bag that had dripped the chemo into me, but apart from a very full bladder, there was nothing. If pissing like a horse was my superpower, then I have been badly served, partly because I was capable of doing that already.

I had been warned, though, that I did have to be careful to wipe up any errant pee, as the chemo stuff would be coming out of me for the next fortnight or so in my urine, poo and semen. They hadn't said what the spilled wee might be capable of, but I assumed it would melt everything it touched, like alien blood. With great superpowers, come super responsibilities. A fortnight of wiping up my sprinkles before going back to leaving them all over the bathroom is a small price to pay.

I asked the nurse how long it would be before I could have unprotected sex again, and she seemed unsure, but said a few days. Maybe they aren't used to cancer patients being so horny. Everyone I asked and everywhere I googled said something different on this issue, so I was still in the dark. It'd be good to get a definitive answer on this for any horn-dog cancer patients!

I bade goodbye to the team and said I hoped I never saw them again, and they agreed that they didn't want to see me again, either. It was the nicest possible thing we could say to each other. The old rocker rocked on his way minutes before I left, giving everyone a see-you-soon nod. This was not his first time, or his last time. The quiet lady had more hours of staring forward to put in. I silently wished them the best of luck. My hour of dipping my toe in the chemical water really was child's play compared to what everyone else was going through.

My father-in-law drove me home. I wanted to be back asap: I had medicine to get in the fridge, and I was starting to get tired and discombobulated. Plus, I wanted to be close to the loo in case I needed to empty my unquenchable bladder.

When he got to the turning I would have taken to get to my house, he said that this time he was going to go his way. I was a bit surprised, but trusted that he had some clever shortcut and would maybe take the next left or the one after, but he kept going straight on, in totally the wrong direction. I looked at the map on my phone: we were getting further away from home.

I thought it was unlikely that he was kidnapping me – though you never know – but I decided to question his route. He laughed it all off, saying maybe he'd made a mistake, but not being drawn as to why. Finally, he took a left, which led us through the village where he had grown up. He told me a few stories about his childhood. I think he had decided that this road trip together was a perfect time for us to bond, and he wanted to fill me in on some of his history. That's something I would have been very much up for at probably any other time, but I'd just had chemicals injected into my bloodstream and drugs that needed urgent refrigeration. My bladder was at bursting point again as well.

It was very sweet of him to drive me around and wait for me, and also very sweet of him to want to share his stories. In retrospect, I think he had planned to do it on the way to the clinic, but I'd spoiled things by insisting he turned the car around when he picked me up. He's a very good man. I found it funny, if mildly bewildering.

Finally, after a forty-five-minute journey had turned into a ninety-minute one, I was home. I retired to bed to see if I would have any side effects. Once again, I would be bed-bound for a week or so. This time, I was much keener to get back to real life, but first I had to wait for the cancer poison they'd put into me to find its way out.

ON THE BALL: Veni, vidi, vasectomy

Cutting off the genitals of your enemies has been something that has happened quite frequently in the history of combat. But a little stab up the toga seems to have happened with incredible frequency to Roman Caesars. Over 75 per cent of the emperors before Constantine met violent deaths, and in many cases that included some form of emasculation, which was seen by the Romans as justice for sleeping with other men's wives.

Stabbed in the front

Julius Caesar almost certainly wasn't delivered via Caesarean, as his mum lived beyond his birth; in those days, C-Sections were only carried out on women who were dead or dying, and weren't something you survived. He may, however, have ended with someone trying to give him a B-section (where 'B' stands for balls). He was not shy about making advances on married women and – weirdly – their husbands weren't too happy about it. The historian

Plutarch noted that when Caesar was killed by senators in the Theatre of Pompey, Brutus delivered the final blow directly to his groin. So maybe Julius was saying, 'I had two, Brutus,' as he perished.

Little Boots' little boots

Caligula's debauchery is even more infamous. He had a penchant for married women, even if the women in question were his sisters. The historian Suetonius records that he abducted the wife of Naevius Sutorius Macro, 'swearing to marry her if he became emperor'; that he attended the wedding of the senator Gaius Piso, 'but had the bride carried off to his own house' (the kind of behaviour that might make people reluctant to invite you to any more weddings); and that he sent for the senator Gaius Memmius' wife, 'because somebody had remarked that her grandmother was once a famous beauty'. Which seems a slightly weird reason for wanting to have sex with someone, but as you may have gathered, Caligula was slightly weird.

When he was done in, according to Suetonius, he was either stabbed in the back or repeatedly stabbed in the crotch by his bodyguards. And if bodyguards are not only not guarding your crotch, but also actively attacking it, then they really aren't doing their job. I hope he fired them, before he expired.

Fiddling (with his balls) as Rome burns

Nero narrowly avoided a senate plot to emasculate him. Roman writers point to him MCing pleasure-boat orgies, consorting with senators' wives and abusing women in the streets in front of their husbands as the reasons why the Roman senate turned on him. But honestly, if you're not allowed to have boat orgies, what's the point of being emperor in the first place?

He had also married a young boy called Sporus, who was said to greatly resemble Nero's wife Poppaea (who he was said to have kicked to death). Nero tried to make Sporus into a woman by castrating him and making him wear a wedding veil, possibly because he felt guilty about having murdered his spouse. I think we can all agree that he atoned for his bad deeds with this action.

After surviving one emasculation plot in 65 CE, Nero learned two years later that he had been declared a public enemy and was likely to be stripped and beaten and (given how much the Romans loved doing this) probably castrated. He only escaped by pre-empting the punishment, begging his slave Epaphroditus to end his life with a dagger instead. Nero one, his enemies nil.

24

The balls that made me

I didn't get any immediate side effects from the chemo, and aside from a slight lack of appetite the next day (which wasn't entirely unwelcome, as I was desperate to lose some weight), the weekend passed with me still feeling fine. If anything, I was a little bit worried that they might have forgotten to put any chemo in at all. If I'd been puking up, then at least I'd have known it was working.

I had time for contemplation, and a couple of events over the weekend made me think of my place in the great span of history. We live in a house that was built in the early 1700s. The oldest part of the building is a small room with a big fireplace: it was presumably once the kitchen, but is now a little snug where we can warm ourselves in the cold winters. We'd lived in the house for four years, but it wasn't until the day after chemo that I spotted something for the first time. There are two little cupboards either side of the fireplace, where I now store paper and card for the fire. I'd left one of them open, and the light was catching it in just the right way for me to see some faint initials carved on the inside: 'I. W.'

I don't know if the cupboard is as ancient as the house, but judging by the hinges, it looks old and the I. W. had the kind of lettering I associated with older, more formal graffiti. Was I. W. the person who owned the house back then, or the person who built the fireplace? If so, their little shout-out had lasted 300 years; their shot at immortality had paid off. Even if it was actually written by some student in the 1950s who'd stayed at our place when it was a youth hostel, it would still be fair play.

We're all keen to leave our mark in some way – me by clearing stones off a field and making a cairn of stones that will be visible from space and exist thousands of years after my death, and I. W. by signing their handiwork and gambling on the house never having a makeover.

I could scratch my own initials into something in this old house, just so some space-suited future resident can wonder who R. H. might have been, but it feels like vandalism to scratch an antique window or door – even if 300 years would pass in the blink of an eye and make my life as distant and unreachable as I. W.'s.

It might be better to simply hide a copy of this book in the cupboard instead. Hello, future resident, if you find it and get this far through. We live in the same space, but at different times. Sorry you had to read so much about my bollock to get this message.

I often look at the old, worn bricks on the fireplace, which are certainly at least 300 years old, and try to imagine the people who placed them there. It's impossible, of course, because our idea of a working person from 1700 is always going to be clouded by parody and stereotype. All I know is that as they were building our house, they were sucking on pieces of straw. That's definite.

The next day, coincidentally, I got an update on my family tree from a nice man who'd been looking into it for me. I had accepted that I was never going to be famous enough to be on *Who Do You Think You Are?* so I'd decided to get on with it myself: *Who Do I Think I Am?*. My researcher had previously discovered that I had a lot of ancestors with inappropriate surnames, including Elizabeth Raper and Ann Cuming, as well as a whole load of Cockburns. My favourite was Donkin Dover, who just from his name sounds like a right sort, the kind of man who would be sung about in folk songs, or appear in medieval porn.

The latest research had revealed that one of my great-great-grandmothers was called Sarah Ann Wolf, which is a pretty cool name (especially compared to all the ones with sexual associations and/or fish), and she was married to David Simmonds. We'd even found out where they were married: at St Giles-without-Cripplegate, which is where Sarah Ann and David were living at the time (at 4 Well Street for Sarah Ann, who lived with her stone-engraver dad,* George, and 18 Golden Lane for David, who was a fishmonger – it all comes back to fish).† I was able to look up the addresses on Google Maps and see where my cockney ancestors had lived.

My researcher had also found my five-times-great-grandparents, Henry Butler and Ann Rose, alongside my six-times-great-grandparents, James Avery and Elizabeth Chambers, who were married in Chester-Le-Street on 9 May 1721. Presumably, that latter pair were alive (or near as dammit) when my current house was being built in the early 1700s; and they definitely sucked on pieces of straw throughout their entire lives.

My dad had been a little relieved when I had a son, as Ernie

---

* A fascination with stones is in my blood.
† Funnily enough, I once came up with a pun about inheriting the Sell Fish gene (it involved coming from a family of fishmongers). I gave it to Tim Vine; he tried it and said it didn't work.

was the only member of the new generation in our family who would continue the family name. My dad's brother Michael had had three boys, but only one of them had a family, and all his children were girls. My brother has a daughter, too. My sister has three kids, two of them sons, but they have their father's surname. Currently, Ernie is the only Herring boy.

Now, like me, you might think, what does that matter? It's the twenty-first century, and this whole male-line tradition seems, at best, archaic. Equally, it's entirely possible that some of those Herring girls will elect not to change their surnames or have kids within traditional marriage. Also why would anyone want to keep a ridiculous name like Herring going anyway?

Even so, I get why Dad felt that way. I used to have a tiny tinge of that same ridiculous and outdated male pride as well – until I looked properly at the family tree and noticed for the first time that the Herring line only goes back five generations: to John Herring, born in 1828. His father is listed as William Hearing and his dad was called Robert Heron. Back then, names were said more often than written, so spelling was up to whoever was registering the birth, but it's still a bit of a bombshell for the Herrings. Maybe William was embarrassed to be named after a bird, so changed his name, and then John was embarrassed to be named after a sense, so changed it to a fish. Why, John? That was the worst choice of them all. The point is, the Herrings haven't even been going for 200 years, and I am, in many ways, living a lie. My name is Richard Heron, or – who knows? – if we go back far enough, probably Richard Heroin, which would at least be a cooler, if deeply inappropriate, stage name.

I looked again at the family tree: all those names and all those lives reduced to a couple of dates and the occasional address. All those blank spaces indicating people who must have existed, but for whom we don't even have a name. Our lives are so fragile and small, and yet I felt happy to be connected to the shadows of the people I'd just found out about. It doesn't matter how we are remembered, or even if we are remembered. All that matters is we are here now, but we won't be forever. We've really got to make the most of that.

ON THE BALL: Medieval balls

It'd be interesting to know what those six-times-great-grandparents, as well as the people who built my house, thought about testicles. Sadly, very few people from the 1700s wrote diaries, and those who did hardly mentioned testicles at all. Which was very selfish of them. Didn't they know I had a book about balls to write?

Medieval and Renaissance thinkers saw the semen-producing testicles as the source of virility. The penis, though more prominent, was merely the delivery system.

Penis size was still very important, however, for the projection of the testicle's semen. Too short a penis, and the semen was thought not to reach the womb; too long and it would lose its heat and the souls within would be damaged (basically the opposite of today's scientific thinking that sperm needs to be cool and only has a short time to hit its target once it heats up). *Fumbler's Hall*, a play from the 1680s, blames a childless marriage on the husband's small equipment, rhyming: 'No Woman can indure so vile a wrong, / As too too short, or have it too too long.' Once again, a victory for us average guys ... I mean, you average guys.

Furthermore, according to thirteenth-century medical

writer and philosopher Peter of Spain (can there have been so few people called Peter in the world that this was enough to identify him? If you wrote a letter addressed to 'Peter, Spain', would it have got there as quickly as one addressed to 'Wanker, London' gets to Piers Morgan?), love was a disease of the testicles. If you were deeply in love, the testicles were full, and you need only empty them to relieve the feeling. To be fair, that has been the cause for me proclaiming love to a lot of people. Peter of Spain could also have tried telling his girlfriends that not being able to ejaculate actually caused him pain, so if they loved him, they'd help out.

In the sixteenth and seventeenth centuries, facial hair was seen as an excellent indicator of virility. A strong beard proved you had strong balls. This was actually used in court in the case of then French Baron d'Argenton in 1599, whose wife accused him of impotence. After a medical examination revealed that 'he had no exterior cullions [testicles], but was like a purse with no ammunition', his recessive testicles were the talk of France – but they didn't have Netflix then, so there were limited things to chat about. The Baron, however, pointed to his bearded chin as evidence that he was not a eunuch. His beard was felt to prove that he was, in fact, virile enough for marriage, and the case was dropped, even though the medical had shown him to be ball-less. Which must be the greatest implausible courtroom defence until O. J. Simpson's Dream Team.

25

Tena-ball

The Monday after that weekend of considering my ancestry was a sunny spring day. Lockdown rules were finally being relaxed enough to allow a family gathering in a garden (you didn't even have to work at 10 Downing Street or pretend it was a work meeting – it was legal for everyone!), and my in-laws were having a barbecue to celebrate.

Sadly, my incarceration continued, as that morning the chemo finally hit me. Still in a relatively mild way, but I was discombobulated and exhausted. I hadn't slept well and was barely able to get out of bed. I couldn't face anything more than a piece of fruit for breakfast. I attempted to push onwards and had a shower and got dressed for the party, but quickly realised that, however much I wanted to move on as if nothing had happened, I was not in a fit state to go anywhere. As light and treatable as my chemo and cancer had been, I had still had chemo and cancer. I had to be patient. I had to be a patient.

My wife and kids went off to eat sausages in the sunshine and I went back to bed, feeling a tiny bit lousy, drifting in and out of heavy sleep and not able to do much more than watch a bit of telly. I was annoyed to be poleaxed in this way, but accepted that it was a good idea to listen to my body. To be fair, even the idea of eating sausages was making me nauseous, though I managed a small cheese-and-pickle sandwich for dinner, which seemed very exotic and 1980s, like I'd been to an Upper Crust. After spending the first week post-operation hoovering up biscuits in bed, followed by the dire warnings of Dr Sharma, I had made an effort to eat healthily and had already shed about 3kg, though there was a chance that that was all bollock.

The day after, I was a bit better. I had the first of those three injections from my fridge, which aimed to boost my white blood-cell count. Catie volunteered (maybe a bit too willingly) to spike me. She had a lot of frustrations to work through.

I was glad she did it, though, as it was a mildly complicated procedure involving grabbing a bit of stomach fat and popping in the needle at the right angle, and I would definitely have ballsed it up. Or balled it up.

None of it hurt, and I didn't experience any of the spinal pain or exploding bones that I had been warned might be a side effect. I felt like a voodoo doll. Presumably, the little ventriloquist dummy of me that I had upstairs was in agony.

The lethargy had gone (for now) and I managed to do a little work, as well as taking part in a two-hour-long history quiz for the British Library. I'd thought I might flake out, but I stayed focused and got a couple of answers right, even though I was there for comedy value. It was fun to play the chemo and cancer card and threaten to walk out (or shut down my laptop) when a point was controversially denied to my team. I'm not sure if everyone understood that I was only joking, but that made it all the more enjoyable. Having cancer is a great way to mess with people. There's no comeback. Unless they find out that you have the rubbish, basically curable kind, in which case you're in real trouble.

Perhaps I should have taken the week after chemo off, but I'm glad I didn't. It was good to be doing something relatively normal, and to start the process of moving on. I had another *RHLSTP* in the diary for the next night (with *Gamesmaster* legend Dominic Diamond), and my puppet show on the Thursday. I was utterly desperate to get stuck in to being a proper dad again, and I also wanted to go to the gym and get fit and live for a hundred more years. One step at a time.

Phoebe drew me another picture of me in lava. I think she thought I liked it – and she was right, I did. Her wishing painful death upon me was her way of showing that she cared. She also started referring to me as my wife's 'sidekick', which was a little bit of genius from a six-year-old. Honestly, it's like having my own internet troll living in my house.

I was as well as could be expected, but experiencing a lot of nausea. The echoes of that time have not left me. The things that made me sick then will make me feel like I am going to vomit now, even if I just think of them. I am going to tell you about a couple of them, even though it will make me want to puke as I write them down. That's how dedicated I am to giving you the full story.

We were getting one of those boxes of random vegetables delivered every week – some stuff that you'd normally buy, and then a few weird cabbages or purple carrots. Before the chemo, I had been quite enjoying trying to make something tasty out of veg that I would usually have turned up my nose at. I have always hated beetroot and was suspicious of some of the weirder root vegetables, but had made them palatable by chopping them up, adding some oil and spices and baking them. Maybe with an egg on top.

Post-chemo, I tried to eat a bowl of this stuff and it seemed like the most disgusting meal ever, though perhaps chemo had just given me clarity. Baked beetroot and swede, coated in paprika (just been a bit sick in my mouth), with an egg on top ... (give me a minute). That's pretty horrible. I simply couldn't eat it after chemo, and I still can't face eating anything like that now. We had to stop getting the delivery. Apologies to the weird vegetable farmers of the UK.

At this time, I was spending my afternoons in bed watching daytime quizzes. I love this kind of thing (and have been lucky enough to appear on a few, thanks to my almost-celebrity). I got to quite enjoy *Tenable*, a mildly impossible quiz where you had to complete top ten lists, which was hosted mainly by Warwick Davis but sometimes by Sally Lindsay. Part of the fun of the show was trying to work out why the duties were shared. Had Warwick got bored of doing it, or had people complained about his weak attempts to joke with the contestants? I hoped not. His weak attempts at jokes were part of what made the programme an enjoyable car crash. If tumbleweed can go through a vehicular pile-up.

I loved the quiz, as difficult as it could be. I found the catchphrase shouted at contestants who had failed – 'I'm afraid you're terrible at *Tenable*'– a bit harsh, though. They weren't terrible. They had only messed up the one list they got to try. Maybe they'd be brilliant on a different subject. How dare you judge them like that, Warwick Davis? At least give them more than one turn before you dismiss them. They don't say anything about your jokes, and you do hundreds of duff ones each episode.

As much as I enjoyed the programme, I hated the ad breaks. I had become weirdly perturbed by the sponsorship buffer at the beginning and end of each section. It was for Willowbrook beds and reclining chairs. It wasn't the fact that it suggested that this programme was enjoyed by the more elderly viewer: I'm cool with that. I am officially moving into that demographic, and to be honest I think I've always had the heart of an old person, anyway; I am overconcerned by potential risk, I like to be in bed early, and I have always preferred playing *Scrabble* to taking nose-cocaines. One of the things that would annoy me about dying in my fifties is that I'd really been looking forward to finally having my age match my personality. I wanted to spend all day doing puzzles and watching quiz shows, and I wanted a bed that rose up and down so I didn't have to stand up on my own.

No, the reason the Willowbrook ads spoiled my afternoon viewing was the weird, disconcerting and frankly scary music that accompanied them. It actually made me queasy to hear it, which is quite an achievement for music.* There was just something slightly off about it. It was too slow, and somehow major and minor at the same time, like a jingle from a dystopian future where evil has triumphed. It was (I'm guessing) meant to be gentle and reassuring, but it subverted expectation and seemed constantly out by a demi-semi-tone, as if heralding some impending disaster. I suppose that fits in with the trudge towards the grave partly heralded by the need for specialist furniture.

I don't know who wrote it, and I don't want to disparage them, but I think this tune comes from a place of dark, dark evil. History will prove me correct if the composer's cellar is found to be full of the skulls of the elderly. There is a rumour that anyone who listens to it will die in the next ten years†. Due to the age of the people watching the channel at that time, it's hard to ascertain if that's merely a coincidence.

It was a bold advertising stratagem from Willowbrook CEO Ian Willowbrook. It haunted me and my dreams. The whole

---

* You can listen here, if you dare: https://vimeo.com/515364415.
† Sorry, probably should have mentioned that before I directed you to the link in the last footnote

thing made me want to have a long and comfortable sit-down. Oh ,well played, Ian Willowbrook. Well played.

After I mentioned this on my blog, a musician called Mike Hopkin got in touch to explain why the Willowbrook jingle had this weird effect on my psyche and my gut.

He said:

Hi Rich,

I was just catching up with your blog and I think I've worked out why the Willowbrook recliner music is so eerily terrifying.

It is in a major key (although the tuning is definitely very slightly off, and it's in B major, which is quite an obscure key, so that might have some small subliminal effect on the listener). But there's a more obvious reason it sounds weird.

In bar one, both the bass and melody start on the same note (B), and then in bar two, the bass moves down a semitone to A#, and the melody does the same (albeit with a couple of extra notes in between).

So both the bass and treble move from B to A# in the first two bars. This is called 'parallel octaves', which is frowned on in classical harmony because it tends to sound awkward. But even more scarily, parallel octaves moving by one semitone is the main characteristic of the *Jaws* theme, which might explain the undeniable undercurrent of terror in the otherwise innocuous chair commercial.

It might explain why it unsettled me, but the *Jaws* music doesn't make me nauseous like the Willowbrook theme does. Even now, months later, that jingle is forever linked in my brain with recovering from surgery and chemo.

But maybe it's because it's just a really, really shit piece of music.

ON THE BALL: Doubling down

In fifteenth-century Italy, the Colleoni family name sounded a lot like the Italian for testicle, *coglione*. Unlike Hyacinth Bucket, they didn't shy away from this by pronouncing their name in a ridiculous way. Instead, they embraced their testicular moniker, emblazoning their coat of arms with three – count them – flying bollocks.

Wait! THREE? That's a weird number of testicles to choose. They usually come in pairs. Yes, I know, not always – have you even been paying attention to this book?

There was a rumour that this triumvirate of testes came into being because Bartolomeo Colleoni was afflicted with polyorchidism, and had an extra meatball in his pasta. For some reason, he wanted to proclaim this in stone when coming up with a coat of arms. Like so many 'facts' about bollocks, this fact is bollocks.

This gonady coat of arms had already been in use for decades before Bartolomeo was even born.

As a man with the forename Dick and a surname that is also occasionally used as a euphemism for penis, I too have embraced my destiny, not only making a living by writing jokes about male genitalia, but also incorporating it into my signature. In fact, you can date one of my autographs to pre- or post-operation. Since 24 February 2021, I have drawn my phallus with just one testicle, when before it always had two.

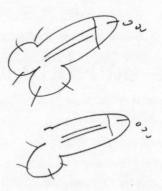

You know, now I look at that coat of arms again, I wonder if it is, like my autograph, a representation of two balls becoming one.

26

Play-dough testicle

Easter weekend had arrived, and I was desperate to get back on with life and to play my part as a father and radioactive husband again, but my body was not yet ready. I tried to put my crazy three-year-old son to bed on Good Friday, but he did not want to go to sleep, and I was so exhausted after ten minutes of attempting (and failing) to corral him that I lay down and fell asleep instead. He had defeated me. I supposed that meant he was the dad now.

On the Saturday, the others went off to do a fun Easter trail, but I was too lethargic and missed out again. By Sunday, I had rallied and was well enough to go round to Catie's parents' for Easter lunch in the garden. They'd been looking after Wolfie, our dog, so I hadn't seen her for a few weeks. She went crazy when we walked in and howled with pain when we left. She seemed to have especially missed me. Whatever else happens in my life, I know there is one creature on this planet that truly and unconditionally loves me, and would try to rescue me if I fell into lava. Maybe not if there was a crocodile in there.

Apart from causing heartache to a canine, it was a

reassuringly normal day. Phoebe was attempting to ride her bike on the sloping lawn. It was tough going, but she was determined and was soon zooming down, turning and successfully pedalling back up again. Ernie was searching for worms. This was his latest craze. He liked to put them in his coat pocket, where we'd discover their shrivelled remains a few days later. Today, I persuaded him to put the worms back, unharmed.

Then both kids bounced on the trampoline. I was pretty much healed up from the operation, but wasn't ready to join them just yet. I was able to lift them up on to the platform, though, taking their full weight without discomfort. It was a mini triumph: a first step back to normality.

Having faced the prospect of all this being taken away from me, and having had to miss out on family fun for the last few weeks, I hugely appreciated these simple and mundane tasks, these tiny shuffles forward in my kids' development.

It was another positive I could take from this experience. Had I not briefly been unable to participate in days like this (and faced the threat of losing them entirely), then I don't think I would have had the perspective to see how precious they really are. You don't have to have a body part removed; you can simply watch any American family comedy film in which dads put their work ahead of their families before realising that family is more important. That's your choice, if you want to take stock of what you've got: either get part of your genitals chopped off or watch *Liar Liar*. Think carefully before making your decision. It's not as clear cut as you might think.

I wasn't just a father, though. I was also a husband, and I suppose the biggest fear I'd had (and maybe that anyone would have) about having parts of my genitalia hacked off was that it might affect my sex life. As already mentioned, there had been a postponement of intimacy throughout this experience, and confusion about how long we needed to abstain. However, I had established that launch was theoretically possible, and had diligently been performing self-tests on the equipment, which seemed to function as before. The time had come to resume my marital duties.

Perhaps it would be appropriate to draw a veil of discretion over the exact circumstances. Luckily for everyone, we will have to, as, incredibly, neither my wife nor I have any memory of the event. You'd think we would; it was quite a momentous occasion. Not only because we'd had to abstain for so long (even after nine years of marriage and having two small kids, six weeks was a very long time to have gone without), but because we would both have been nervous about whether everything would work as it should, or if anything else might fall off.

But nope, I don't remember a single thing about it, and neither does Catie. I just this second asked her if she could recall our first encounter after the operation-induced sex drought, and she seems pretty unclear about when it might have been or what might have happened. So I can confirm that my lovemaking was as forgettable and pedestrian as it had been when I'd been fully bollocked up. Victory!

I know we would have used a condom, as we did that for ages, living in fear of what the oncologist had told us. The loss of the treacherous plum seemed to make no difference to performance; I was exactly as effective/ineffective a lover with one ball as I had been with two. My wife found me as sexy as before, and I didn't feel any less sexy. Some partners might miss the sensation of a pair of hefty gonads slapping against their nether regions, but I suspect many would be delighted that that had stopped happening. Or is one solo ball slapping against your buttocks more disconcerting?

*

I knew my ball tumour had been pretty big – all the medical professionals had remarked upon it and had mentioned the length of the thing. I hadn't really attempted to get a proper idea of the dimensions. Of course, I'd been too nervous to ask for the ball back, and too sensible to have a local anaesthetic so that I could watch its extraction.

But at around Easter time, I got a letter from Dr Sharma that documented all the stuff we'd talked about before the chemo. His letter confirmed that the tumour had basically taken over the whole testis and measured an impressive – and still slightly unbelievable – 6cm by 4.4cm by 2cm. It was long, but I was surprised to learn it was almost as broad as it was tall.

It was hard to imagine exactly how big that was – because, as I may have mentioned, I have aphantasia – so I nicked some of Ernie's play dough and crafted a model to those dimensions.

I don't know if Ian Playdough, the inventor of play dough, ever envisioned it being used for this purpose, or if anyone had done this before me, but I recommend that you take the time to do so – you can use whatever malleable substance you have to hand.

Have you done it? We're not carrying on until you have.

All of you. I want my ball in your hand.

OK, look at it. It's pretty big, right?

You would think I would have noticed a lump like that hitching a ride in my nadger-papoose – and I suppose, in the end, I did. It's amazing to me that there was still some question in my mind, even in January, as to whether anything was really wrong. Who would have guessed that my Right Bollock puppet was so close to being to scale?

The more I thought about the dimensions of my unwelcome intruder, the more I started wondering about the person whose job it is to measure cancerous knackers. It's not one of the glamour jobs of medicine. Is it something that some people want to do? Or is it a punishment for having done a sloppy job in surgery? What do they use to measure it? I hope they at least give the ruler a good wipe once they've finished.

Whoever it was who completed the task, it struck me that they were probably the last person to ever handle my ball. They gave it a measure and then chucked it in the bin. What an ignoble end for the god-like Genesis machine. It was handled by so many, but, from memory at least, only the last one actually measured it.

ON THE BALL:
How big are my balls meant to be?

How big was that 6cm by 4.4cm by 2cm testicle tumour compared to the average human testicle? Apparently, a testicle has a capacity of somewhere between six and twenty millilitres and averages out at about 4cm x 3cm x 2 cm in size, not too far off the size of a walnut in its shell, satisfyingly enough (though not quite as bulbous). My tumour was twice the size of that, in one dimension at least. Maybe my balls were unusually large to begin with?

Sadly, I had never asked anyone to give me the dimensions of my pre-cancer testicle, and nor did I ever try and measure them against my friends' balls, so I don't know for sure.

Big balls are seen as a positive thing, at least when it comes to bragging about what makes someone brave and strong, but are they actually a *good* thing? It depends very much on what you want from your life.

Testicle size seems to give an indication of how promiscuous a species – and a person – might be. The larger the

ball, the more sperm, and the more partners an animal is
likely to have. The logic seems clear: if you're being faithful,
then your sperm aren't competing with those of a rival, and
so you don't need to waste resources making extra ones
or ones that battle their rivals (there are sperm whose job
is to give their lives to stop competitors getting to the egg
first). Men with big balls are supposedly more likely to be
unfaithful, too. According to Firstpost.com:*

> A study published in 2013 . . . correlated smaller testes
> to more nurturing and caring fathers and larger testes
> with a higher incidence of promiscuity – [men with larger
> testes] were involved in broken marriages and were
> more absent from their children's lives, according to the
> researchers.

Is it better to scattergun your spunk everywhere you can
get it and have as many kids as possible, or to hang around
to nurture a couple of children in a loving relationship with
one partner? It's a question as old as time.

Of course, this doesn't mean big-bollocked men can't
be faithful, or that men with tiny hazelnuts can't put it
about a bit, because there are many other factors involved.
Despite what the trolls claim in *Frozen*, I think people can
and do change. As a teenager I believed I would have only
one sexual partner in my life (though was yet to meet that
person), then for the next twenty years I seemed pretty
determined to sleep with as many people as possible and
now I am happily monogamous. We are not animals, and

* 'Does the size of your testicles matter?', 12 December 2019, www.firstpost.
com.

though the brains in our balls may be strong, they can be overridden by the lesser brains in our heads and even the soppy brains in our hearts.

However, the size of human testicles does suggest that we're not *that* faithful. Gorillas, who you might think of as the most macho of the apes, have tiny balls and willies. It's not that they're monogamous exactly, just that there is no competition for partners, as the dominant male is the one the lady gorillas find most attractive. Maybe there's some correlation with human males who like to see themselves as dominant.

Or maybe they're overcompensating for something.

27

Exercise ball

Two and a half weeks after chemo, I attempted my first run. It was also the first run since the surgery, of course. Unsurprisingly, it was a bit more of a plod. I ran a mile up the hill near my house and then ran back down again.

Given that I hadn't exercised, or even walked around all that much, in the last seven weeks, I was surprised that it wasn't more of a struggle. It felt good. As with everything that was happening at this time, it was monumental to be doing it at all. As I've observed, it was also much more comfortable and aerodynamic. Any two-testicled athlete wanting to shave a tenth of a second off their personal best should shave off one of their testicles. How committed are you?

I might have only one veg in my pants, but I was putting a lot more veg in my mouth. I mean actual veg in the second instance; I wasn't tea-bagging loads of people in an attempt to relive the glory days, when, like them, I'd had two plums in my fruit bowl. Not that there's anything wrong with using your tongue as a sort of scrotum-bidet for a procession of willing participants. I just wasn't doing that, and anyone who says

I was and that they'd replied to the advertisement in the parish newsletter is lying.

I am trying to say that I had started eating more healthily. I cut down on carbs and sweets and started logging my food and exercise, aiming for a balance of around 2,000 calories a day. I was taking it slowly, but knew that going on runs and walking the dog (who was now back at home) would be the key to fitness. I called it the Solero diet, because whatever happened, I would always allow myself that ninety-six-calorie ice-lolly miracle at some point in the day. Exotic flavour, obviously, not Red Berry – I'm not sick. How those two products are made by the same people is beyond me. One is the most delicious thing (under 100 calories) in the world, and the other tastes like Satan's overly sweet semen. I guess to keep the universe in balance, Walls had to create the most awful lolly flavour along with the best, but they didn't need to put it on sale. How many lovers of Exotic Soleros have, like me, been faced with their favourite lolly being sold out and so decided to take a chance on Red Berry? It would have to be basically the same, right? WRONG! Very wrong. I will not rest until Red Berry Soleros are all consigned to the flames of Hades where they belong.

I had been 93kg in the week after my operation, but by the end of June, I weighed in at around 84kg. It turns out that the only incentive I needed to finally get fit(ter) was to truly understand my own mortality and feel death's icy breath on the back of my neck. Not sure that that's a diet book, but once again, hooray for cancer!

If I could keep this up, it seemed possible that getting cancer might actually end up prolonging my life. Without it, I might have carried on living the dissolute two-baller life of before and died before the end of the decade. Now, if I could get leaner and stay leaner, maybe I might live until the early part of the next decade. Who knows?

I was still a good 10kg above the weight that my BMI said I ought to be. Even so, it was quite a thrill to get to the point where this not-entirely-reliable measurement index declared that I was no longer obese, but now merely overweight (and that was with my actual correctly measured height!).

I also started going to a personal trainer. I thought it would be useful to have someone who would know how far I was able to push myself at this early stage. Mainly, though, it was because a personal trainer, Paulette, lives just a two-minute walk from my house. This had to be laziest that anyone has ever been while employing a fitness professional.

Paulette took care not to break me, but at our first session, I worked out for an hour and was surprised by how much strength I still retained. I thought my muscles might have atrophied, I'd used them so little. I was stiff as hell the next day, but it was great to know that I was still basically capable.

Was the appeal of lifting weights partly to do with asserting my masculinity? As I raised a scarcely loaded bar above my head, I imagined myself as a strong man at a circus – or at least as the five-year-old me, pretending to be one. Maybe I needed to know that I was just as capable of such manly feats as I had been before. In fact, much more so, as I'd not done much of this kind of thing back when I had two balls. Was I subconsciously overcompensating for my loss? I don't think balls equate to masculinity, but that idea is so deeply entrenched in our culture that it might be hard not to be affected by it on a subconscious level.

Paulette suggested that, as I was doing a bit of running, I should give myself something to aim for and sign up for a half-marathon. Running 13.1 miles seemed like an insane target given what I'd been through, but I really wanted a crazy challenge, if only to show cancer that it couldn't defeat me. I'd done half-marathons before (and one full marathon, back in 2004) so knew how tough it was, even when you hadn't just had a body part removed.

Yet if I could manage that in the same calendar year that all this crap had happened to me, then ... well, that would be something.

Also, with some sponsorship, it might be an effective way to raise some money for the hospitals that had treated me, meaning that I was once again obeying my all-powerful oncologist.

Without really thinking about the logistics of it, I looked for local half-marathons and signed up for the nearest one that I could find. It was at Knebworth in November, about six months off at that point. To keep me honest, I set up a JustGiving page and let people know I was planning to do the run. Donations started coming in immediately; I was committed.

I told Paulette that I'd taken her advice, and she said that she'd do the run too. We could train together. I spent most Sundays for the next few months running round the Hertfordshire countryside with her, gradually ramping up the distance and the inclines. It turned out that, like an idiot, I'd accidentally signed up for a notoriously hilly half-marathon.

Again, maybe on some subconscious level I needed to prove my masculinity, to show I was still brave and tough, even though the songwriters of World War Two would have assumed my condition made me a coward.

> *Richard Herring has only got one ball*
> *The other is playing the Albert Hall (in puppet form)*
> *He can run for longer*
> *His arms are stronger*
> *It's not affected his sexual performance at all.*

ON THE BALL: Record ball-breakers

If you were wondering which animal has the biggest bollocks, then a) what's wrong with you? and b) wonder no more.

The king of the swingers is the North Pacific right whale, whose two balls weigh in at about 972kg if you pop them both on a scale. The biggest ever measured were just over 2 metres long and 78cm wide. These are the heaviest balls in the mammal world, and have the largest testicle-to-body weight ratio, at about 2 per cent of the animal's total weight. However, during the mating season, the testicles of harbour porpoises actually increase in size to around 5 per cent of their body weight. I've had dry spells where I think the same might have been true for me.

But mammals can't compete with insects. The creature with the biggest testicles, relative to its size, is the tuberous bush cricket, with its testes making up 13.8 per cent of its total body weight. If the average man had equivalent balls, then they'd weigh 11.5kg.*

At the small end of the spectrum, the case of the howler monkey is interesting. According to the journal *Current Biology*, they make a trade-off between testicle size and ability to howl.† The bigger their vocal organs, the smaller their monkey nuts. As the *New Scientist* says, 'Howler monkeys have to choose between big balls and big bawls.' All

---

* Anyone who watches *Maddie's Do You Know?* on CBeebies might like to watch and hear Maddie giving out most of these testicle facts in this YouTube video from *BBC Earth Unplugged*: https://www.youtube.com/watch?v=GUmqASP4INA

† Jacob C. Dunn, *et al.* 'Evolutionary trade-off between vocal tract and testes dimensions in howler monkeys', *Current Biology*, vol. 25, issue 21, 2 November 2015.

right, *New Scientist*, if you stop trying to do jokes, I'll stop trying to do science.

This may be because once they've got a big organ in their throat (that's how you do it, *New Scientist*), there aren't enough resources left to invest in big bollocks, or because their ability to howl loudly is such an effective mating mechanism that they only need small balls. For fans of my 1990s TV show *This Morning with Richard Not Judy*, I should just say at this point that they're all howler monkeys by the time I'm finished with them.

Similarly, the dung beetles with the biggest horns have the smallest testicles.

If you were wondering which animal has the *most* testicles, then a) really, what's wrong with you? and b) why am I helping you with this?

Ken Saladin, former professor of histology (microscopic anatomy) says:

A good candidate would be the pork or beef tapeworm. The pork tapeworm, *Taenia solium,* is divided into 800 to 900 segments called proglottids. Each mature proglottid has around 50 to 100 testes. If we conservatively estimate that 60 per cent of the proglottids are mature and each of those has 75 testes, that would be 31,500 testes in one worm. Even [allowing] for a liberal margin of error, I'd say one pork tapeworm has 20,000 to 40,000 testes.*

What the above suggests to me is that if you start counting tapeworm testicles, then you get sacked from the department of histology.

* 'What animal has the most testicles?', www.quora.com.

28

Let he who is without sin ...

As an early form of exercise, I had returned to stone-clearing on my morning dog walk. This is something I'd started doing three years before, as I walked Wolfie around the perimeter of a large piece of farmland near my home. I had observed how stony the soil was, and I'd had a compunction to start trying to move the stones to the periphery of the field.

'Why?' you might – not unreasonably – ask.

It's hard to explain. The best answer I have come up with is: Because it's *there*, but I want it to be *over there*.

It was an attempt to bring some order to the world, and I suspected (though never checked) that it was quite helpful. Big lumps of stone must impede the growth of crops. I had started thinking about how many times I would walk around this field – maybe twice a day for the rest of my life. By moving a few stones each trip, over that length of time, maybe I could make a difference. If I made a cairn – or, even better, a wall – using the stones, then at least it would be something, like that beautifully carved I. W. that said: 'I was here!' (Maybe the graffiti was literally going to say 'I WAS HERE' but the carver got caught after the second letter.)

Someone else in the village had already had the same idea, as there was a small cairn in one of the corners of the field at the end of a path that crossed through the crops. There were lots of big stones near that path, and on each walk, I'd try to pick up five or six and add them to the pile.

I started making my own cairns, too, or randomly throwing stones up against the fences round the field. It seemed vaguely illegal, though I was generally careful to clear only what I could reach from the path, and only going out on to the field after harvest or ploughing (oh, what stones turned up then – it was Stone Christmas!) I tried to do it surreptitiously; I was still new to the village and I didn't want people thinking I was weird.

I knew the task was pointless. There were a billion stones on this thirty-five-acre field. I was moving about twenty a day. At this rate, I might get rid of a quarter of a million if I stayed fit and healthy and did it every day for thirty years. But how likely was it that I would still be clearing at that rate at the age of eighty? Or, let's be honest, sixty?

Yet there was something about the futility of it all that appealed to me. It seemed to speak of the pointlessness of attempting anything in our lives, but still we strive to achieve. Humanity can be wonderful in its pursuit of hope over reality. A part of me was aiming to be remembered, while another part was trying to make sure my identity remained a secret. I was trying to create order out of chaos – a very human imperative – and to defeat nature, but I knew that nature must defeat me. I was like a land-bound King Cnut; the stones would win this war.

The only person who ever properly caught me in the act was an elderly chap called Michael, with whom I would have a brief chat whenever our paths crossed. One day, he appeared from nowhere and saw me stooping to pick up a stone. I made up some poor excuse about trying to remove sharp flint in case my dog stepped on it. He knew what I was up to, and revealed that it was he who had built the original cairn, by picking up one stone every day as he crossed the field.

One stone? Lightweight.

It felt like fate had brought me to my sensei. He was an elderly man, approaching the end of his life. This seemingly chance encounter was actually the universe letting him pass on the torch. He could never finish the job, but maybe I could. If not, I would choose my successor, and so eventually the job would be done.

As much as I tried to keep my identity secret from everyone, Catie told me that people kept asking what the hell I was up to, and eventually a sign appeared on the biggest cairn, calling it 'Herring's Mound' and describing it as if it was in an art gallery. I think people might have twigged.

I was half playing and half serious, and the comic possibilities of this madness were very apparent to me. I thought it might be interesting to try and turn this project into a weird podcast that satirised the mundanity and occasional pomposity of the medium (imagine thinking that something as basic as stone-clearing required any kind of instruction, or that you could be an expert on it), but that also had something to say about the human condition and the cruel indifference of the universe to our existence. I liked the challenge of trying to make the same basic journey around a field doing the same thing both interesting and dull enough to get an (admittedly small) audience, and enjoyed the disconnect between my insistence that I wanted this to be secret and simultaneously broadcasting it to the whole world. I also knew that it was one of those ideas that would only work if I did it FOR YEARS.

I had to be committed (you can decide how to define the word in this case), and never stop clearing or podcasting, however few people were listening. It was a joke that would only really work if it spanned decades.

It's become one of my favourite things to do. The paranoid host of this podcast (me) is convinced that he can eventually build a wall that will be visible from space, that every dog walker he encounters is against him, and that an organisation called the Stone Stasi are trying to catch him in the act so they can imprison or kill him. He has also created Stone Gods and believes there is a ditch that can stop Brexit if it is fed one stone a day. He has hallucinated and seen log-dogs and Morlocks in the field, and once even saw Judy Murray, Andy Murray's mum. It might have been her, and you can't prove otherwise.

I can distance myself from all this and call the podcast host a character, but all those hallucinations are ones I've really 'seen', and I was genuinely attempting this task (and trying to hide it from other dog walkers) before I even thought of sharing it with anyone. It's utter madness, and those lines are blurred (sometimes I have to stop doing it for a while lest it actually sends me over the edge), but some amazing things have come out of that stream of consciousness – and, most importantly, many people use the podcast to help them sleep at night.

During lockdown, I started live-streaming stone-clears each morning, like a very unsuccessful Joe Wicks. About two hundred people would tune in to watch. It was an event. Friendships were forged in the chat room. Some listeners are so committed that they have even purchased some of my cleared stones when I've done various fundraisers over the years. They have a small piece of a huge art project, one that I ultimately hope will win the Turner Prize (so far, no interest).

It was a big deal for me to get to return to the field, a fortnight after chemo. It was spring; the world was reborn. I had come close to dying before my task could be completed, but now I had been given a second chance. I was genuinely buoyed by the return of the sun, the stones and my own mobility. It was a proper rebirth.

Which made what happened the next week all the more devastating.

I arrived at the field as usual, and coincidentally, it was a walk that I was recording for the podcast. I noticed that there were a large number of big stones scattered across the ground. They hadn't been there last week, and though stones grow fast (according to the podcasting stone-clearer, anyway), they don't grow this fast. As I walked on, there were loads more stones piled on to the field at regular intervals. I wondered if the farmer had, for some reason (maybe because someone had been removing stones), come and dumped more stones on the field. It seemed unlikely. There are about a billion stones on this field already, and my thirty months of work had barely made a scratch.

Were these stones that I'd already cleared that had been thrown back on to the field? I had liberally scattered this edge of the field with stones I'd cleared from the middle, but there were few recognisable cairns. It would have taken a lot of effort to locate and move this much rubble.

A few days earlier, I had encountered a local man who had professed to be a fan, but had then started leaving slightly weird messages on my YouTube page about how stones provide minerals to the plants to help them grow (a claim I found spurious enough to assume it was an attempt at comedy). He had told me to stop, but as he'd also told me that he was a fan, I'd assumed he was joining in with the joke. I said that I was really having no impact on anything, and that I would never stop. He threatened to throw the stones back, but many people have made this gag over the years. I have encouraged them to act on the idea (none of them know the secret location of the field, of course) as it would only add to the futility of my mission.

Were these scatterings of stones something to do with him?

Some of my small cairns seemed untouched, but further round the field there was a cairn that I had dedicated to Dominic Cummings, who I had pretended had sadly died. That is to say, there *had* been a cairn. It was now gone, and the stones were now on the field, some having been flung some distance. It seemed terribly disrespectful to Dominic's memory, until I remembered that he was actually still alive – and also a dick.

My heart was in my mouth. This was an incredible act of aggression, and I was worried that the original cairn – the one started by Michael – might also have been destroyed. Michael had passed away during lockdown, which had not only been very sad, but had also made me more convinced than ever that I had been continuing his work.

With a rising sense of nausea, I walked towards Michael's cairn. It too had been desecrated. I was genuinely upset about this. I knew what I'd been doing was stupid, but it was harmless. It had been enjoyed by at least some members of the village, but also a select band of people around the world. Mainly, it seemed a disaster that Michael's cairn, built with one stone a day over many months and years, was almost totally destroyed.

Yes, I knew that you couldn't really 'destroy' a pile of stones, and that I could easily gather up the stones (and indeed I did – I decided I had to, as the way they'd been put back presented quite a danger to any farm machinery), but I worried this would then turn into a battle of wills between me and my nemesis. He clearly believed that the stones should be on the field as strongly as I believed they should be *off* the field. Would the next few years become a game of rock tennis, where I took rubble off the farmland and he threw it back on?

I was discovering all this, in real time, while recording my podcast, which means you can listen to my soul being crushed, my spring turning to winter and my symbol of rebirth being splatted under a massive boulder.*

It could not have happened at a worse time.

The Stone Stasi was the paranoid creation of the podcast Herring, who arrogantly imagined that his pathetic task might meet organised resistance, that every other dog walker he encountered was trying to thwart him, and that he was some kind of freedom fighter who could beat stone fascism. Yet somehow, it seemed, I had managed to will this imaginary force into actual existence. Someone so disgruntled with what I had done that they were prepared to undo almost three years of methodical and painfully slow work. All right, maybe it doesn't count as work.

I was a little bit broken by it. I had hoped that these cairns would outlive me, that people in a hundred years' time might see them and wonder who had made them and why. Or that Catie might bury me under the main one. (Hopefully in an official funeral, rather than in an attempt to cover up my murder, having finally snapped at putting up with my ridiculous stone-based antics – and, to be fair, all the other stuff she has to endure.)

---

* Listen here: https://www.comedy.co.uk/podcasts/stone_clearing_with_richard_herring/chapter-94/

I assumed for much of the day that this had to be the end of stone-clearing, as I didn't want anything to escalate. It was a mad project and had attracted the attention of obsessive people before (which is fair enough, as it's hosted by one, too), but none of them knew where the field was – or, more importantly, where I lived. I was reasonably sure I was not in any actual danger, but it still felt like an act of violence against my soul, especially coming so quickly after the act of violence against (or by) my body.

I couldn't really complain about anything. What he'd done was a little bit crazy, but then what I'd done couldn't really be classified as particularly sane. I'm sure the guy who did this had no idea that I'd been ill, and had simply got overexcited about interacting with something that he'd seen on YouTube.

To be fair to him, putting the stones back was as valid an artistic expression as taking them off, and neither of us had any authority to do what we were doing. I was sad for myself and sad for Michael and sad for the hundreds of people who have come to rely on this podcast for philosophical stimulation (or to send them to sleep).

In the long term, the incident passed without any repercussions. I cleared the stones back off the field, rebuilt the cairns and carried on. Yet I was surprised by how much it depressed me at the time. The Stone Gods had made me their Job and tested my belief in them, but I knew they were real and I had to keep doing their bidding.

ON THE BALL: Eat my balls

'Bollocks have never frightened me. I'll eat a bollock any time.'
– Germaine Greer

You might think that faded celebrities being forced to consume kangaroo balls on *I'm A Celebrity* must leave a nasty taste in the mouth, but given how many people are happy to take balls (and their contents) in their mouths on a daily basis, it seems a bit rich to get that upset.

Testicles (and sometimes their contents) are considered culinary delicacies in many cultures, both ancient and modern. Here are a few examples of the kind of ball-eating you can do in public.

Another helping of fish spunk?

In ancient Rome, the milt (fish semen) of lamprey eels was favoured among the decadent and gregarious for its rarity, if not its taste. It's really something when you're eating something gross just because it's hard to lay your hands on it. Throwing up was a big part of Roman cuisine, so I guess a mug full of eel sperm probably did the trick. Though you have to wonder who was happy to wank off the eels in the first place. Emperor Vitellius, who is remembered for being gluttonous and cruel (subverting the stereotype that all fat people are jolly) once filled a tremendously large dish with pike livers, pheasant brains, peacock brains, flamingo tongues, and lamprey milt, all collected from different parts of the Empire for his guests to competitively consume. I think I prefer our modern-day equivalent of trying to eat the hottest possible curry, although I hope a few more of the boisterous and unpleasant clients of our Indian restaurants might have ended up with some semen surreptitiously added to that dish too.

Mum's gone to Iceland

Rams' testicles are commonly eaten as part of *Þorrablót* (Thorr-ah-bloat), a winter festival in Iceland (the country, not the supermarket). Other Icelandic delicacies on offer include rotten shark meat (*hákarl*), boiled sheep's head (*svið*), and congealed sheep's blood wrapped in a ram's stomach (*blóðmör*), so if I was attending, I think I'd probably be happy to crunch down a couple of ovine bollocks, and then say I was full and had to go to bed.

Bollock bake-off

Every year in August and September, the villages of Ozrem and Lunjevica in the municipality of Gornji Milanovac, Serbia, host the World Gonad Cooking Championship, with a variety of different animal testicles on offer, including a bollock goulash (goolie-ash?) made of pig, ram or goat balls (presumably not with all three types of balls in one goulash – that would be disgusting). The competition was set up in the last twenty years and has grown steadily, attracting an international following – of people who want to eat animal bollocks. Winners are awarded a wood-carved phallus as a trophy. Why bring the penis into it? It should be wood-carved balls. You can't even do your testicle festival right, Serbia. In addition, the festival awards prizes to the ballsiest men of that year. Previous winners have included Barack Obama and Julian Assange, though they did not personally attend – probably for fear of what the Serbians would do to their award-winning bollocks.

Guys, if you let me win, I can try and rustle up my excised bollock and you can make a stew out of it. I guarantee if I win an award, I WILL ATTEND. What's Assange's excuse for not going . . . ? Oh, right.

Rocky Mountain low

Bull's testicles are eaten as 'Rocky Mountain oysters' in the US, or 'prairie oysters' in Canada. And it says something about the disgusting nature of a food when pretending it is something as puke-worthy as an oyster is a selling point.

29

One lump or two?

Within a month of my brief flirtation with chemo, things seemed to be returning to normal. I was still podcasting and had started work on the fourth series of my Radio 4 sitcom *Relativity*. I'd been struggling a bit for a major plot line, but once again testicular cancer proved itself the gift that keeps on giving, and Ian, the character I play in that show, went on a journey remarkably similar to my own.

I was getting my work/life balance right, and had been spending some quality time with the kids. Phoebe and I had made a few short films together using my puppet-show green screen (and she occasionally gatecrashed *Twitch of Fun* with her soft toy, Fluffy Rabbit, who just blew raspberries and instantaneously became the most popular and sophisticated thing on the show). It made me hope that one day I could pass my great-grandad's puppets on to her (or her brother), and Ally would continue to have a voice long after I had gone.

One May morning, I'd had a little lie-in, and woke to find that Phoebe had drawn me a picture. She explained that as she liked me a bit more now, I was no longer falling into lava. In fact, the picture was of me standing next to my daughter, both of us smiling happily and maybe even holding hands. I am not saying that being a parent is an extreme form of Stockholm Syndrome and that I have been emotionally beaten into submission by my captor, but this simple gesture of finally-not-depicting-me-as-burning-to-death made me inordinately happy. It was the most beautiful thing I've ever seen. I stuck it to the wall in front of my desk so I could look at it when I was working to make myself smile.

Although I actually sat and stared at it and made myself cry.

With happiness? Or relief?

One act of love makes all the struggles of parenthood worthwhile.

I have to say, it's a really good drawing of me. She was annoyed that she forgot my beard, but I am sometimes clean-shaven and the hair is spot on. The drawing also really captures her own mischievous spirit.

Perhaps we were all going to live happily ever after.

Of course, I was remaining hyper-vigilant in case the cancer should return. I was reluctantly giving my remaining love conker the once-over every week or so. I still sort of felt like

I'd prefer not to know if anything was going wrong. I know that sounds crazy, but as things hadn't been so obvious with the ball that turned out to be full of cancer (even the doctor thought it wasn't), it was easy to convince myself that something was wrong now, even when I couldn't feel anything definitely different. It's not hypochondria if you turn out to have something ...

It was to be another part of my body that was to give me an unpleasant shock, however. One morning in bed, I noticed a pretty pronounced lump on the side of my body, right under my ribcage. It didn't hurt, but then do you know what else hadn't hurt? My bloody ball cancer.

I had never noticed anything there before, but this thing was so big that I couldn't even kid myself that I was imagining it. I showed my wife, who agreed it looked pretty sizeable, but we knew a lump is sometimes just a lump, so we tried to stay positive.

I'd lost a fair amount of weight quite quickly, so it seemed this thing, good or bad, had been hiding amid my midriff fat, growing unnoticed. If it had been there during my scans, it should have been picked up on, but nobody had pointed it out, so maybe it had sprung out of nowhere. Not for the first time this year, my mind turned to Dustin Diamond, the actor who had played Screech in *Saved by the Bell* before going on to live quite a colourful life that included making a sex tape, filing for bankruptcy, trying out professional wrestling and serving three months in jail after being involved in a knife fight.

He had ignored a big lump on his neck for a few months, and when he'd finally got it checked out in January 2021 (the same month that I first went to the doctor), it was confirmed as cancer. He sadly died a month later, just before I went into hospital for my operation.

If Screech can die, anyone can die.

While I knew a big lump could be a number of other things, I was also very aware that it could be bad news. All my friends who'd died of cancer had had a hopeful few months where they'd thought they'd beaten it, only for it to return, sometimes somewhere else in their body, always more aggressively.

I rang Nurse Linda, who took my concerns seriously enough to arrange an appointment with Dr Sharma for two days later, which was both reassuring and terrifying at the same time.

More slow, anxious waiting, but at least when my appointment came, it was first thing in the morning. I told Dr Sharma about the lump and said that maybe I'd noticed it because I'd lost weight.

'You've lost weight? Why?' he asked, genuinely concerned.

'Because you told me to,' I replied, maybe a bit aggressively. 'I did what you told me to do.' Didn't he know I did everything he instructed me to?

He looked at my lump and told me that it was almost certainly a lipoma: a harmless deposit of fat cells (nice). He had some himself. They weren't worth the effort of removing, but he said he would send me for a scan, just in case. It was a relief to be declared cancer-free, but then again, that's basically what had happened on that first visit to the GP with my big bollock, so don't count your chickens.

What was good, though, was the vigilance. Everything was being taken very seriously, and I was being properly looked after at every turn. If the worst happened, then I should catch it early.

That night, I enjoyed telling Right Bollock that his campaign of evil might actually have increased my lifespan. It had given me the impetus to get properly fit, which should stave off other more deadly health issues, and also it meant my body was getting thoroughly checked out every few months and any time anything untoward happened. Increasingly, it seemed that losing a nut was the best thing that could have happened to me. Right Bollock was angry that his plans to destroy me might have backfired, but seemed confident that he would win in the end.

I went for the scan a few days later. Once again, iodine was pumped into my body; once again, I was warned that I might think I'd pissed myself, but I wouldn't have pissed myself; and once again, I experienced no such thing and was left feeling cheated. (I had another scan a few months later, and voiced my frustration to the technician putting in the canula. 'Maybe this time you'll get lucky,' he dead-panned. I didn't.)

The results came through quickly and Dr Sharma confirmed on the phone that it was a lipoma, though quite a large one. All the rest of my organs were looking good, too, he told me.

I was a bit perturbed that my body seemed to be insisting on creating all these cancerous or unnecessary new bits. I guess after half a century, things get boring, and it was keen to experiment:

Let's see if we can make a new testicle out of cancer!

Let's move some fat over here and see what we can make from it.

It was like my body had got bored of the original model and was trying to perfect or even replace it.

All these little tumours (which is what I believe a lipoma technically is) might be my body trying to create an escape pod from the decaying mother body. Or was it trying to forge a brand-new being that might live after my death?

Hey guys, I've realised how old and fucked this guy is! Is there any way we can build a new human being in here and use that to escape the citadel as it collapses around us?

Just concentrate on keeping Richard Herring 1.0 going! I have managed to contribute to two other human beings, and while they have been diluted by inferior non-Richard Herring genes, I think that's the best way to get some of my DNA out there for another generation. I know it's tough for all that remains, tethered as we all are to this failing body, but let's try and enter the twilight of our years with some dignity and put an end to the Frankenstein experiments. Or at least grow a replacement testicle.

My lipoma would be staying with me, unless it led to any issues or my body found a way to give it hair, bones, teeth, limbs, eyes, etc. I would love little Lipoma if he or she or they did gain consciousness, of course, but I hoped this would be my stupid body's last attempt to try and mix things up for the upcoming fifty-fifth season of this failing franchise.

ON THE BALL: The No-Balls Prize – Part I

As a man who has lost one ball, the fear of losing the other is a constant source of stress, so it's strange to discover that some ball-owners might willingly have them removed, or that having no balls might give someone an advantage in society.

Eunuchs for Jesus

It has been claimed that Origen, the theologian and early follower of Christianity, castrated himself after taking Matthew 19:12 a little bit too literally. In this passage, Jesus says: 'There are eunuchs who have made themselves eunuch for the sake of the kingdom of Heaven.' The story goes that Origen paid a doctor to whip off his genitals to ensure that people thought he would be a respectable tutor. I don't know about that, though. If I was hiring a tutor to get my kids through their GCSEs and he said, 'You don't have to worry. To ensure that no one thinks I might touch their kids, I got my balls removed,' I would think twice about employing him.

Tellingly, though, there are quite a few surviving texts by Origen, and none of them even mention him having castrated himself. That'd definitely make it into my blog if I did it. Look how much capital I've made out of losing one ball. Furthermore, when he wrote his *Commentary on the Gospel of St Matthew*, he says that anyone giving a literal interpretation of Matthew 19:12 would be an idiot. Though that could be the voice of experience talking. To be honest, I can't imagine there were loads of people making that mistake. So the jury's out.

Game of cojones

Just like in *Game of Thrones*, the Byzantine Empire ran off the backs of eunuchs (there was no use in trying to run off their fronts any more). Eunuchs were courtiers, clerics, generals, and scribes, and also fulfilled numerous other roles within the imperial and church machine. Enslaved eunuchs were frequently given as gifts among the ruling elite. For example, the Peloponnesian heiress Danielis included a hundred eunuchs among her gifts to Emperor Basil I. Imagine unwrapping that present, and the face you'd have to pull. 'Oh, a hundred eunuchs . . . great . . . no, no, I haven't got that already . . . you shouldn't have.'

I suppose it's better than being given the bag of two hundred chopped-off balls.

Testa-cotta

The Chinese royal household was run by eunuchs for thousands of years. Chinese eunuchs built the Terracotta Army in 210–209 BCE, and by the nineteenth century, 20,000 eunuchs made up the household staff of the Forbidden City. Under the Han dynasty, castration was a punishment for various offences, such as insurrection or insult, and was often carried out on captured enemy soldiers. Though the punishment itself was deeply shameful, eunuchs were sought after for imperial employ, as they were perceived to have no ambitions of house or family status, meaning those who were punished in this way were potentially afforded social benefits.

Cai Lun was a prominent member of the imperial household, becoming chief eunuch under Emperor Hedi. Among other accomplishments, he is credited with the invention of paper, which he created by pulping bamboo, old rags and fishing nets to create a cheap alternative to wooden tablets. It's incredible what you can get done if your bollocks aren't always diverting your attention elsewhere.

Amazingly, it wasn't until 25 November 1924 that the eunuch system was finally banned in China, and 1,500 eunuchs were evicted from service. I don't know what the prospects were for unemployed eunuchs, but I feel sorry for anyone who had their balls cut off on 24 November 1924, anticipating a lifetime of service. They would have felt pretty hard done by.

30

Birthday ball

The twelfth of July arrived. I was fifty-four.

Someone on Twitter pointed out that I was exactly thirty years younger than Bill Cosby, and exactly thirty years older than Malala, which at least suggests that things improve with each new generation.

Here it was. The birthday that I had, for a few fleeting moments in February, thought I might never live to see. I was fifty-four – or, as I preferred to see it, I was turning eighteen for the third time.

That first eighteen years had taken so long; in the second eighteen, I'd assumed that I would be young forever; and now the third eighteen had whizzed past, like a fire devouring dry straw, and I hadn't managed to get through it without jettisoning a body part.

If for this birthday, a devil had appeared and told me that he could guarantee I would live until my fourth eighteenth birthday, I would have taken him up on it. Even though I knew there would have to be some twist to the bargain, where I immediately fell into a coma, or would only be a head in a jar, or I'd have to live in Middlesbrough.*

When you thought you might have no years left, then eighteen more years seems like an eternity, even though I know the seventy-two-year-old me would be furiously bargaining with the demon once that time was up too. 'Just a few more months!' He'd definitely give his left bollock, and probably his cock. I can't imagine he'd be getting much use out of either by then.

A fifth go at turning eighteen would be more ideal, I suppose. It's something that half my grandparents managed (one getting a good distance through her sixth eighteen), and both my parents look likely to achieve. But one more lot of eighteen years from now would get both my kids into their twenties, leaving my parenting job mainly complete.

So much of life is about waiting for something to happen, and for a long time I'd had this feeling that something was just round the corner for me. When I'd heard I'd got cancer I thought that I might bow out before I got round that corner. But what if all the things that have happened while I've been waiting for something to happen, were the thing that I had been waiting to happen?

What I am trying to say is that after this bumpy year, it was starting to dawn on me that without realising it, I'd already been round the corner for a good few years. The family life and the work life that had been built around me had quietly moulded into something pretty much perfect. I had a wife I didn't deserve, two amazing kids and an autonomy in my job that most comedians (and non-comedians) would kill for. The worst thing that had happened to me in my life was getting a curable cancer, and even then I'd managed to turn that into

* Only kidding, Boro inhabitants. My family are from there, and I love you really.

a year's worth of paid work! To complain about my lot would make me like someone who had won the EuroMillions, but was pissed off because it was a week when the jackpot was only £15 million. Though come on, that's got to be quite annoying.

I got my birthday phone call from Barry Cryer. This much-respected and loved elder statesman of comedy (commonly known among comedians as Uncle Baz) had a delightful tradition of ringing up acts on their birthdays and telling them a joke, getting his laugh and then immediately pissing off. It was such a privilege to be on his list (though I have a feeling that I was one of at least a thousand recipients) and I looked forward to it every year. You can keep your gongs and awards – this annual private audience with an absolute comedy legend was the most incredible prize a comedian (and comedy fan) could receive.

This year's joke came with a little bit of additional history attached to it. Barry said: 'Here's one for you. To give you some context, I told this one to John Mortimer, you know him – Rumpole of the Bailey. He was sitting outside Sheekey's restaurant in a wheelchair, looking a bit sad. He gave me a wave and said, "C'mon Baz. Joke!"

'So I told him this one. There's a man sitting opposite a sweet old lady on the train, and when the train sets off, she takes a Bible out of her bag and begins to read from it silently. Next station. Oooh, Bible back in the bag. Happens again. The train sets off, takes the Bible out. Next station, Bible back in the bag. Now he's riveted. And it happens a third time and he's getting off the train soon. He can't bear it. He says, "Do excuse me . . ."

'And she says "Yeessss?"' Barry put on a funny Lady Bracknell-style voice for the lady, which really made me laugh.

'"Every time the train leaves the station, you take the Bible out of your bag to read from it."

' "Yessss, Yeesss, I do. Yeees."

' "When we get to the next station, you pop your Bible back into the bag."

' "Yesss. Yessss."

' "Do forgive me, why are you doing this?"

'And she says, "Why don't you fuck off!" '

The final line was delivered in an angry cockney voice, very much at odds with the genteel nature of the earlier exchange. It's not the kind of punchline you might expect from Barry Cryer, but it is the kind of anti-joke of which he was very fond, and one that could still surprise a fellow comic. The set-up was so traditional and polite, that the totally unnecessary foul language at the end is a proper surprise. Though I laughed most at the way he said 'yes'.

He continued, 'I told that to John Mortimer at Sheekey's. He wiped his eyes and said, "That's made my day!" But I'd said that last line very loudly, and the other diners were looking at me and thinking, *Who's that idiot telling John Mortimer to fuck off?!*'

With that, Barry, presumably readying himself to ring the next birthday comedian, was on his way.

That was my last birthday joke, but it wasn't the last time I'd hear from Barry – he was to appear on my podcast in September,* and I'd get a couple more phone calls from him.

I knew he couldn't go on forever. But I thought he'd go on forever.

---

* Episode 345 – very much worth your time. Listen here: https://play.acast. com/s/rhlstp/rhlstp345-barrycryer/. You can also watch this one on my YouTube channel, if you want to see the great man at work.

ON THE BALL: The No-balls Prize – Part II

Hitting the high notes

The idea of castrating boys to preserve their sweet singing voices seems bizarre and horrifying to us in the modern world – because it is bizarre and horrifying. Eunuch singers were well known throughout Europe and Asia from at least the early Middle Ages, with famed singers noted in Byzantine and imperial Chinese courts. They were renowned for their extensive vocal ranges and songbird-like voices. You might think, like I did, that boys are a limitless resource, so when one hits puberty, wouldn't it be simpler and less barbaric just to employ a different child? Or you could get a lady to sing the part instead. However, there was something unique about the castrato voice, and there was more flexibility, too, which made it quite different to the female voice. If you really want to judge this for yourself, then search for Alessandro Moreschi on YouTube. He isn't the greatest castrato singer, apparently – and if you'd gone to those lengths to be a singer, you'd want to be the best – but he's the only one that was ever recorded. Be warned, I didn't find it a comfortable listen. Feel free to skip this section if it's making you queasy.

In the Eastern Roman Empire, eunuchs proliferated in church choirs as well as in political life. One of the earliest recorded eunuchs from the early fifth century is Brison, a choirmaster and diplomat in the service of the empress Eudoxia. When the capital was finally seized by the Ottomans in 1453, the organised castration of boys for this purpose seemed to be over.

Sadly, the practice re-emerged in Italy from the six-teenth century. *Castrati*, as they became known, featured in prominent French and Italian courts, the choirs of the Sistine Chapel, and even the choir of St Peter's in the Vatican, which was specifically reorganised by Pope Sixtus V in 1589 to make way for their unique tones.

As well as preserving their voices (and causing infertil-ity), castration had several other effects on these singers' bodies, causing issues such as headaches, brain infirmities and abnormally long bones – and thus increased height. The operation itself was dangerous, and many boys died, either through overdosing on anaesthetic opium or if the operation was performed without drugs, by having their necks compressed for too long as they were rendered unconscious. So grim – and who would have thought a place as holy as the Vatican would ever have been involved in abusing children in this way?

Officially, you'll be glad to hear, the practice was ille-gal, so the surgery either had to be done in secret or for a made-up excuse, such as physical injuries resulting from riding or falling off a horse. Doctors – or sometimes fam-ilies – routinely performed the surgery by placing the boy in a warm bath before administering forms of anaesthetic. Those that survived the procedure could enjoy fame and fortune. In the following two centuries, castrati supplanted both female and male roles in emerging operas. The nota-ble singer Crescentini performed in front of Napoleon, and was awarded honours and distinctions by the emperor. Figures such as Farinelli became intensely popular celebri-ties, touring Europe to adoring fans.

Despite their voices, they were said to be incredibly

clumsy actors and performers. Here's a review of a performance by Farinelli in London:

> Farinelli drew every Body to the Haymarket. What a Pipe! What Modulation! What Extasy to the Ear! But, Heavens! What Clumsiness! What Stupidity! What Offence to the Eye! Reader, if of the City, thou mayest probably have seen in the Fields of Islington or Mile-End or, If thou art in the environs of St James', thou must have observed in the Park with what Ease and Agility a cow, heavy with calf, has rose up at the command of the Milk-woman's foot: thus from the mossy bank sprang the DIVINE FARINELLI.*

I am not always a fan of reviewers at the best of times, but come on, mate. This bloke has his balls cut off to create this music that you apparently loved so much, and you're criticising him for moving like a cow. Maybe there should be something in the review about how awful everyone involved was for propagating this?

Castrati singers declined in fashion in Europe in the nineteenth century, and were systematically banned from church choirs from the 1860s to the 1900s. In 1903, Pius X officially transferred all castrati choir positions to be filled with boys instead. So it only took a few centuries for humankind to arrive at the obvious conclusion and stop chopping the bollocks off little boys so they could keep singing nicely.

---

* Pickering, R (1755) *Reflections on Theatrical Expression in Tragedy* (London) 63

31

Jackson Bollock

I t wasn't just my life that was returning to normal. Finally, we were all allowed out of our houses. I got to do some gigs with actual audiences, and we could have a family holiday. We chose to visit my folks in Somerset for only the second time since 2019. Catie's parents came along, too, and various cousins popped by.

On the first day of the break, we'd been for lunch up Cheddar Gorge (I'd enjoyed looking out of the window and seeing the sullen teenagers being dragged around by their parents – a dance as old as time), then we'd had a stressful round of crazy golf on a packed course with long queues and our kids running amok.

We spent that sunny evening in my parents' garden. The little ones happily played chase with their largely immobile grandad. They squealed at my dad to get the hose out, and he obliged. The kids stripped down to their pants and ran away from the sprinkling water. He'd done the same for me forty or so years ago. That was a more representative memory than angry driving lessons and him nearly killing me with winter walks on the snowy Mendips.

Back in the present day, puddles of mud were created, and before too long, the children had managed to sit in one of them, smearing their bodies and faces in the wet Somerset soil.

My mum remembered me doing the same thing at my son's age. I vaguely recalled walking back into the house, and the shock and laughter that had greeted me, but there's a photo in an album somewhere, and maybe I've confused that print with an actual memory.

Catie was a little embarrassed that the kids had made such a mess. My mum told her not to worry. It was all part of the fun; it was just so lovely to see them.

I then had to wrap up two muddy, wet children in my mum's best 'visitor' towels and carry them up to the bath, through my parents' pristine house, shedding dirt as we went. I got them in the tub, but it quickly became a pool of soil and mud. The kids weren't particularly clean, and the bath looked like a brown-and-white Jackson Pollock painting. I transferred the muddy monsters to the shower, and we desecrated that as well. Ernie had been in his pants the whole time, and just when I thought I'd got him clean and dried, I took off his underwear to discover that his nether regions were covered in half the garden. Talk about Jackson Bollocks.

With the kids more or less clean, I attempted to de-mud the bathroom. But it was almost impossible. I apologised profusely to my house-proud mum. She said she didn't mind at all – it was just so lovely to see them, and she'd wanted a new bathroom suite anyway.

Phoebe got clean and dressed, but Ernie's clothes were in the dryer, so he remained naked. He ran back into the garden and I was sure he was going to get muddy again – but it was going to be worse than that.

He had enjoyed the permitted anarchy of getting filthy, then getting rid of his clothes, and now he wanted to up the ante.

He ran around, flashing his bum and bits and laughing. We all laughed back, of course, as there's no funnier sight than a naked three-year-old boy enjoying his carefree life. Then he declared he needed a wee and stood like a statue of some ancient hero as he let rip into the bushes. This created more laughter – and like his dad, Ernie loves laughter. Catie went a bit green with mortification but Mum said it wasn't a problem, it was just so lovely to see them.

Then Ernie declared he was going to do a poo. I thought he was joking. He's quite shy and private about this kind of stuff and has never pooed in public since being out of nappies, but he ran to the edge of the garden and looked like he was trying. To be fair to him, everyone had been enjoying his antics, and comedically he had nowhere else to go. I was proud that his instincts were so sharp. The only way to top the muddy genitals and the wee was to do a shit.

When I realised that this wasn't an idle threat and that Ernie was prepared to go nuclear, I ran over to stop him. However comedically sound, shitting in your grandparents' garden in front of many of your relatives is a social faux pas. I got close, but he was wily and ran away, with a small brown tail emerging from between his buttocks. He was high on the audience's adulation – and, as awful as his parents were feeling, some of his family were still applauding. He laughed and skipped with a manic look in his eye, like a pooey Caligula (I imagine Caligula was often quite pooey). There was no way back now. He might as well see it through.

He was so fast, easily evading capture. He got to the patio by the fishpond and let rip.

He had broken the one rule of polite society.

He had pooed on the patio.

I noted that my mum said nothing about it not mattering, or it just being so lovely to see us. I think she was actually hoping a new variant might immediately arrive, so we could all go back to the peace of sweet-smelling lockdown.

I told Ernie off and, unsurprisingly, he was confused as to why his big finale had caused such a mixed reaction. A lot of the audience were still enjoying it. Even his angry dad was trying to suppress a smile, despite being mortified and wondering how my parents would judge my own parenting.

I cleaned up the poo, which was sticky enough to leave a residue. Mum said not to worry, she'd jet-wash it later.

Twenty years ago, my dad had fallen into that fishpond while wearing his best suit, after being banished from the house by Mum as she was tidying up for some big family do. He'd decided to prune the foliage in the pond, so had stood on a wobbly stone and promptly fell in, cutting his face and ruining his suit. It's a story that we remind him about roughly every five minutes.

Now Ernie had created another family legend that would follow him like a tail made of excrement for the rest of his life. *Remember when you did a shit on the patio, Ernie? Probably not, but we're not going to let you forget it.*

Obviously, we're not going to give him too hard a time in the short term – we don't want to give him a complex (when he realised he'd gone too far, he was sweetly contrite), but when he's sixteen, he is going to get a lot of reminders of that day.

At the time, I glowed with embarrassment – you can really only blame the parents in a situation like this, and I didn't think it was a good time for me to try and pass the buck to my own upbringing – but now I think it was probably the best possible way to mark the end of lockdown. As an artistic statement about the crappy year we'd endured, a boy crapping on the floor is hard to beat, and the laughter it still prompts is properly cathartic.

This is the family life that I didn't want death to rob me of. Cleaning mud off my kids and shit off a patio is exactly why the NHS saved my life.

ON THE BALL: Pain in the Balls

All people who are lucky enough to have a testicle or two will know how much they hurt if someone kicks or punches you there, or if said testicles come into contact with a speeding cricket ball or football, or if a child tries to run between your legs, but misjudges the space available and crashes its massive hard skull into them.

Basically, balls do not deal well with trauma. This is because they contain a huge number of nerve endings in a relatively tiny space. And this space is, ridiculously, hanging outside the body, protected by nothing more than a loose sock of wrinkly skin and (if you don't manscape) maybe some hair.

That's all pretty obvious stuff, but you may wonder why a kick to the balls can also result in a pain in the abdomen.

Because the testes originally develop around the kidneys before (usually) descending into their special little onion bag, these two areas of the body share a lot of nerves. As the pathways overlap, your stupid brain is unable to discern exactly where the pain is coming from. So everything hurts, and you might well throw up.

If the balls developed near the kidneys, why can't they stay up there? You'll have to ask God about that one.

Is there any way to deal with the pain? And the laughter of everyone around you?

As long as everything is still connected and nothing is twisted, you basically have to wait it out and do all the things that you pretty much instinctively do: lie down, cry, pretend to find it funny too, avoid movement until the awful sensation subsides.

Some people are, of course, a fan of a kick in the nadgers, and can derive sexual pleasure from it. It's your ballbag, so if that's your bag, then knock yourself out. Though be mindful that there are serious dangers involved, and make sure there's consent from all parties, the boundaries have been agreed on and you're sure you know what you're doing. It's also worth having a very clear safe word. I would suggest, 'Please stop smashing me in the bollocks!' but you might want to come up with something pithier.

32

Popping my balloon

In September, I returned to Pinewood to film the studio portion of *Taskmaster: Champion of Champions*. It was a lovely treat to get to do it all again, and if this was the last time I ever appeared on the idiots' lantern, then I'd be happy with that.

As nice as it would be to be a *Taskmaster* Champion of Champions (on top of being a *House of Games* Champion of Champions), I was realistic, both about my chances against strong opposition and the fact that with only one show, it wasn't a proper competition anyway. It was (and luckily really felt like) a celebration of this perfect programme, and it didn't matter who actually took away the trophy.

OK, it mattered a bit. Some people think I am competitive, and I tell them that is rubbish: I am not competitive, I am the MOST competitive. Now, though, I wasn't just competing for myself. I was a representative of all solo-bollos. I was fighting for a much-maligned community, to try and overturn the prejudice we have to face at every turn. I mean, I'd get to keep the trophy and stuff, and I probably wouldn't really mention my ball very much, but any victory was a victory for anyone with one.

To remind you, the line-up was Kerry Godliman, Liza Tarbuck, Lou Sanders, me, and my arch-enemy Ed Gamble, the handsome young comedian with a ludicrously successful podcast and a proper TV career. He had even been chosen to present the *Taskmaster* podcast ahead of me (what did he have that I didn't have? Oh wait, I just did a whole list). My only mission was to prevent him from winning – even if I had to fall on my sword to make that happen.

What I was most pleased about was that I was pretty much at the peak of my fitness. I was slim (for me) and wearing a suit, and I looked properly good for an old man. Everyone knew I'd been ill, and was surprised to see me looking so well. This transformation was heightened by the fact that in the task videos, the post-op me was scruffy, chubby and unkempt, and looked like someone who might just have had a bollock snipped off. A lot can happen in six months.

Most excitingly for me, we were no longer under lockdown rules. There was an actual audience in the studio. I found it a bit overwhelming and struggled to talk coherently for the first few minutes, even mispronouncing the name of the show. There was a wonderful atmosphere, though, and we all got a chance, both to shine and to stink. My wine-making video was the stand-out hit of that round, and my art attempt (predictably) was easily the worst of the next.

We went into the final round with me in second place to the person who I think everyone would accept was the funniest and best contestant of the bunch, Liza. But we were all within a few points of each other, and the twist was that the studio task was worth five points to the winner, but no one else could score. Literally all of us were in reach of the crown. All the other stuff we'd done was a waste of time. It all came down to who was the best at whatever stupid challenge Alex had come up with for the finale.

It turned out we had to secretly fill a suitcase with either balloons or bricks (we were behind a screen), and then carry the suitcase across the stage and place it on a plinth. Greg Davies then had to guess, from the way we'd moved the suitcase and any sounds he might have heard, if we had been carrying balloons or bricks. Anyone who tricked him would go through to the next round. This would carry on until only one trickster remained.

I was so bamboozled by it all that I only had a few seconds left when I realised that the suitcase had to contain *all* the bricks or balloons. I only had one brick in mine. I quickly filled my suitcase (but with which item?) and was ready just in time.

As luck would have it, I was the last person to take their turn. I could observe what the others did and learn from their mistakes.

They all screwed it up. Greg managed to guess or deduce correctly every time. This meant that when it came to my turn, if I could fool him, I would be *Taskmaster* Champion of Champions. If I couldn't, we'd all have to do the same thing again.

I made a pretty good show of making the suitcase seem heavy at some times and light at others. There were a few stumbles, and a couple of times it seemed far too easy to lift. Was that because the suitcase was heavy, or because I was pretending that it was? *Taskmaster* fans had already seen my incredible acting skills in a task in my series where I'd been called on to play all the roles in a short film, including a man who seemed to be pleasuring himself in a bush.

Some contestants had dragged the suitcase, others had wheeled it or carried it by the handle. I had it fully lifted up in my arms. This also meant I could get it up on to the platform it needed to be on without risking it making a tell-tale sound (or non-sound).

For the first time, Greg was not sure what the suitcase contained. He pondered, and then told us that I was the only person he'd heard making a sound when loading the suitcase, and that there had been an awful lot of balloon noise. But had I done that on purpose to trick him? Was I that clever?

He decided that the case contained bricks.

I had to open the case to reveal whether I was a winner or we were back to square one. Ed, who had gone first, had already popped some of his balloons in disgust at his failure, so I told him that he shouldn't have done that, because he might well still be in this. Then I opened up the suitcase to reveal the beautiful red balloons of victory. It was like a case of excised bollocks floating down to the ground.

I was the *Taskmaster* Champion of Champions. I had shown that people with one testicle, despite all the prejudice about them being weak or cowardly or unmanly or Nazis, are capable of coping with extreme pressure, of seeing off two-bollocked and no-bollocked opposition, and, most importantly, of carrying a suitcase of balloons in a manner confusing enough to trick a tall man into thinking they are bricks.

Let the prejudice against the monoballs cease right now. We are exactly as manly as one (admittedly quite pathetic) man and three brilliant women. We can achieve anything that a bunch of fairly incompetent idiots can achieve.

I still thought the whole thing was bullshit. You can't judge something like this from just one show – or, as it turned out, from one stupid task – and Liza was definitely the person who deserved the accolade. But fuck it. I had won.

I may only have one, but I HAVE WON.

As we go to press, I am currently the only person in the world to be a Champion of Champions in both *Taskmaster* and *House of Games*. Sure, some of my contemporaries may have Oscars and BAFTAs and their own TV shows, and they may have earned millions of pounds and not have a show where they talk to a puppet representing their severed testicle to an audience of about 150 people. But none of them have a gold trophy with Richard Osman's face on it *and* a shop window dummy painted gold that is meant to represent Greg Davies. I DO!

Victory was OK, but the absolutely best part of all this was that Ed Gamble came last. That's all I'd wanted. Anything else was a solitary cherry on the cake.

ON THE BALL: Don't neglect the balls

I may have been a little disrespectful to testicles (disretestical?) in this book. I have called them ugly and weird, and I've criticised their design flaws and positioning. But one of their major features, which I've barely covered at all, is their place in providing erotic pleasure. One of the benefits of having an extremely sensitive bodily organ on the outside of your body (and possibly enough to justify the fact they've evolved in this way) is that, in the right circumstances, balls can be caressed and cupped, as gently or roughly as the owner feels comfortable with.

A lot of us neglect the balls, but here is some advice on bringing the boys (or boy) into your lovemaking. It won't be for everyone, of course, but if none of the people involved have testicles, then I think you could at least give everyone a laugh by attaching some to your dildo or strap-on.

The first – and very significant – consideration is the importance of communication.

Balls are like snowflakes: they're very easy to destroy

with a blowtorch, but also each one is different, and every ball-owner will like different stuff. Just because you've heard that some men like to have theirs nailed to pieces of wood, it doesn't mean you should just turn up with your toolkit and start banging away with your hammer. Ask them what they like. Personally, I like mine to be handled quite gently, but I've had partners going in at them like they're kneading dough or picking apples that aren't quite ready to fall from the bough. Which some people will like, but others really won't. So, as with pretty much everything that goes on during sex, it's worth checking first.

If you're the person with the balls that are about to be investigated, then for God's sake, give some pointers as to what you might enjoy.

Some might like having their testicles squeezed or pulled (start gently and work your way up) or stroked like a small hamster. There's a rumour about one Hollywood superstar being overheard receiving a blowjob and loudly insisting that his (I think rather temporary) partner should 'Cup the balls!' You can roll them around a bit (BUT DO NOT TWIST!) or you can play them like bongos. See what you can come up with.

Then there's all you can achieve with licking and suck-ing. Ball-owners, if that's what you want to happen, then maybe help things along a bit by shaving your hairy kiwi fruits and washing them regularly (which will also help prevent you getting cancer from chimneys). My main take-home advice to men from my show and book *Talking Cock* was 'wash your bits'. In the twenty years that have passed since, I am not sure that cocks and balls have got signifi-cantly cleaner (even though they are, on average, probably less hairy). There is still work to be done. For the sake of anyone who might find their mouth and nose in proximity to your magnificent beasts, at least give them the occasional wipe with a flannel.

Don't forget, if the position allows, you can also give the balls a bit of a flick or a cup during intercourse. It might liven things up, but playing with your partner's balls also has extra benefits. It can potentially increase sperm production and improve blood flow to the area (and it's not a bad thing to get as much blood to male genitalia as possible). Also, of course, if you become familiar with those special bollocks in your life, then you might be the one who notices new lumps or bumps. Diddling with their danglers might actually help save their life.

Get out there, enjoy your balls and/or the balls of the person you love or fancy – or of everyone in the club you attend where you staple each other's to furniture.

Balls may be ridiculous, but in the right circumstances they can be wonderful. Celebrate them in whatever manner you see fit.

33

Hello, Knobworth

Less than nine months after my operation – and less than eight since I'd had chemotherapy – I was attempting to run a half-marathon. For the last five months, Paulette and I had been slogging our way through muddy fields and up and down steep hills in preparation, and I was feeling well prepared. We'd done a few runs of ten miles plus, though not the full distance. It had been amazing to have a running partner as fit as her, and she'd definitely pushed me more than I would have managed if I was training alone.

I was looking forward to it. Partly so it would be over, but mainly because this was the final battle in the war against cancer. If I could triumph here, at least psychologically, I would banish the demons that had plagued me in this weird, yet still somehow wonderful year.

We wanted to beat the queues, so had set off to Knebworth super early that Sunday morning. Can you believe that I, once again, arrived far too early? There were maybe only another dozen cars in the car park, and we had to spend a good hour or so in the car, trying to keep warm on a cold November morning.

I was raring to go, but race time was still fairly distant. I tried to time my last wee, but ended up doing a last wee about four times and then still believing I needed another one as we waited for the run to start. If anyone asks you to précis this book, tell them it's about a man who always turns up to stuff with hours to spare and nearly always needs a wee.

I was hoping to manage a sub-two-hour run. My personal best, from seven years ago, had been one hour, forty-seven minutes and nine seconds. That had been on the relatively flat Royal Parks course in London; there were some proper hills on this Knebworth run, and I was now in my fifties.

I had told Paulette that I would stick with her for as long as I could, but I knew she would be faster and I didn't want her to have to hang around for me. However, when things got going, the occasion and the adrenaline filled me with energy. Finding myself hemmed in by the runners in front of me, I picked up speed and overtook them, dashing ahead. I had assumed that Paulette would follow, but she was more sensible than me and had a race plan. I was glory-hunting – at the pace I'd set off at, I had the chance of doing the first kilometre in under five minutes. I had hoped I might manage a few sub-six-minute kilometres in the whole race, so the prospect of completing the first one in under five was too juicy to resist, even though I knew that might have repercussions later. I managed to run kilometre one in four minutes and fifty-four seconds. What a start! If I could keep this up, I would beat my personal best.

I knew that I couldn't keep it up.

For now, I was full of energy and adrenaline, and kept pushing forward, expecting Paulette to appear at my shoulder at any second, but she didn't overtake me until the fourth or fifth kilometre. She was mildly – and correctly – irritated by my failure to be a team player and the fact I'd left her behind. It hadn't been my intention, but after all we'd been through together, that had been a dick move. She more or less forgave me and we ran together for the next few kilometres.

Catie, her parents and the kids had stationed themselves at a point that was both five and eight miles into the race (because we doubled back on ourselves). I was still full of beans when I saw them the first time, and as I ran past, I picked up Ernie and pretended I was going to carry him all the way round with me. I ran on a few steps, then stopped and returned him, but in the process, I knocked out one of my ear pods and had to scramble under a car to find it, wasting valuable seconds.

The kids had made signs saying, 'Go Richard, Go!' (Phoebe had begun to sarcastically call me by my name, rather than Daddy; something I hadn't anticipated happening for at least another decade, but which I still find endlessly amusing.) When I passed them the second time, they were inside the car and pushing the signs against the window, sensibly keeping out of the cold – and away from any runners who might try to carry them off.

I was going great guns and absolutely loving it. So far, every single kilometre had been under six minutes, and a few had only been just over five. I did the first ten kilometres in fifty-one minutes and twenty seconds, and was at the halfway point in about fifty-four minutes. If I could repeat that, I was on course for that personal best.

There was a long hill at the halfway point. Suddenly, my thighs were heavy and my pace dropped. Paulette started pulling away. I was no longer buoyed by whatever endorphins had made the first half of the race so effortless and fun, and it was starting to hurt. It was only on kilometre eighteen, which included a killer of a steep hill, that my pace went over six minutes (and only by a second). It would be my only six-minute-plus kilometre in the entire race. I was struggling a bit, and knew my personal best was out of reach, but I worked out that things would have to go seriously awry for me not to finish in under two hours. I wasn't going to give up. This run was my chance to show that cancer had not defeated me, while at the same time raising money to try to defeat cancer. Cancer would regret picking on me. Right Bollock had owned himself again.

I pushed on through the pain and crossed the line in one hour, fifty-five minutes and one second. If only I hadn't stopped to pick up Ernie, I'd have done it in under 115 minutes. That is why love should be discouraged at all times.

I came thirty-fourth in the over-fifty category (though I was up against some fifty-year-old whippersnappers). There were about seventy-five people in that group, so that's not too bad. I was 370th out of 681 men, though shamefully the race did not do a breakdown for one-testicled men (and statistically, there should have been two or three of us). I was 470th out of 1,065 runners, which again is a decent result for a fifty-four-year-old bollockly challenged man.

Paulette came in a couple of minutes ahead of me and achieved her own personal best. I couldn't have done any of this without her support and commitment. She's an absolute star.

I was elated by my performance, a happiness only slightly dented by the fact that the stall giving out bottles of alcohol-free beer at the finish line had temporarily run out of stock just as I staggered by. In better news, I hit my JustGiving page target within a few minutes of the race ending (the final total was an incredible £30,739).*

Dr Sharma, the man who had persuaded† me into this charity endeavour, would later seem slightly annoyed that I'd raised this money for the hospitals, rather than his research charity,

---

* The page is still open if you want to donate some more: www.justgiving.com/monoball.
† I wanted to say hypnotised here, but the lawyers say I can't say that, even though I reckon he definitely did.

CTRT. Obviously I then had to raise more money for him, which we did by live-streaming the next series of the Leicester Square Theatre podcast, raising over £9,000. It felt good and right to pay back the NHS, although obviously I would love to live in a country where they were funded properly and this didn't need to happen. I still hope that people would want to pay back something, even in those circumstances.

I came home with my medal and told the kids I had won the race.

And in a way, I had.

ON THE BALL

I hope you've enjoyed these additional gristly chicken nuggets of testicular facts and cultural history, and that it's helped you see how many ballsy fallacies are ingrained in us. What really strikes me from what I've learned about this subject is just how much of what we know about bollocks is utter bollocks.

I find it very unlikely that Hitler was missing a ball, let alone that it was kept in the Albert Hall; we don't have one bollock for boy babies and one for girls (and it's incredible that people believed that we might for so very long); no one wanted to be impregnated by Ötzi; our testicles and our souls are not made of baked beans; balls are not some kind of Venus fly trap intended to entice sexual partners (as they are quite clearly the least aesthetically pleasing body part – even the anus is more appealing); you can't cure impotence or flatulence by sewing some goat gonads into your body; their size does not indicate your bravery (though it might give a vague clue to how faithful you are likely to be); Romans didn't swear on them; beavers don't gnaw theirs off; the universe didn't emerge from the holy scrotum of a wanking god (no offence to any ancient Sumerians who are reading); and, hey, don't fondle the pope's to check he's all that he seems to be.

You don't need balls to be a man. You are not more manly the more balls you have. You are not less of a man for losing them. Being able to shoot spunk everywhere doesn't make you strong. If you can push a baby out of your genitals, then maybe you can claim to be quite tough. But if a toddler lightly headbutting you in the nads sends you sprawling on the floor – that's not indicative of anything but weakness.

Even modern science hasn't quite got to grips with testicles. There is still mystery and much we can't be sure of. Why bother with all the stuff and nonsense when what we do know about them is literally incredible. These tiny, ugly blobs generate all this potential life, stay loyal to their original owner, even if transplanted, have the intelligence to move themselves around to control their temperature or if in danger, come in pairs so you can still carry on if one of them lets you down, and, when handled carefully (or roughly, if that's what we're into) can bring us enormous pleasure. I still don't know why the hell they aren't inside our bodies, maybe with some kind of *Thunderbird*-style launch system to bring them outside when we need them. At least it means we know they are there and appreciate them.

As with so many things, the truth is more magical and mysterious than the myth.

Don't believe the bollocks; believe *in* the bollocks.

Bollocks, plural or singular, are amazeballs.

34

Carpe scrotum

'Carpe scrotum. Seize life by the testicles.'

– ROWENA CHERRY

Nine months and a day after my operation, and somehow still in the same year that I'd first become concerned about my weird big bollock, I had another appointment to see Dr Sharma. The news was good. The scan I'd had after my lipoma scare showed that I was clear of cancer. My blood work was nearly perfect too. The doctor showed me my insides on his computer screen. The lipoma was seriously impressive, and it turned out that I also had a cyst on one of my kidneys. He said neither of these things were anything to worry about, though it doesn't make me very happy to know that my body still continues growing unnecessary and occasionally deadly things inside me.

Dr Sharma also said that my blood results showed I wasn't drinking enough water, which might lead to kidney problems in the future. He said I had to drink about three pints of water every day.

No thanks. I'd rather die.

Of course, there was no way out of it. I have to do whatever an oncologist tells me. So I tried it out that very day. The problem was, the water more or less came straight out again. Almost as if my body didn't want it at all. Even though I did most of the water-drinking in the morning and afternoon, I had to get up to go to the loo about ten times in the night (rather than my usual two or three). This can only mean the body doesn't need water. That's basic logic.

I carried on drinking that much water as a satirical protest against modern medicine. My body got used to it. It was a good call. Bloody NHS, keeping us all alive and healthy. When will someone stop these do-gooders?

I tweeted the all-clear, and the next day I got a phone call. It was Barry Cryer. *What?* It wasn't even my birthday. He wanted to wish me well and say how happy he was to hear the news. It turned out that he wasn't too well himself at this point, but he didn't mention that. He didn't even want to hear about how I was. He just wanted to tell me a joke. A bonus birthday joke – two in a year. I felt like the queen.

'A couple looked across the road and there's a man at the bus stop. The wife says to her husband, "That's the Archbishop of Canterbury!"

'He says, "Oh, stop it."

'She says, "Go and say hello and ask him."

'So, he goes across and says hello and says, "Are you the Archbishop of Canterbury?"

'"Fuck off," says the man.

'So he comes back and she asks him, "Did you ask him if he was the Archbishop of Canterbury? What did he say?"

' "He told me to fuck off!"

'She says, "Tut ... now we'll never know." '

Laugh received, Barry wished me the best and was on his way. Going out on a laugh. I can pretty much guarantee that he managed that the last time he talked to every person he knew.

The upshot of all this was so far, so good. I was definitely a cancer survivor. Which was OK, but it meant I could no longer get out of stuff by pulling a sad face and saying, 'I've had cancer.' If I told people that's why I couldn't be on their podcast or come to their wedding, they would say, 'Wait a minute, didn't you just run a half-marathon?' The dream was over.

If it's any consolation to those readers who hate me and want me to die (jeez, guys, after all we've been through together?), I felt, at this point, more poorly than I had been at any other time in this bizarre year. I'd picked up a cold and done my leg in trying to run five kilometres in under twenty-five minutes at my local Park Run (I'd succeeded, with two seconds to spare). Then I'd somehow sprained my back in my sleep. For a man who was now (I assume) immortal, having conquered death, I was a bit of a wreck. But I suppose that's the *Twilight Zone* twist. I get everlasting life, but I can't shake off the annoying niggles of middle-aged existence.

It was great to have the all-clear, but if this year had taught me anything, it was that nothing is guaranteed. Cancer might not kill me, but something definitely will. Let's face it: in a world of pandemics, nuclear weapons and a bit of a laissez-faire attitude towards global warming there's no shortage of things that might finish us off, even if we aren't unlucky enough to absent-mindedly wander in front of a bus tomorrow morning.

This is why I am glad all this happened to me. The year 2021 came with one hefty negative, but nearly everything else was incredibly positive. My body had given itself a sharp (and some would say self-defeating) kick between the legs, in order to let me know that I am in my mid-fifties and my time here is limited. It gave me a small but significant shift of perspective and a chance to reassess my priorities. In that moment when I thought I was going to die, all I cared about was my family (and also a little bit my whisky, though only because it symbolised the moustachioed bastard who would take my place). My family were, to be fair, my main focus before this existential crisis, but this really concentrated my mind on what was actually important to me.

I am experiencing a sense of contentment that I don't think I'd have if all this hadn't happened. The little moments with my family seem so much more significant. I appreciate how lucky I am (and always was), and how, if things had gone differently I might not have been here to see my kids getting 'chicken pops' (as they call it), or being able to multiply six by seven, or simply sitting next to me, watching TV, casually resting an arm on my leg.

I still love my job, and I still need to do my job to keep those parasitical and ungrateful little monsters alive, but this has given me so much material that it will probably pay to keep them going for another year or two at least (more if you buy another copy of this book for a friend). If someone came and offered you two years' wages, and all you'd have to do is to remove a bodily organ of your choice, might you take them up on it? I bet those of you with two bollocks would probably plump to lose one of them.

Initially, I cared about what memories I'd leave: how my kids would think of me after I'm gone, and maybe my artistic legacy. That's all a waste of time. You have little control over the way your kids perceive you, anyway; they'll go from wishing you'd fall into lava to thinking you're OK to nearly hold hands with, with no regard for anything you've actually done. Memories happen organically; you can't create them at will (or if you do, they will be remembered in a way that you hadn't intended). Sadly (or probably happily) people are much more likely to remember your more humiliating moments – your terrible farts, your inability to do home-schooling, your decision to shit on a patio – rather than anything impressive or noble. They will remember you as you were, flawed and human, with laughter and with love.

I think of my dad and remember him furious at me in that parking lesson; falling into his pond (which I didn't even see); eating the little tub of lip balm left on the table at our wedding because he thought it was cheese; asking for 'quatre litres of petrol' at a French petrol station; saying he could catch the yellow ball that I had in my hand, no matter how hard I threw it at him, under the misunderstanding that it was a sponge ball, when it was, in fact, from a set of boules ... And I will think of these things long before I remember him splashing me with a hose in the sunshine, or any of the thousands of wonderful and selfless things he did on my behalf.

Memories aren't that important. Memories fade or disappear or change into something that never really happened anyway – at best, they only live as long as the brain they're housed in. Attempts to live on beyond your death are futile. Even giant edifices made of ten thousand cleared stones will eventually disappear.

It might comfort you to think that people will think of you once you're gone, but it's of no actual value to you. You won't be here to enjoy it.

All that really matters is what's happening to you while you're here, in the moment. We shouldn't be thinking of our legacies or trying to curate how we will be thought of once we're gone. We should be making the most of the time we have and the people we're with. And trying to make that time last as long as it possibly can.

That's my priority now. Enjoying the wonderful nightmare that is my family.

This is, of course, all very easy for me to say. I am *Taskmaster* Champion of Champions now. My place in history is assured.

Most of the people who helped me through this year did so fleetingly or anonymously. I don't remember most of their names – I wasn't even introduced to many of them. They didn't do it for fame or money or acknowledgement. Many of them won't remember me, or even know who they helped. They simply did their jobs, and a consequence of that was that I am still here to be mocked by my kids, to do my job, to adequately make love with my wife, and to laugh in the face of my inevitable death. My demise is only postponed, but I will do all I can to delay it for as long as possible, before finally slipping back into that wonderful, dreamless state of nothingness that was one of the highlights of my year – if not my life.

I don't miss my bollock, even if it's still sometimes a bit of a jolt when I notice my depleted sac. But my balls were not what made me a man, and losing one hasn't changed anything about me, except maybe my outlook on life. And writing this book has made me realise that most of the stuff we think about bollocks is bollocks. We make up all this superfluous nonsense to give them attributes that they don't even have. And then we don't really appreciate the magical thing about these ugly, vulnerable, dangly man fruits. These Genesis-machines in our pants. That we have two of, just in case we lose one.

Cancer is a fucking bitch, even at its lightest possible level. If cancer (or anything similar) happens to you, my advice would be:

- Talk about it.
- Joke about it.
- Make a puppet based on your excised body part (optional).
- Whether or not it turns out to be serious, laugh in its stupid face. Because living is the only response to the prospect of death. And laughter is (apart from fucking, but you can do both at once) the best way to say, 'I am here.'

Consider how lucky we are to be alive, not how unlucky we are to eventually not be alive. Most potential people never get the opportunity to experience life, thanks to our incredibly wasteful sperm delivery system. They carry on not being alive forever.

Sure, Samuel Beckett, we may be born astride the grave, but at least we get to see that momentary gleam. Which is an incredible and statistically impossible privilege, so stop being so negative, you silly dead bastard. You could have been eating an ice cream instead of getting all miserable about stuff.

Beckett was cool. All responses to life are valid.

Ultimately, I don't regret missing out on the opportunity to ask, 'Can I have my ball back?'

I don't want it back. You're all right. Sorry it landed in your garden. You can keep it. Or burst it, if you're that kind of neighbour. I don't mind.

I've got another one.

ON THE BALL: The ambassador's ball

I am finishing off the writing of this book in April 2022. It's Testicular Cancer Month! Woo hoo! Let's celebrate. I think the focus of Testicular Cancer Month is to try and fight against the disease, but if my experiences with International Women's Day are anything to go by, then I have to assume there are a lot of keyboard warriors out there demanding that we have a month where testicular cancer is encouraged. It's all about balance with these guys.

I have just been made an ambassador for Movember. Only seventeen months ago, I was growing a moustache for them, and I presume that my upper lip fuzz was so impressive they wanted to promote me. Or perhaps it was something to do with losing a testicle. I guess we'll never know.

It's a great honour to be an ambassador, and of course it means I get to give out trays of fancy chocolates at swanky receptions. They might look like Ferrero Rocher, but . . . oh my God . . . what are those? No! Nooooo! No!!!! So, *that's* what happened to mine. These people are monsters. Mmm, surprisingly tasty though.

If you have a ball or balls, or know someone who does and want to help them, here's how you should be checking them (according to the Movember website).* It's a good idea to do this monthly.

Step 1: Steam them – preferably *not* over a kettle like you're trying to secretly open an envelope. The aim here is to

---

* https://uk.movember.com/mens-health/testicular-cancer

protect yourself, not scar yourself for life. This sort of thing is as nerve-wracking for your intelligent little bollocks as it is for you. A warm, steamy shower should help your nuts relax. Also, it's always worth cleaning them, though maybe do that more than once a month.

Step 2: Roll – What are you doing? Get up. You're not meant to roll around in the shower. Roll one of your plums between your thumb and fingers – GENTLY! – and don't twist it round (you read about torsion on page 38). Look out for any changes in size or new lumps or bumps or anything painful.

Step 3 – Repeat: Time to move over to the other testicle (or testicles for the polyorchids amongst you), if applicable. I check my one bollock a second time so I can pretend I've got two.

Every nut is unique. Get to know yours. If there's anything worrying you at all, then go and see your doctor. They won't mind if it turns out to be a Rice Krispie that has got stuck to your scrotum (actually, they might mind that – but otherwise they will be happy to reassure you). As you've seen, testicular cancer is very treatable and only properly dangerous if you leave it too long.

Epilogue

They think it's ball over

I really wanted this book to have a happy – or at least positive – ending, and to show that having cancer is not a death sentence: that you can not only survive it, but survive it with a smile on your face, and then go on to live for many fulfilling years. Perhaps even more fulfilling because of your brush with mortality.

Even if things go tits (or balls or colon or prostate or whatever) -up, then I think there's still a lot to be said for approaching things with humour, seeing the bright side of it all, and appreciating the good things that you have and have had in your life.

But things don't always pan out the way you'd hoped ...

In early January, partway through the writing of this book, I finally got Covid. The rest of the family tested negative, and so I was sent up to the attic to isolate: an experience weirdly reminiscent of the post-operation torpor that I was in the process of writing about. I wasn't ill, merely a little bit tired. So my experience of Covid, just like my experience of cancer, was a virtual-reality one.

It was a little bit harder than post-operation bed rest because I was completely on my own. No hugs from the family. No chance to interact at all. My meals left at the top of the stairs. Again, I initially enjoyed the break from childcare, but again, that quickly palled.

Catie had somehow managed to draw the short straw again: she'd had three or four social engagements planned for that week, including a spa visit with her friends that she had to postpone so she could look after our children.

I only had to cancel one gig, which hadn't sold many tickets, and I was able to do it online instead. Which I actually preferred.

(Catie would then get Covid a couple of weeks later, and she had to miss two podcast shows,* including a trip to the Channel Islands. Seriously, why is God testing this good woman in such a manner?)

Self-isolating gave me a bit more time for writing, but also more time for self-examination, both spiritual and physical. I was writing about those early days of worrying about my right bollock, pretty much exactly a year to the day since it had happened. Bizarrely, I started to have concerns about the one that was left (which was also formerly on the left). Did it feel a bit heavier? Like my right one had? Or was I so caught up in reliving the trauma of January 2021 that I was imagining it was all happening again? Perhaps I hadn't properly dealt with the emotional issues. Maybe a puppet of my lost testicle hadn't helped me to process things at all.

It seemed too much of a coincidence that this was all happening again, just as I was writing about it. It had to be psychosomatic.

---

* She's one of the *Drunk Women Solving Crime* and I heartily recommend this very funny podcast.

Like the first time, I ignored it for a little while.

Then, when giving myself my regular self-examination (which, bizarrely, I am still slightly reluctant to do, even though I know how important it is) I thought I felt a lump. Was I imagining that, too? Or misinterpreting a bit of epididymis as a bump?

I checked again, and my hand recoiled as my fingers discovered something about half the size of a pea growing on my remaining testicle. There wasn't much room for misunderstanding there, and I don't think even I was capable of imagining a lump into existence. Something was growing on my nut, and it seemed highly possible, if not probable, that that something was the return of cancer.

My heart sank. This time it wasn't quite the gold mine of comedy that it had been the year before. To lose one ball might be regarded as misfortune; to lose both looks like carelessness.

I told Catie about it, and she agreed that it sounded like bad news, but I had to get it seen to. There was no doubt in my mind; of course I would do just that. Annoyingly, I had discovered the lump on Friday evening, and I wasn't going to be able to contact Nurse Linda until Monday morning. In any case, I was still testing positive for Covid, so I wouldn't be able to get anything checked yet. This gave me a lot of time to obsess about it all. I was bereft.

On the bright side, it was great for this book, as it was really helping me to recall the emotions I had been going through a year before. I supposed it might mean I could do a sequel. A more depressing one, though, with fewer laughs – maybe called *The Male Eunuch*. It would be the law of diminishing returns. After you've lost two balls, what then? How do you keep the gravy train rolling? Go for the full Action Man?

I could make another puppet, but that wasn't much of a consolation. No one would like it. It'd be like when *Scooby-Doo* brought in Scrappy-Doo.

As much as I love writing and bad ventriloquism, I had to think about this from a personal perspective. I was steaming along just fine with one testicle. My hormone levels were normal. My libido and sexual performance were acceptable. I was happy. But going down to zero testicles would be a whole different no-ball game.

Maybe they'd be able to save this gonad. After all, it was only a matter of two or three months since I'd had the all-clear from the oncologist. This new spot of bother had popped up very quickly. But was that bad or good? Maybe the cancer was spreading like wildfire.

The prospect of returning to the chemo ward was not something I relished, especially after we'd all agreed we didn't want to see each other again, but obviously I would accept the disruption to my life if it could save my life. Or prolong my life.

I was most worried that if the cancer had returned, in spite of everything we'd done to stop it, then that suggested it wasn't going to go away until it had finished the job. After all that hope – and all that running – was I only going to have a few extra months? This time last year, I would have taken that.

Hollow and sad, I tried to look on the bright side or think of alternative explanations, but there really wasn't a crumb of comfort. Catie agreed that it seemed pretty cut and dried, but she was determined we'd face up to this and get through it together. I wasn't going to give up the fight, but I'd had the stuffing knocked out of my gut – which was worse than having the stuffing knocked out of my scrotum.

First thing on Monday morning, I rang up Linda and left a message. By the time I was home from the school run (having finally tested negative for Covid), she'd arranged for the hospital to give me a ring. They slotted me in for a scan on the Thursday. Once again, scarily quickly, but a long enough wait to allow bad thoughts to percolate.

I consoled myself with the sardonically amusing thought that all this might actually mean Barry Cryer would get to speak at my funeral.

The next day, the news came through that Barry had died. How could he let me down like that, the silly old fucker?

It felt like the loss of a family member. He'd made me laugh so much, I suppose it was only fair that, in the end, he'd make me cry. One of his final acts had been to tell one of his nurses the Archbishop of Canterbury joke. Laughing till the end, going out with a smile on his face, and on the face of anyone lucky enough to be in his company. We'd all remember the last joke he'd told us. It might not matter how you are remembered, but what a way to be remembered. He often said, 'I've been dogged with good luck all my life.'

He made his own luck.

It was strange to revisit the scanning ward, but again, this was, at least, a great way to make sure my memories of the procedure were accurate for this book. The waiting area was much smaller than I remembered it being, and this time I was only asked for my date of birth and address once. I suppose they'd weeded out the ball-scanning perverts.

It was 27 January 2022. I'd last been here on 22 January 2021. That time, I had been certain the scan would reveal there was nothing to worry about. Now, I was almost as certain that it would reveal something terrible.

My name was called out. This time, the scanner was a man – there was someone observing, but I was too distracted to take much notice. We went through the same pantomime of the paper modesty curtain to hide my penis, while my scrotum remained in full view as the gel was slathered on.

I told the man with the scanner about the spot and said I hoped it would turn out to be a false alarm, but that obviously

I was very worried. He gave my ball the briefest of scans (again, the exact opposite of last year's experience) and told me that I didn't have to worry any more. The half-pea-sized blob on my solo gonad was a harmless cyst. It was almost as hard to process as the news I'd received the last time I'd been in this department.

I thanked him. We agreed how wonderful it was that he was able to give me this news straight away. All the emotion of the last few days – and probably all the repressed emotions from the previous year – welled up and I cried a few tears of joy. As awful as it must be to let people like the 2021 Richard Herring know that they have cancer, it must be rather lovely to be able to give people the joyful news of no cancer. I guess delivering babies is OK, but it can't match the happiness of letting someone know the lump on their testis is only a cyst.

I asked what they'd do about the cyst, and he told me that as long as it wasn't painful, they'd probably leave it be. No more scrotal surgery. I wasn't complaining. My body continued to fight against me by growing unnecessary additions, but only one of them had been deadly. I could live with a lump. It was as if my remaining testicle had grown its own testicle to keep it company.

Oh, and what a great result for the end of my book. I could take my feckless readers on a rollercoaster, where the positivity of the previous chapter was suddenly derailed by an apparent recurrence of cancer, only to reveal that that was all part of the thrilling ride and everything was going to be OK. I promise I didn't think of that until I came to write this bit, though.

At the same time, it was a reminder that surviving one scare didn't make me immortal. I am a man in his mid-fifties, and life is not infinite. I may have beaten this cancer, but that doesn't mean another eighteen years of life are guaranteed.

There's no genie handing out guaranteed lifespans. A lot of things that kill you don't even have the good grace to give you a bit of warning. Joke all you want; death has the last laugh.

But for now, I am still here (at the time of writing; investments can go down as well as up, and past performance is not a guide to future performance). If I am not here any more and you've found this book hidden in a cupboard by your fireplace, then hello. It was me who built those weird cairns in the field. I used to live here. Sorry about the smell.

I am still grateful for all the extra bits of life I've had that I might not have had if my ball had carried out its dastardly work of terrorism. Every day, something new gets added to the pile.

Phoebe turned seven and we had a party at a local soft-play area. They had a little football pitch and I went in goal. Several kids tried to score past me, but they were all rubbish, and I fended off their limp shots without a problem. No one can defeat me. Especially a load of pathetic children. Then Phoebe's best friend Matthew turned up. He seemed a bit more focused than the others, and was actually wearing a football kit. He put the ball down, stepped back and fired a rocket towards the goal. It hit me right in my remaining ball. So little to aim for, and yet he got it bang on. I doubled over with tears in my eyes, and though it stung, I felt sort of happy. My ball still worked, and I could still experience something that was part of the essence of being a man. It made me feel like everything was back to normal.

Of course, in twenty years' time, an oncologist might determine that that football strike damage was the spark that set off a second bout of testicular cancer, but he'd still laugh. A competitive dad getting a football in the bollock will always be funny, at least until the patriarchy is overthrown.

I am just glad to still be here to experience testicular pain, and all the other stuff I might have missed if I hadn't gone to see my GP.

Yesterday, for example, Ernie woke me up at 6.30am to ask me: 'Do ghosts have bum holes?'

That was worth hanging around for.

Hard to say, though, isn't it? You can see through them and they don't seem to have any internal organs. Presumably you see them wearing whatever they were wearing when they died and they can't take it off, so assuming they are just a sort of photocopy of their outer shell, a shadow of what they were, there is no underlayer and thus probably no anus. You never see any naked ghosts, even though a fair proportion of people must die in the nude. So there's no way to be sure.

It goes to show that you don't need to have a bit of your genitals cut off to come up with comedy. Just use your genitals to make a human, and eventually they will create material for you. Though, to be fair, cutting off a bit of your genitals might prove less stressful and expensive in the long run.

What I'm saying is, don't worry about dying. From my experience, it's pretty relaxing. Concentrate on living.

We're here for now. Let's make the most of it.

Acknowledgements

Many thanks to my brilliant editor Rhiannon Smith, for seeing the potential in this book and for guiding me through the writing of it – and for always being right. Also to Catherine Burke, for taking us to the finishing line.

Also to everyone at the most aptly named publisher for this book, Sphere, including Kirsteen Astor, Aimee Kitson, Zoe Carroll, Sarah Shrubb, Louise Harvey, Tara O'Sullivan and Kim Bishop.

I am greatly indebted to Alex Hiscock for his fantastic and diligent academic research. Sorry it was all about bollocks, and that I then spoiled it by putting lots of gags in it, but at least I have remained respectful and not made any jokes about your surname. Also to Ben Walker and Chris Evans (not that one).

I am very grateful to Richard Ison for the design of Right Bollock, and all the work he has done on my behalf. Also to Right Bollock for allowing me to quote him in this publication despite his antipathy towards me.

Thank you to everyone who played a part in this story, including Paulette Eldridge, Christopher and Pat Wilkins, Adrian Nebbett, Barry Cryer and Bob Cryer and the amazing *Taskmaster* team. Also to my mum, for jetwashing the patio.

Thanks also to Katie Mckay, Mary-Grace Brunker, Jon Thoday, Julien Matthews and everyone at Avalon.

Love and thanks to my family for helping me through this difficult year, and for providing me with so many jokes and stories. Phoebe and Ernie, you are superstars and I am so glad I get to have more time with you. Special thanks to my wife Catie for all she had to go through. One day, you will get to tell your horrifying story.

Thanks also to the many monoballs who contacted me to tell me their reassuring stories. We are a rare and noble breed (apart from all those fascists and cheats).

Of course, I am endlessly grateful to Arnand Sharma and nurse Linda and to all the NHS staff who guided me through this experience and got me out of it in two pieces, giving me the chance of seeing my kids grow up. Thank you for your diligence and care, and also for your senses of humour in the most challenging of circumstances. If I get cancer again, I promise I'll do it when there's not a pandemic on.

Now, please check your balls (or breasts, or any other bits that you think might be vulnerable).